William Lloyd Garrison and
American Abolitionism in
Literature and Memory

# William Lloyd Garrison and American Abolitionism in Literature and Memory

Brian Allen Santana

McFarland & Company, Inc., Publishers
*Jefferson, North Carolina*

LIBRARY OF CONGRESS CATALOGUING-IN-PUBLICATION DATA

Names: Santana, Brian Allen, 1979– author.
Title: William Lloyd Garrison and American abolitionism in
    literature and memory / Brian Allen Santana.
Description: Jefferson, North Carolina : McFarland & Company, Inc.,
    Publishers, 2016. | Includes bibliographical references and index.
Identifiers: LCCN 2016008312 | ISBN 9780786498284
    (softcover : acid free paper) ∞
Subjects: LCSH: Garrison, William Lloyd, 1805–1879. | Garrison, William
Lloyd, 1805–1879—Influence. | Garrison, William Lloyd, 1805–1879—In
literature. | Antislavery movements—United States—History. |
    Abolitionists—United States—Biography.
Classification: LCC E449.G25 S26 2016 | DDC 326/.8092—dc23
LC record available at http://lccn.loc.gov/2016008312

BRITISH LIBRARY CATALOGUING DATA ARE AVAILABLE

ISBN (print) 978-0-7864-9828-4
ISBN (ebook) 978-1-4766-2452-5

© 2016 Brian Allen Santana. All rights reserved

*No part of this book may be reproduced or transmitted in any form
or by any means, electronic or mechanical, including photocopying
or recording, or by any information storage and retrieval system,
without permission in writing from the publisher.*

Front cover image: William Lloyd Garrison (Library of Congress)

Printed in the United States of America

*McFarland & Company, Inc., Publishers
Box 611, Jefferson, North Carolina 28640
www.mcfarlandpub.com*

For Erin, my partner in all things

# Table of Contents

*Acknowledgments* ix

*Introduction: William Lloyd Garrison and the Birth of American Abolitionism in History and Popular Culture* 1

1. The Construction and Evolution of Garrisonian Narratives of Abolitionist Sacrifice in Antebellum America, 1834–1857 25

2. Commemorating Garrison: Origins of the Garrison Revival in Post-Bellum American Memory, 1867–1910 56

3. "For Future Generations": Garrison's Children, Massachusetts Educational Reform and the Institutionalization of the Garrison Narrative in Boston Schools, 1880–1922 88

4. Ross Lockridge's *Raintree County*: American Abolitionism as Epic Origin Narrative 117

*Epilogue: William Lloyd Garrison in the Mid–20th Century and Beyond* 153

*Chapter Notes* 157

*Bibliography* 187

*Index* 199

# Acknowledgments

I began researching this book in 2006 while completing my doctorate in American studies at George Washington University. Almost a decade later I find it impossible to fully convey the gratitude I feel towards the many people who contributed to the conceptualizing, researching, writing, and completion of this project. I am particularly indebted to Dr. Jennifer James for setting aside years of her life to see this project through from start to finish. Her voice of encouragement and her model of intellectual camaraderie made this entire process a rich and valuable experience. My debts to her are too numerous to list here. She will always be my teacher, my mentor, and my friend.

Dr. James Miller was the co-director of the doctoral dissertation that inspired this book. We worked together for six years and he consistently provided detailed feedback and warm support that made my final analysis both richer and stronger. Sadly, Jim passed away in 2015 before this final manuscript could be published. I hope that this book will reflect positively on the strong influence he had on my development as a scholar and thinker.

Dr. Kip Kosek and Dr. Elaine Peña provided thoughtful responses to earlier drafts of this manuscript. I am very grateful for their time, detailed notes, and critical questions. Their comments and advice helped to make this book better.

Of all my teachers my father, Victor Santana, was my first and he remains my favorite. His enthusiasm for early American life and culture led to the development of my own academic interests in this same period of history. However, it is the spirit of intellectual curiosity that animates his entire life that I find most inspiring. It is this quality that I work to impart to my own students.

The archivists at the Boston Public Library, the Library of Congress, and the University of North Carolina at Chapel Hill were generous with their resources and knowledge. They saved me countless hours by locating and suggesting materials that they thought would be helpful to this project.

At my own institution, George Washington University, Tricia Greenstein and the interlibrary loan officers at Gelman Library became familiar faces. Their prompt assistance helped me to keep moving forward.

Very special thanks go to Tom Guglielmo and the faculty of the American Studies Department at George Washington University for providing generous institutional support in the form of research stipends and summer funding that alleviated the costs associated with undertaking a project of this size. Both Tom Guglielmo and Chap Heap worked tirelessly to protect the integrity of student funding and research support. They created an atmosphere that facilitated my ability to pursue this project.

During the fall 2011 semester I designed and taught a seminar course at George Washington titled, "The Civil War and American Popular Culture." In preparing for this course, I read widely and this experience stimulated me to think in new ways about the abolitionist memoirs I analyze here. I wish to thank all of my students for the wonderful time we shared together. Julie Hyman, Thomas Nicholas, Amanda Castroverde, Susannah Glick, and Kelsey Johnston, in particular, always ensured lively and intellectually rich discussions. These discussions helped keep my interest and enthusiasm for this book strong.

My family has sustained me emotionally, logistically, and financially from this project's conception to its completion. My mother, Elizabeth Santana, has cheered me on for years and has always been ready to talk me off a ledge with kind words of support when I encountered obstacles. My brother, Cameron Santana, has always shown enthusiasm for this book and for all my projects.

My grandmother, Sarah Connor, died in 2014 and would be extremely proud to know that this book achieved publication. I owe her more than I can possibly describe and I miss her dearly.

My in-laws, Edward and Toni Fife, provided support and encouragement as I finished this project. Indeed, a draft of at least one chapter of this book was completed while living with them during the summer of 2009.

My wife, Erin Santana, is my partner in life and my very best friend. She has been living with some variation of this book for almost seven years now. When we married in 2009 she became my greatest emotional support system and a consistent voice of optimistic enthusiasm. When I began working on the book version of this manuscript she took on a much more active role when technical difficulties arose that resulted in the loss of hundreds of pages of manuscript and research files. Armed with a copy of my original dissertation she literally spent months painstakingly typing and reformatting hundreds of original manuscript pages for me to edit and prepare for book publication. To say that this book would not be possible without her is a supreme understatement. She is the reason that this permutation of the project exists and she will always have my love and gratitude for the sacrifices that she made to ensure its publication.

# Introduction: William Lloyd Garrison and the Birth of American Abolitionism in History and Popular Culture

On a cool afternoon on April 17, 1830, a young abolitionist named William Lloyd Garrison anxiously paced the confines of his twenty-foot prison cell in Baltimore, Maryland. Publicly he worked to make light of his incarceration and to project an image of stoic resolve and indifference. In a May 25, 1830, letter to Joseph T. Buckingham, the editor of the *Boston Courier*, he humorously mocked the severity of his situation: "it is true, I am not the owner of this huge pile, nor the grave lord-keeper of it; but then, I pay no rent—am bound to make no repairs—and enjoy the luxury of independence divested of its cares."[1] Privately, however, he struggled to comprehend the events that led to his incarceration and searched for the meaning of his unjust punishment. In a letter to his childhood friend Harriet Farnham Horton he expressed a more melancholic tone that he reserved for those closest to him: "the tyranny of the court has triumphed over every principle of justice, and even over the law—and here I am in limbo."[2]

Weeks earlier a Maryland court convicted Garrison for criminal libel for a story that he published in the November 29, 1829, issue of the abolitionist periodical the *Genius of Universal Emancipation*.[3] He wrote the article roughly three months into his tenure as a member of the Quaker abolitionist Benjamin Lundy's editorial staff and in it he accused Francis Todd, a Newburyport merchant, of using his ship to transport slaves from Baltimore to New Orleans. A criminal and civil suit quickly followed that resulted in the dissolution of the paper and a six-month prison sentence for Garrison.

Garrison would only serve seven weeks of his original sentence, but during this time glimpses of his new conception of the relationship between abolitionism, persecution, and suffering slowly fermented. He wrote at least three letters a day from his Baltimore prison cell for seven weeks, he composed several sonnets and other works of poetry that were inspired by his ordeal, and he authored an eight page pamphlet titled, *A Brief Sketch of the Trial of William Lloyd Garrison, for an Alleged Libel of Francis Todd of Massachusetts*, that vividly recounted the story of his wrongful imprisonment.[4] Garrison's "brief sketch" also included sonnets like "To the Victim of Tyranny" in which he equates his suffering to the wrongful suffering of Christ and encourages all those who will inhabit his cell to the future to "bear nobly up against thy punishment" because such pain leads to greater rewards: "A martyr's crown is richer than a king's!/ Think it an honor with thy Lord to bleed,/ And glory midst th' intensest sufferings!"[5]

Garrison's incarceration and the heated printed debates that his conviction inspired reinforced his belief that the press offered an avenue for rallying public support for his antislavery cause and that it could also provide him with a means to counteract the negative publicity that men of wealth and resources, like Francis Todd, were capable of generating.[6] His 1830 letters from the Baltimore prison and his published sketch of his criminal trial represent his first efforts to assume control of his public image and to reframe the attacks levied at him by detractors into a new narrative of exemplary and redemptive abolitionist witnessing and suffering.[7]

This book examines the role of suffering in Garrison's antebellum anti-slavery theology, the rhetorical strategies that these religious beliefs inspired, and the influence of these ideas and images on the late 19th and early 20th century popular culture transformation of William Lloyd Garrison into a representative symbol of Massachusetts and American abolitionism, moral fortitude, and sacrifice.[8] It shows that the dramatic shift that occurs between 1831 and 1900 in how audiences remember, represent, and write about Garrison is indicative of a broader cultural transformation of perceptions about American abolitionism. By 1850, Garrison was considered a religiously heretical and socially dangerous madman by both northern and southern audiences.[9] Northern newspapers compared him to controversial religious leaders like Joseph Smith, southern papers threatened his life, and prominent intellectuals like Unitarian minister William Ellery Channing publicly voiced disapproval of the violent images and fantasies of death found in Garrison's paper *The Liberator*.[10] Even amongst Massachusetts abolitionists the term "Garrison man" was considered a derisive label.[11] Garrison fiercely responded by denouncing other abolitionist efforts and reserved his harshest words for New England churches and citizens, whom he threatened with divine retribution.[12] His controversial appeals and his fiery rhetoric attracted a great deal of public attention but not necessarily admiration. His friends and allies often expressed reservations about the less than conciliatory temperament that he eagerly displayed with little provocation. Garrison's friend, one-time employer, and fellow abolitionist Benjamin Lundy expressed the frustration of many who engaged in lengthy debates with Garrison when he wrote to Elizabeth M. Chandler, a member of his Quaker meeting, following just such an argument over the use of grotesque stories of violence and disfigurement in *The Liberator* and, more broadly, their place in Christian activism. On this particular occasion Lundy's frustration led him to denounce his friend as "vain and egotistical," "too much to be endured," and he asked Chandler to pray that one day his friend would cultivate a greater sense of "modesty in such matters."[13]

However, by the late 19th century, and especially by the time of his 1879 death, the dominant trend within Massachusetts popular culture was to discuss Garrison as *the* symbol of American abolitionism and *the* representative example of New England's past anti-slavery activism. Far from being dangerous, he is instead widely represented as embodying the region's best virtues.[14] *Harper's* describes him as a "moral inspiration" and credits his influence with turning "the whole country into an anti-slavery society."[15] Former colleagues like Samuel May and Parker Pillsbury published memoirs that remembered Garrison as the founder and leader of a unified American abolitionist movement.[16] Poems and eulogies by black and white authors celebrated his sacrifices and courage.[17] Boston in 1886 and Newburyport in 1893 constructed Garrison monuments.[18] State-sponsored festivals and commemorative events were held throughout Massachusetts that celebrated his birthday.[19] Civil War novels dramatized fictional meetings between Garrison and Abraham Lincoln in which the young Garrison convinces Lincoln to adopt an anti-slavery stance.[20] By the early 20th century Boston even adopted textbooks for the city's standardized educational curriculum that celebrated Garrison's suffering and his activist work as the enduring historical and cultural legacy of the Civil War.[21]

In doing so, the popular celebration of Garrison moved into the realm of official history.

By the mid–20th century Garrison is so associated with American abolitionism that it becomes near impossible to discuss or depict his historical anti-slavery activities without drawing on popular narrative conventions and literary tropes of suffering and sacrifice that were intrinsically linked with his antislavery theology. This dominant sentiment, I argue, participated in the rise and popularization of the literary trope of the "suffering abolitionist," which post–Civil War novelists used throughout the early and mid–20th century and which reached a zenith of visibility and expression in Ross Lockridge's 1948 epic, *Raintree County*.

A guiding principle of this book is that heroic and sentimental narratives of suffering and their relationship to the historical and symbolic William Lloyd Garrison should be framed within the same debates that scholars of Civil War memory have similarly engaged other battles over the racial, political, and cultural meanings of the war's causes, outcomes, and legacies. Scholars like David Blight, W. Fitzhugh Brundage, and Nina Silber have all extensively considered the way in which post-bellum northerners and southerners constructed different cultural memories about this traumatic national event.[22] What is not discussed is how the link between William Garrison and literary tropes of the suffering and self-sacrificial abolitionist have helped to make America's complicated and problematic relationship to slavery intellectually, emotionally, and morally comprehensible to a wide array of different audiences.

The various ways that Garrison was invoked and celebrated throughout the post-bellum years is a scathing omission from Civil War memory scholarship. This is, of course, despite the fact these celebrations were central to construction of the dominant historical and popular understanding of American abolitionism. Perhaps, as David Blight points out, the very process of remembering and commemorating discourages such reflections because the process of transmitting historical narratives is linked with the impulse to enshrine them "as a sacred set of absolute meanings and stories, possessed as the heritage or identity of a community."[23]

Attempting to locate Garrison in history and memory is further complicated by the remarkable degree of continuity between commemorative works of popular culture and the major "professional" histories of the early 20th century. Trained historians did not appear until the late 19th century and their emergence coincided with the major period of Garrison commemorative activities and, as the work W. Fitzhugh Brundage shows, the majority of the "professional" histories produced during these early years carefully adhered to the popular "interpretive conventions" and narratives of the previous generations.[24] This book's focus on the active labor of selecting, structuring, and interpreting the history of American abolitionism around the story of William Lloyd Garrison also questions the extent to which the perpetuation of these dominant literary conventions of celebrating abolitionist suffering and witnessing displaced black suffering and protest from the official "emancipationist" history of the war that emerges in the 19th and early 20th century.

My approach to the historical, cultural, political, and literary phenomenon of William Lloyd Garrison is also informed by a growing body of scholarship that grapples with discourses of suffering and sympathy and their relationship to personal and national self-definition. Such works offer a vocabulary by which to consider the dynamics of dependency between reformers' identities and objects of compassion in antebellum America. Elizabeth Clark's arguments in "The Sacred Rights of the Weak: Pain Sympathy, and the Culture of Individual Rights in Antebellum America" provided a useful starting point to consider the role of suffering in the legal construction of human rights."[25] Clark's history of the antebellum literary trope of the "suffering slave" in the 1840s, for instance, stresses the importance and popularity of eyewitness testimony in antislavery discourses.[26] However, whereas Clark's study focuses on the way some popular antislavery narratives emphasized "the slave's subjective experience of pain," this book is more interested in the way Garrisonian discourses complicate her argument—not, as she suggests as "as a way to understand the other's experiences"—but instead as a means of abolitionist self-exploration in which witnessing and suffering simultaneously exist as an emotional appeal, as a form of self-definition, and as a central component of political protest.[27]

Scholarship that analyzes the politics of sympathetic mediation encouraged me to think about the relationship between rhetorical figures embodied for readers, antislavery discourses, and later efforts to commemorate and remember William Lloyd Garrison. Karen Sanchez-Eppler's *Touching Liberty: Abolition, Feminism, and the Politics of the Body*, for instance, demonstrates the limits and dangers of sympathetic identification in antislavery discourses that seek to erase difference by asking the reader to identify with the pain of another.[28] She argues that within such traditions of abolitionist thought: "the rhetorical effaces and contains the real" and rather than interpreting such histories as part of a movement towards a more democratic society, she views them as remnants of a long history of progressive "exploitation, appropriation, and displacement."[29] Elizabeth Barnes' *States of Sympathy: Seduction and Democracy in the American Novel* similarly considers the relationship between subjectivity, authenticity, and the other's materiality.[30] Her understanding of sympathetic appeals as "a projection of one's one sentiments" provides a useful way to consider the dependent relationship between slave subjectivity, materiality, and the rhetorical abolitionist figure that witnesses and relates the experience of their suffering.[31] Lastly, Julia Stern in *The Plight of Feeling: Sympathy and Dissent in the Early American Novel,* like Sanchez-Eppler and Barnes, examines the violence of altruism in antislavery discourses and its investment in perpetuating "the ongoing suffering of another."[32] Stern provocatively argues, "that the political power of sympathy is touted as a liberating force ... but often denigrates into self-affirmation and the social death of those who are supposed to be uplifted."[33] By examining the role of suffering and abolitionist subjectivity in Garrison's discourses and by revealing its political, cultural, and literary traces this book begins the work of approaching a story that continues to be retold and reinvented by each new generation of Americans.

Garrison's story and the dominant history of American abolitionism is not, as John Stauffer suggests, about the effort to "embrace an ethic of a black heart."[34] As this book shows, sympathetic identification through the witnessing of black pain (and not embodying it) became the quintessential way of expressing the Garrisonian abolitionist's internal pain, reformer identity, and conception of activism. Rather than "blurring and remaking racial lines," the study of William Lloyd Garrison in history, memory, and literature is about the way such boundaries have been reinforced and, as a result of the Garrison revival of the late 19th century, become virtually impermeable.

We continue to invoke Garrison's narrative of righteous abolitionist suffering, witnessing, and sacrificing as a way to come to terms with the death, destruction, and divisiveness of the Civil War. Politicians, novelists, and audiences have done so since the war officially ended in 1865. Suffering and sacrifice were also, however, themes that permeated post-war narratives penned by former soldiers, politicians, as thinkers as diverse as Jefferson Davis, Jubal Early, and Frederick Douglass.[35] Retelling events of the past helped post–Civil War audiences to reconcile the deaths of close to 620,000 Americans during the four-year conflict. Drew Gilpin Faust's *This Republic of Suffering: Death and the American Civil War* convincingly shows that unprecedented levels of suffering during the Civil War inspired sweeping changes in American religious and cultural conceptions of death, dying, and pain. She writes that, "at the war's end this shared suffering would override persisting differences about the meanings of race, citizenship, and nationhood to establish sacrifice and its memorialization as the ground on which north and south would ultimately reunite."[36] According to Faust, bearing witness to and disseminating stories of suffering took on increased importance during the mid–19th century.[37] The Garrison narrative is part of this larger cultural trend, but it also stands outside of it since it has long escaped serious critical attention.

My desire to excavate the relationship between William Lloyd Garrison, discourses of suffering, and efforts to narrate and mythologize the history of American abolitionism repeatedly led me back to the image of the young Garrison nervously pacing and writing in his Baltimore cell in 1830. The legal arguments against slavery that characterized Garrison's earliest activism are abandoned in Baltimore in favor of a type of anti-slavery rhetoric that stressed the redemptive nature of abolitionist suffering.[38]

Even at this moment, which precedes the January 1, 1831, publication of the first issue of *The Liberator*, he wrestles with an idea that will come to dominate his later appeals: that abolitionist suffering is the only protest and sacrifice grand that is enough to spiritually redeem the nation, the American church, and the moral corruption at the heart of the perpetuation of slavery. In time, Garrison comes to not only accept suffering, but to embrace and seek it out as a marker of righteousness. In an early letter to Ebenezer Dole that he later reprinted as an address to "Garrison's Free Color Supporters in Boston," in the August 27, 1831, edition of *The Liberator*, he bluntly expresses his awareness of the burden that he assumed when he became a Christian abolitionist reformer:

> The martyr's blood's the seed of freedom ... I am well aware that the path which I am destined to tread, is full of briers and thorns. Foes are on my right hand and on my left. The tongue of detraction is busy against me. I have no communion with the world-and the world none with me ... 'tis the cause, and not the punishment, that makes the martyr. 'Tis not the what, but the why of a man's suffering, which gives him the credit on' t. He only is the brave man that mortifies upon principle; that chooses rather to suffer than to misbehave himself ... believe me I shall remain until death.[39]

Garrison's paper, *The Liberator*, from its first issue in 1831, rhetorically linked abolitionist suffering and sacrifice to a larger tradition of Christian suffering and persecution. Between 1831 and 1865 Garrison filled the pages of his paper with stories of abolitionist persecution, eye witness testimonies of slave lynchings and executions, and brave pledges from himself and his followers to die a martyr's death for their noble cause. Exploring abolitionist spiritual and physical torment allowed Garrison to empathize with slave pain, to set himself apart from other abolitionist groups, and to imagine his entire struggle as part of a grander spiritual narrative of progress. Many of Garrison's personal letters from these formative years are dramatically signed with "yours to the grave" or similar remarks that stress his own potential martyrdom and his willingness to suffer.[40] Thoughts of relinquishing his life for the anti-slavery cause repeatedly led him back to meditations on the death and suffering of Christ and his apostles. "My duty is plain," Garrison writes matter-of-factly in a letter to George Benson in August of 1832, "my path is without embarrassment. I shall still continue to expose the criminality of slavery, be the consequences what they may to myself. I hold my life at a cheap rate: I know it is in constant imminent danger: but if the assassin take it away, the Lord will raise me and make me up as a better advocate."[41] The constant threat of danger and the need to be at peace with the prospect of forfeiting his life at any moment gave Garrison's writings an ecstatic and urgent tone.

Garrison's meditations on his and his follower's efforts repeatedly imagine their potential victimization in an attempt to re-enact Christ's original suffering and death, which he believed would bring them into a more direct union with God. "The likelihood that I will be assassinated or abducted, seems more than probable," writes Garrison in another letter to George Benson, but he finds refuge in such a scenario because, "he who loses his life for Christ's sake shall find it. To die is to gain. The soul, secured in her existence, smiles."[42] Such words are more than mere rhetorical flourishes. Here and elsewhere Garrison is carefully producing and narrating the history of his personal efforts and his antislavery movement and works to situate both in relation to an authentic "primitive Christian" context that is far removed from the religious debates that characterized his contemporary Massachusetts context. In an October 11, 1834 letter to Amos Phelps, Garrison stresses to his friend that their "strict obedience to God" and the restoration of his church will bring them into conflict with religious leaders and publications.[43] He cites their recent public spat with the *Christian Mir-*

*ror* as one such example and encourages Phelps to "never keep anything back, merely for the sake of conciliation."[44] He reminds him that "obedience" and not "equal justice" is their ultimate goal and concludes by expressing his pity "for any man who has God as his antagonist."[45]

Throughout the antebellum era Garrison looked to past Christian suffering as a way to legitimate and differentiate the nature and scope of his efforts from those around him. This private and public habit expresses a tendency that David Blight observes about the very nature of writing or narrating history: "history forces us to interpret, explain, and imagine ourselves into the events of the past."[46] In other words, historical memory is an important component of self-definition and empowerment. Historical Christian narratives offered Garrison a way to vividly dramatize and to understand his own irreconcilable worldviews in the present.

Garrison's unrelenting fixation on redemptive suffering in the 1830s came from his renewed interested in studying New Testament scriptures that address why "righteous men" experience unjust persecution and why good works can lead to punishment, pain, and death. He concluded that suffering-and not prosperity-was the earthly reward for faithful service to God.[47] Religion scholar Bart Ehrman describes this very New Testament understanding of suffering in simple but concise terms: "sometimes God brings good out of evil, a good that would not have been possible if evil had not existed."[48] Ehrman explains that suffering is a prerequisite of salvation within the Hebrew and New Testament traditions. In the Hebrew tradition the book of Isaiah speaks of a "suffering servant" (meaning Israel and the suffering of exile) and suggests that Israelite suffering is necessary to ensure the prosperity of future generations.[49] Within the New Testament tradition, Ehrman points out that early Christians, like Paul, in passages like Romans 3:24–25, interpreted Isaiah 53 as a prophecy that the messiah would come to earth to suffer and die in order to atone for the sins of humankind.[50] Within this theological view, Christ's sacrifice and death were essential for humankind to attain salvation and eternal life. Paul encouraged early Christians to sacrifice their life and to relinquish their attachment to worldly concerns of the flesh in order to attain eternal blessings and salvation.

As early Christians experienced persecution in Asia Minor and other regions the term "martyr" evolved to signify any believer who died "like Christ."[51] By the third century martyrdom became an honorary title reserved for those who willingly put themselves in danger and forfeited their life for the spiritual nourishment of their community. The early Christian theologian Origen underscored this point when he wrote to gatherings of believers under persecution and attempted to strengthen their resolve with stories of noble suffering: "among the brethren, inspired by their reverence those who resisted even to death, the custom was established of calling martyrs only those who witnessed to the mystery of faith with the spilling of their blood."[52] This tradition looked to Jesus as the prototypical martyr, as an example of a person who *chose* persecution and suffering and who remained in control of his destiny despite (or perhaps because of) the violent threats and efforts of those around him. Within this theological view, Christ's suffering and death are vindicated through his resurrection, which is a moment that results in a literal victory over death and suffering, the spiritual redemption of humankind, and the birth of his church.

William Garrison actively read stories of early Christian martyrs and rhetorically positioned his anti-slavery movement as an extension of their efforts to purify the church. Beginning in 1834 Garrison even created a column titled, "The Refuge of Oppression," which linked abolitionist persecution and reform efforts with other historically persecuted Christians.[53] The necessity of suffering for righteousness would have been readily familiar to him growing up in a region where Foxe's *Book of Martyrs* remained the most widely owned and read text since the first days of republic.[54] In a April 5, 1834, letter to Helen Benson, who would shortly after become his wife, Garrison writes about reading Foxe's accounts of Christian martyrs and being humbled by a "full realization of the sacrifice they made and the faith and strength that sustained their last days."[55]

What Garrison found in Foxe's book were stories of dramatic confrontations between believers, government authorities, and hostile pagans who threatened Christians with torture and death. A common narrative convention found in this collection is the martyr's decision to embrace death. The martyr is not a victim and by embracing death he attains and taps into Christ's power by mimicking his example. The martyr's persecution, according to Foxe, is part of a necessary fulfillment of Christ's prophecies. Foxe outlines in his first chapter the three prophecies that should guide a Christian's understanding of suffering: that a Church will be established; that the Church and its members will be impugned and attacked by hostile forces from this world and the next; and that through faithful devotion, suffering, and sacrifice the church will continue.[56]

Foxe's book provided Garrison with a way to relate the threats against his life to the harrowing trials faced by early Christians. For instance, when a small mob menacingly "pelted" the window of the Brooklyn home where he slept on September 15, 1834, with rocks and a brick he wrote to Henry Benson and drew parallels between this incident and the death of Mathias, one of Christ's twelve apostles (who was stoned to death), whose story is told in Foxe's book, and he enthusiastically remarks: "shades of Mathias, arise!"[57] He prayed for the strength to live a faithful life and the courage to die as nobly as early Christians.[58]

By 1834 Garrison viewed abolitionist persecution and potential death as a central part of his faith and his activism. In a May 31, 1834, Garrison writes of welcoming affliction and death: "affliction is welcome! Come the hour of release! Come death to this body-this burdened, tempted, frail, failing, dying body!-and to the soul, come freedom, light and joy unceasing! Come the immortal life!"[59] This religious belief led Garrison to view suffering as an important part of the abolitionist project and, more importantly, it situated the literal emancipation of the slave with the physical and spiritual suffering of the abolitionist. In this narrative, the abolitionist became the key figure in the redemption of the nation.

Garrison imagined himself at the center of the American antislavery movement and the culture of commemoration that developed in the post-bellum years widely adopted and disseminated this narrative to such an extent that it continues to influence the approach and major themes of scholarly histories of Garrison and American abolitionism today. Comparing Garrison's private correspondence, published editorials, and speeches from the 1830s to late 19th and early 20th century eulogies, memoirs, biographies, fictional representations, and educational textbooks, reminds of the longevity, cultural capital, and power of the historical memory of the antislavery movement that he played an active role in shaping. And textual traces of Garrison's vision of the suffering abolitionist permeate the genealogy of our "professional" historical narratives and frame the very borders by which we approach the subject of American abolitionism.

The major historical biographies of Garrison, for instance, emphasize his leadership of the American anti-slavery movement and his singular outspoken willingness to die for this cause. This scholarly trend began the same year that Garrison died, with the publication of Oliver Johnson's *William Lloyd Garrison and His Times* (1879).[60] Johnson, a friend of Garrison's from his activist days, paints a portrait of a man whose faith gave him the strength to confront near constant threats of violence and death.[61] Johnson stresses Garrison's interpersonal domestic dynamics with his wife and children as a means to heighten the reader's awareness of the blissful household existence that he risked for the sake of the slave.[62]

Godwin Smith's *The Moral Crusader: William Lloyd Garrison* (1892) follows Johnson's history and produces a similar narrative that emphasizes Garrison's sacrifice and heroic efforts.[63] Smith describes Garrison as one of the "few people who cared" about the plight of the slave and he credits Garrison's efforts with the legal eradication of slavery and with what he perceived to be the public's new willingness to envision a more egalitarian society.[64]

In *William Lloyd Garrison* (1913, 1921), John Jay Chapman goes further than his predecessors and turns Garrison into a demigod worthy of lavish public commemorations and recognition because his sacrifices led to a new and more modem America.[65] In the preface to the 1921 edition of his Garrison biography he expresses continued frustration with the lack of national fervor around Garrison's image, which he deems an unconscionable offense:

> It is easy to explain why Garrison has never been adopted as one of the most popular heroes in America. He gave a purge to his countrymen, and the bitter taste of it remained in our mouths ever after. Moreover, the odium of slavery, which he branded on America's brow, seemed to survive in the very name Garrison, and we would have willingly forgotten the man. After the Civil War there was not, apparently, time for our scholars to think about him. And yet equally certain is it that the history of the United States between 1800 and 1860 will someday be re-written with this man as its central figure.[66]

Such passages are representative of the major Garrison biographies of his era, but Chapman takes this rhetoric further by describing Garrison in ecstatic religious language:

> If one could see a mystical presentation of the epoch, one would see Garrison as a Titan, turning a giant grindstone or electrical power-wheel, from which radiated vibrations in larger and in ever larger, more communicative circles and spheres of agitation, till there was not a man, woman, or child in America who was not a-tremble.[67]

Chapman's vivid image of Garrison "turning a giant grindstone or electrical power-wheel" betrays the language of Progressive-era scientific and industrial advancements. It is within this reform-minded era, which was guided by scientific and evangelical values, that Chapman situates Garrison as an example of humble sacrifice and unbending and uncompromising morality.

The tone of these early histories mirrored the commemorative enthusiasms found in popular contemporary prose and poetry. Works like Henrietta Cordelia Ray's 1905 poem "William Lloyd Garrison," viewed Garrison's life as symbolic of a change in American race perceptions and part of a larger historical turn towards fully embracing a uniquely American democratic spirit.[68] Garrison became, for Ray, a historical and symbolic marker by which the nation's movement towards democratic renewal could be measured and encouraged. An anonymous review printed in the *Atlantic Monthly* of Frank and Wendell Garrison's voluminous history of their father and his abolitionist movement begins with a succinct expression of this overwhelmingly dominant popular and historical consensus: "the great personal qualities of Mr. Garrison and his leadership of the American antislavery enterprise are now generally conceded."[69]

Of the major scholarly abolitionist histories produced before the mid–20th century only Gilbert H. Barnes's *The Antislavery Impulse: 1830–1844* (1933) challenged the widespread acceptance of Garrison's singular leadership of the anti-slavery movement and the corresponding thesis that abolitionism was a product of Massachusetts culture.[70] Barnes argues that Theodore D. Weld, and not Garrison, should be remembered as the leader of American abolitionist efforts and he also claims that the movement emanated from New York and not from Massachusetts.[71] Barnes' book also offers the provocative suggestion that Garrison became an obstacle that other abolitionists were forced to confront in order to realize the task of emancipation. He writes that Garrison's principle liability rested in his arrogance and "his promiscuous vilification of all individuals, institutions, and beliefs with which at the moment he did not agree."[72] Twenty-eight years later Dwight L. Dumond's *Antislavery: The Crusade for Freedom in America* (1961) affirmed Barnes' controversial thesis and expanded on it by lamenting the widespread praise of Garrison and suggesting that amongst the great abolitionists, Garrison lacked the moral clarity and strength of the others.[73] Dumond describes Garrison as "a man of distinctly narrow limitations among the giants of the antislavery movement."[74] Dumond reserved his sharpest criticism for the conceited nature of Garrison's antislavery appeals and takes particular offense with Garrison's postbellum efforts "to claim credit for almost everything that was done in the movement before 1840."[75] "He made contributions," Dumond concedes but Garrison's role in the larger movement "was neither a large nor an overpowering one, and sometimes it was a negative one."[76]

The growth of the modem Civil Rights movement in the 1950s seemed to encourage scholars to move away from Gilbert Barnes' critiques and to once again embrace Garrison as an exemplary symbol of the unbending self-sacrificial social reformer. Civil rights activists nostalgically looked back to the Civil War as an era marked by violent racial conflict, but also as a period in which dramatic social advancements were inspired by reformers who devoted themselves to a grander moral cause.[77] The Rev. Al Sharpton's November 3, 2006, appearance on CNN's *The Glenn Beck Show* to discuss the civil rights-era captures this tendency.[78] During this interview he cites Garrison as a forefather of the later movement and a model of "someone who stood up" and who "made great statements" that not only inspired the 19th century abolitionist movement, but also the work of later reformers like himself and Martin Luther King.[79] Garrison and the Civil War provided civil rights activists with a vivid and dramatic parallel between the sacrifices made by reformers fighting (or suffering) for emancipation and their own contemporary calls for racial equality. According to Robert Bellah the Civil War provided the major themes of American civil religion: death, sacrifice, and rebirth.[80] The popular understanding of Garrison's life, especially the emphasis on his single-handed leadership of a movement that could induce such sweeping legal and social changes, transformed him into a symbol that was capable of legitimating and inspiring contemporary civil rights activism.

Russel B. Nye's *William Lloyd Garrison and the Humanitarian Reformers* (1955), which was published during this era, is representative of the scholarly return to a focus on the self-sacrificial aspects of Garrison's character and to an emphasis on his leadership of American abolitionist efforts.[81] Nye's book appeared within six months of the Montgomery Bus Boycott and his prefatory comments concerning America's need in 1830 for strong leadership, spiritual communion with God, and reformers willing to sacrifice to "create a better world" must have resonated with contemporary reform-minded audiences.[82] Nye discusses Garrison's religious faith in the Bible as "the central fact of his life" and goes on to situate him within a longer Christian tradition: "he had the zeal and fanaticism of a Biblical prophet, combined with apostolic dedication."[83] Nye's major study served as a catalyst for other scholars who sought to re-focus discussions of American abolitionism back to William Garrison.

By 1962 scholars largely abandoned the Barnes-Dumond critiques of Garrison and even attacked both these authors' conclusions, particularly those related to Garrison's "negative" impact on the antislavery movement. Writing in the Spring 1962 issue of *The American Scholar,* southern historian C. Vann Woodward took aim at Dumond's work and dismissed the author's conclusions for "admitting no complexities and ambiguities" that might allow for a fair assessment of Garrison's work.[84] A significant outpouring of new Garrison scholarship soon followed in the 1960s. Walter M. Merrill published *Against the Wind and Tide: A Biography of William Lloyd Garrison* (1963) and in it he adopts a Freudian analytical approach that allows him to understand the psyche of Garrison as a young "rebellious son."[85] John L. Thomas's *The Liberator: William Lloyd Garrison, A Biography* (1963) appeared that same year and heavily focuses on Garrison's work with *The Liberator* as the beginning of American abolitionist efforts.[86] George M. Frederickson's *William Lloyd Garrison* (1968) similarly emphasizes Garrison and Massachusetts abolitionism as the epicenter of 19th century American reform efforts.[87]

Understanding this textual genealogy is important because present day scholarly efforts continue to explicitly and implicitly historicize American abolitionism around the symbol and work of William Garrison. Lawrence J. Friendman's *Gregarious Saints: Self and Community in American Abolitionism, 1830–1870* (1982) principally examines American abolitionism through a detailed study of Garrison and his "Boston Clique."[88] James Brewster Stewart's *William Lloyd Garrison and the Challenge of Emancipation* (1992) demonstrates Garrison's public leadership of the abolitionist movement while also departing from other scholars by asserting that his prominent anti-slavery work often overshadows his important role in other reform movements like women's rights.[89] Henry Mayer's recent *All on Fire: William Lloyd Garrison and the Abolition of Slavery* (1998), which was a popular finalist for the National Book Award, examines Garrison's childhood and home life in an attempt to explain his subject's selfless character.[90] Mayer begins his book with a concisely distilled thesis that bears a startling rhetorical resemblance to the major biographies and nostalgic newspaper profiles produced in the late 19th century. Mayer writes: *"All on Fire* is a book about an agitator, and its argument can be simply stated. William Lloyd Garrison (1805–1879) is an authentic American hero who, with a Biblical prophet's power and a propagandist's skill, forced the nation to confront the most crucial moral issue its history."[91]

Other works on the history of American abolitionism, like Louis Filler's *The Crusade Against Slavery, 1830–1860* (1960) and Aileen S. Kraditor's *Means and Ends in American Abolitionism: Garrison and his Critics on Strategy and Tactics* (1967), reinforce the centrality of the Garrison narrative by producing a time line of the historical anti-slavery movement that begins with the 1831 publication of *The Liberator*.[92] Even Richard S. Newman's justly heralded *The Transformation of American Abolitionism: Fighting Slavery in the Early Republic* (2002) participates in this tradition even as it complicates it by offering significant insight into the tangled religious and economic factors that made 1831 a pivotal moment of reinvention or "transformation" for American anti-slavery activists.[93] Newman begins with the year 1831 as a point of investigation because "in both the popular imagination and in many scholarly accounts, Garrison's debut remains *the* benchmark of abolitionism."[94] As Newman directly concedes and as other works inadvertently argue, modern popular and scholarly treatments of this movement most frequently link its origins to William Garrison. In this model, remembering abolitionism is intrinsically linked to remembering the work of Garrison and to bestowing upon Massachusetts culture a privileged place in the evolution of American democratic principles of equality.

A smaller number of scholarly histories challenge the "Garrison narrative" of American abolitionism by asserting the active role of African Americans and other non-white reformers in the historical efforts to eradicate slavery.[95] Benjamin Quarles' *Black Abolitionists* (1969) is the most important work to date that addresses the myriad of ideological problems with American abolitionist histories that view the movement as a predominantly white, Massachusetts, and Garrisonian phenomenon. However, Quarles' book does express a belief common to abolitionist histories of his and our current era: that antebellum abolitionist activism should be remembered as a noble narrative of struggle that was punctuated by short bursts of progress that were achieved despite obstacles presented by both northern and southern peoples. He opens with prefatory comments that stress slavery as one of the "distinctive themes of the American Experience" and like other antislavery narratives he characterizes abolitionists as a "dramatic expression" of noble American ideals of freedom.[96] But Quarles seeks to move beyond merely stressing black participation and instead presents an argument about why the figure of the black abolitionist should be remembered as a "symbol of the struggle" for emancipation.[97] He explains that this idea never fully developed in the north or the south because the process of imagining black abolitionists would require both northern and southern audiences to discard their shared racial conceptions of black passivity and acquiescence to slavery.

For Quarles, the celebration of Garrison to the exclusion of black abolitionists from the broader national antislavery narrative becomes a way that white northern audiences participate in the trafficking of "southern ideas."[98] Quarles also goes to great lengths to discuss the objections of some black abolitionists to Garrison's religious beliefs and especially to the tenuous boundaries between Garrison's public theology and activism that implicitly encouraged his supporters to place him in an exalted position. The author quotes one black abolitionist's remarks that he (and other black abolitionists) would support Garrison on the issue of abolition, "but on religious points we follow Jesus."[99]

While books and articles on Garrison are numerous, they are, as these titles suggest, typically concerned with one of two projects: reinforcing narratives of Garrison's sacrifices, his capacity to empathize with slave pain, and his formal (or informal) leadership of the abolitionist movement *or* they devalue Garrison's historical and cultural role in favor of relocating the regional center of the movement and recasting its leadership. Absent in both scenarios is a serious effort to historicize the origins and evolutions of popular and scholarly narratives of American abolitionism that perpetuate the historical memory of Garrison as a representative symbol of American sacrifice and righteous suffering.

My desire to highlight the origins of the links between Garrison and discourses of suffering and to trace the circulation of the "suffering abolitionist" literary trope emerges from an interest in what Stephen Greenblatt describes as "the circulation of social energy."[100] Greenblatt's conception of "social energy" encourages scholars to view textual creation and historical-cultural influences as a *reciprocal* process.[101] This analytical approach allows one to see traces of texts in works that might otherwise appear unrelated. A major part of this book similarly involves revealing how ideas about Garrison and his relationship to American abolitionism have been translated, adapted, and re-shaped across a variety of temporal and generic boundaries. I believe that the scope of Garrison's influence on histories and representations of American abolitionism can only be appreciated by studying both explicit sites of transmission and traces of this story in other texts. The irresistible and popular portrait of Garrison as the messiah of American abolitionism did not always exist and it required a considerable effort on the part of many disparate people to transmit and maintain it.

The perpetuation of Garrison narratives has not only informed the vocabulary of past representations of abolitionists in works of popular culture but, as I just demonstrated, these stories continue to shape the way historians of the present imagine Garrison. In some cases, the traces of past Garrison narratives are explicit. For instance, Robert Abzug's *Cosmos Crumbling: American Reform and the Religious Imagination* discusses the "radical religious calling of William Garrison," but the principle source of his stories and his understanding of Garrison's religious views derive from a lengthy multi-volume biography that Garrison's sons Frank and Wendell wrote in 1885 titled, *William Lloyd Garrison, 1805–1879: The Story of His Life Told by His Children*.[102] The author disproportionately relies on this text to approach Garrison.[103] Frank and Wendell's book appeared during the Garrison commemoration and was part of a concerted effort to resuscitate and preserve their father's memory and to celebrate his sacrifices. In this context, Azbug's ideas about Garrison are linked to earlier stories, which exist as revisions or traces of Garrison's original self-narration. This book provides a framework by which to historicize the popular and scholarly arena of Garrisonian literature by excavating the emergence and transformation of past ideas, expressions, and representations of Garrison and his relationship to American abolitionism.

Garrison's story matters because it is the dominant regional and national narrative that Americans have continuously retold to understand the singularly most important era of our country's history. After the Civil War, Americans from different regions produced stories, poems, novels, festivals, monuments, histories, and rituals that encouraged them to participate in collective commemorative efforts that promoted specific visions of the past and the present. Accordingly, Garrison's story must be understood within such a specific regional context. In the post-bellum years Garrison's story inspired fiction, poetry, historical biographies, monuments, school textbooks, and public festivals that stressed his personal suffering and the heroic efforts of Massachusetts abolitionists as the catalyst for the national eradication of slavery. Garrison's individual identity and Massachusetts's regional identity depended upon how Americans would remember and write about their past. Former Garrisonians, historians, politicians, intellectuals, and novelists reacted by composing narratives of Garrison's life that stressed his difficult sacrifices and used them to argue that Massachusetts played a pivotal role in the survival of the union. The memory of the sharp disagreements that characterized the contentious religious and political debates between Garrison and other Massachusetts abolitionists slowly transformed into a more general celebration of Garrison and a national association between him and abolitionism.

This emancipationist narrative placed the abolition of slavery as a central event in the nation's past and it followed that New England's reform efforts would, therefore, assume a fundamental level of importance in the Union's victorious interpretation of the war. By highlighting New England's moral leadership on the issue of slavery the region claimed Garrison's vivid 1830 observation that, despite its problems, Massachusetts stood as "a paradise of our fallen world."[104] This popular image animates the language that leading white and black intellectuals like W.E.B. Dubois would later use to fondly remember the region's influence on advancements in racial justice.[105] DuBois lamented the obstacles to black voting rights, he decried the racism of the handling of the Sacco and Vanzetti case, and he decried the state of the Boston school system.[106] Nevertheless, he looked to reformers like William Garrison as an example of why Massachusetts, despite its faults, remained the "glory and hope of America."[107]

The popular tendency to commemorate William Lloyd Garrison is also, however, a part of a national story of America's historical efforts to acknowledge the evils of slavery and to atone for past wrongs. By repeatedly invoking the image of the suffering Garrison and by mapping this heroic language onto more general representations of American abolitionists emancipation becomes the seminal moment in our nation's past. In this view, the focus on Garrison seems to represent a progressive move forward. It appears to stand in sharp contrast to romantic stories of the Old South that depict the benign nature of plantation life and it also diverges from the fraternal military narratives that emphasize common valor to such an extent that slavery is displaced as a general evil and as a cause of the war.[108]

Yet, as this book shows, efforts to commemorate Garrison and the work of New England abolitionists do not necessarily lead to a fuller understanding of the horrors of slavery, especially when the spectacle of slave violence is most vividly rendered and understood through the mystical sacrifices and reports of the abolitionist witness. As Walter Johnson effectively argues in *Soul by Soul: Life Inside the Antebellum*

*Slave Market,* the transformation of the antislavery movement from a regional into a national debate occurred through abolitionist efforts to expose the horrors of the slave market.[109] That nationalization, however, was only made possible through the vivid and violent accounts of the spectacle of slavery that were offered by abolitionists like Garrison who simultaneously stressed the spiritual or physical harm that they endured by witnessing such events.

Garrison's religious beliefs led him to frame his own internal pain and anguish through a language of suffering that placed himself as a moral reference for his reading audience and ascribed redemptive possibilities, for both the nation and for the slave, to the abolitionist's willingness to endure and witness persecution. The popular transmission of this narrative forces us to consider the extent to which remembering Garrison is related to a tendency to contain the horrors of slavery and the movement towards emancipation within the abolitionist's subjectivity. Here it is instructive to pose the question that Sadiya Hartman raises in *Scenes of Subjection: Terror and Self-Making in Nineteenth Century America:* "can the white witness of the spectacle of suffering affirm the materiality of black sentience only by feeling himself?"[110] Hartman here is pointing to the trouble with antislavery rhetorical appeals that feature a white "proxy" who empathizes with slave pain and who facilitates a transformation in his or her audience.

This book is informed by Hartman's understanding of empathy as a violent response that threatens to obliterate the presence of the slave. The "other's pain," in this scenario, "is acknowledged to the degree that it can be imagined, yet by virtue of this substitution the object of identification threatens to disappear … for in making the other's suffering one's own, this suffering is occluded by the other's obliteration."[111] As a literary moral reference in his *Liberator* articles, as a historical figure with religious beliefs that advocated the redemptive work of abolitionist pain, and as a symbolic presence who inspired the image of the "suffering abolitionist" in popular, scholarly, and educational memoirs, Garrison's narrative becomes so pervasive that the war becomes his story and the nation's history, while abolitionist pain, and not slave suffering, becomes the emancipationist history of the war. The repetition of this narrative in post-bellum Massachusetts celebrated the region's righteous role in ending slavery and as Garrison's story became a nationally representative story of American abolitionism the symbolic blood and sacrifices of abolitionists became a way for the Union to atone for its past moral transgressions with slavery.

The first chapter, "The Construction and Evolution of Garrisonian Narratives of Abolitionist Sacrifice in Antebellum America, 1834–1857," examines the role of sacrifice and suffering in Garrison's religious beliefs and in his antebellum anti-slavery appeals. By looking at extensive personal correspondence, pamphlets, and newspaper articles I excavate the origins of Garrison's violent and controversial antislavery theology and demonstrate the way these beliefs led him to emphasize abolitionist witnessing, persecution, and spiritual torment as key components of his antislavery appeals in the pages of *The Liberator*. Since the late 19th century historians have either attributed to Garrison's activism a more generalized religious sentiment, neglected its theological complexities, or ignored it altogether.[112] His religious beliefs have become almost pat and no study has provided an in-depth consideration of the divisive turmoil that his theological emphasis on abolitionist suffering sparked. This chapter analyzes Garrison's investment in discourses of suffering and their relationship to how he publicly and privately narrates his own life and the history of his reform efforts. Such a focus provides an appropriate and needed context to appreciate the late 19th century popular culture reinvention that turns him into a representative symbol of Massachusetts antebellum reform and, within the broader American collective memory, into a symbol of the type of patriotic values and sacrifices that preserved the Union.

The second chapter, "Commemorating Garrison: Origins of the Garrison Revival in Post-Bellum American Memory, 1867–1910," examines the social, political, and cultural forces that converged to produce what I describe as a late 19th century "culture of commemoration" that transformed William Lloyd Garrison from a controversial fringe religious figure into an ideal patriotic symbol of Massachusetts and the reunited nation. This broad cultural transformation was initially aided through the tireless efforts of former Garrisonians like Samuel May who, as early as 1867, begin the work of writing formal histories of abolitionism in an attempt to defend the nobility of Garrisonian work and to preserve their historical role in the increasingly diverse national marketplace of post–Civil War narratives. These early accounts represented Garrison as the leader of an organized and cohesive abolitionist movement. Newspapers, novels, and other popular mediums in New England widely disseminated this story but they also tempered the fervent Christian theology of suffering that historically underscored Garrison's efforts and set him apart (both literally and rhetorically) from his contemporaries. Instead, this chapter traces the birth of a more general understanding of suffering that became the basis by which Massachusetts and New England audiences were encouraged to emphasize their historical triumph and exceptional sacrifice. Within this period, Garrison's story becomes the region's story of their participation in the great events of the Civil War.

The third chapter, "'For Future Generations': Garrison's Children, Massachusetts Educational Reform and the Institutionalization of the Garrison Narrative in Boston Schools, 1880–1922," explores the emergence and implementation of the Garrison narrative within the standardized curriculum of Boston schools in turn-of-the-century Massachusetts. This chapter is especially interested in the work of Garrison's children in the late 19th and early 20th century to narrate the history of their father's activism through formally published histories and through their participation in official Boston city committees that, amidst the wider northern celebration of Garrison, were charged with the task of finding a way for the city to commemorate their father's antislavery work. These efforts, I show, intersected with educational reform discourses and transformed stories of Garrison's suffering and sacrifices into "official" history and, in doing so, they aided in the production of a coherent narrative of the state's historical relationship to antislavery activism and, culturally, used Garrison as a vehicle by which to imagine a stable Massachusetts identity. The previous chapters largely focus on Garrison's commemoration within the popular culture, but this one demonstrates that efforts to transmit his story of exemplary abolitionist witnessing and suffering also took place at the institutional level.

Finally, the fourth chapter continues the engagement with the effects of the Garrison revival by examining how this widespread literary emphasis on abolitionist suffering appeared in late 19th and 20th century fiction. The fourth chapter is titled, "Ross Lockridge's *Raintree County*: American Abolitionism as Epic Origin Narrative" and it looks to the way Lockridge's 1948 novel *Raintree County* places the American abolitionist and his personal suffering (and desire) at the heart of a mythological national rebirth. As the major epic abolitionist novel of the 20th century Lockridge's text provides an ideal example of the way abolitionist narratives become part of a new national mythology. At the time of its original publication, Lockridge's novel provided a counter-narrative to the southern Lost Cause histories of the Civil War that experienced a surge in popularity during the first part of the 20th century. Works of literature like Allen Tate's *Stonewall Jackson: The Good*

*Soldier* (1928), Robert Penn Warren's *John Brown: The Making of a Martyr* (1929), F. Scott Fitzgerald's "The Night at Chancellorville" (1935) and "The End of Hate" (1940), and Margaret Mitchell's *Gone with the Wind* (1936) either romanticized the agrarian south and the plight of the confederate soldier, or, in the case of Warren's book, specifically dissented with the northern celebration of abolitionist "martyrs."[113] However, in the years following World War II the publication of abolitionist-centered fiction experienced its biggest boom since the late 19th century.

Novels like *Raintree County* framed the abolitionist's selfless spiritual and physical sacrifice for African slaves and for Union ideals as part of the patriotic legacy of all Americans. These stories proved to be enormously popular during a period in which the United States found itself in a new position of worldwide moral leadership and as contemporary audiences framed this new war within a broader genealogy of American sacrifice. The close readings of Lockridge's novel in this chapter demonstrates the extent to which the Garrison revival informed how future novelists imagined the nature and scope of abolitionist activism. The Garrison revival of the late 19th century aided in the production of distinct historical narratives of the abolitionist's suffering and its role in the eradication of slavery. By the mid–20th century, traces of these narrative conventions are found in the popular tropes that authors like Lockridge utilize to tell a national story of sacrifice. In doing so, the abolitionist becomes the central part of a new American mythological and sentimental narrative of progress.

Stories of William Garrison's redemptive suffering and the later efforts of politicians, reformers, artists, educators, and scholars to invoke and circulate this narrative to generations born after the Thirteenth Amendment offer a powerful and emotionally charged memory of selfless, progressive, abolitionist sacrifice as an enduring legacy of the Civil War. This narrative created a public sensation that inspired (and continues to inspire) reactions in prose, poetry, and public commemorations. William Garrison and Garrisonian-inspired antislavery rhetoric explicitly and implicitly inform our major understandings and representations of abolitionist protest of this era. This book creates a narrative history that brings Garrison's antislavery theology forward while also revealing the ways that these beliefs were later transformed, re-circulated, and invoked within popular and educational narratives of the war. There is no question that the history of the abolitionist movement is an essential part of New England history and U.S. history.

Since 1867 William Garrison has been the symbol of American abolitionism for popular audiences and the historical starting point of antislavery efforts for 19th century scholars. By examining the historical and the mythological Garrison this book examines the possibilities, limitations, and legacies of this rendering of American abolitionism.

# 1

# The Construction and Evolution of Garrisonian Narratives of Abolitionist Sacrifice in Antebellum America, 1834–1857

Between 1834 and 1857 William Garrison constructed a language of Christian suffering and abolitionist sacrifice as a rhetorical challenge to the institution of slavery. In doing so, he broke away from contemporary New England reformers and from British abolitionists who considered the eradication of slavery to be a political debate that should be approached through a language of Union and republicanism.[1] Even William Wilberforce, the famed British parliament member and Christian reformer was not exempt from Garrison's criticism. While Garrison admired Wilberforce's work on the construction of what would become the Slavery Abolition Act of 1833 he nevertheless felt that legislative reforms inevitably failed to address the sinful nature at the heart of slaveholding's moral corruption.[2] Garrison's presence at Wilberforce's July 26, 1833, funeral in Westminster Abbey is an image that retrospectively contrasts the differences between the implicitly Christian but largely secular rhetorical appeals of the most famous British abolitionist and the violent anti-slavery theology that comes to dominate the language of the man who, in the late 19th and early 20th century, becomes *the* symbol of American anti-slavery discourses.[3]

When Garrison returned from his trip to England in 1833 he arrived in New York with a renewed sense of purpose and leadership, giving countless anti-slavery lectures in churches, and providing organizational aid and encouragement to local New York anti-slavery groups.[4] His activist work during the mid–1830s, however, coincided with a widespread outbreak of violence directed towards abolitionists throughout New England and other northeastern states. It is within this environment that Garrison crafted an antislavery appeal that drew on a language, imagery, and history of Christian suffering as a way to rhetorically express, reclaim, and to transform slave and abolitionist pain into sacred acts of martyrdom with spiritual significance.

Public controversies over the *The Liberator's* appeals for immediate slave emancipation brought Garrison widespread fame in the early 1830s and also made him a prominent target of northern abolitionist and southern slaveholder animosity. This new recognition led to public acts of symbolic violence against his namesake: in 1835 mobs burned a mannequin that bore his likeness in the streets of Charleston, South Carolina.[5] Later that same year in Boston, on September 10, 1835, anti-Garrison mobs placed a gallows with his name engraved on it outside of his rented home.[6] Acts of symbolic violence and protest quickly transformed into real physical violence: on October 21, 1835, Garrison counted himself fortunate to receive only minor injuries as he narrowly escaped a violent group of protestors outside a meeting of the Boston Female Anti-slavery Society.[7] Garrison appeared at the meeting as a last-minute replacement for the night's guest speaker: the famed abolitionist George Thompson. The transference of violent physical aggression from Thompson to Garrison is consistent with the latter's growing prominence as the most controversial religious radical in the New England anti-slavery movement.

This chapter draws on Garrison's private correspondence, his public editorials, and his anti-slavery appeals in *The Liberator* in order to examine the real violence, the potential violence, and the perceived violence directed at William Garrison and Garrisonian abolitionists between 1834 and 1857. It explores how Garrison's fantasies of abolitionist suffering and the desire to experience righteous persecution informed the construction of a new antislavery theology, which placed a primacy on abolitionist witnessing, persecution, and spiritual torment in the pages of *The Liberator*. It shows that these Christian martyr narratives realigned the relationship between the Garrisonian abolitionist and the subjugated slave by linking the abolitionist desire for physical and spiritual suffering with the political emancipation and the spiritual salvation of slaves in the American south. By fully exploring Garrison's anti-slavery theology this chapter diverges from the dominant assumptions of past scholarship that either dilutes Garrison's religious beliefs, like James Brewster Stewart's *William Lloyd Garrison and the Challenge of Emancipation* (1992) or clumsily attributes them to part of a general mainline New England Protestant reform tradition, like Russel B. Nye's *William Lloyd Garrison and the Humanitarian Reformers* (1955) or ignores them altogether, as in *Walter M Merrill's Against the Wind and Tide: A Biography of William Lloyd Garrison* (1963).[8] The staggering scope of the popular post-bellum Garrison revival in New England can only be appreciated by first understanding the enormous theological and rhetorical distance between Garrison and his Massachusetts contemporaries.

Early public traces of Garrison's martyr narratives occur within a historical context of political animosity between northern anti-slavery organizations and southern congressional leaders. Beginning in the early 1830s a broad coalition of anti-slavery societies collected signatures for congressional petitions that called for the immediate abolition of slavery. William Lloyd Garrison remained skeptical of this strategy because of its long record of failing to produce significant results with other religious groups. His letters during this year repeatedly cite the Quaker's historic use of petitions as an indicator of their ineffectiveness.[9] Pennsylvania Quakers used this tactic throughout the 1790s as a way to peacefully protest the American slave trade and to advocate the gradual emancipation of all slaves.[10] Late 18th century Quaker petitions rarely attracted the attention of congressional leaders who typically received them "without comment" and then passed them on to a committee for review, where they were died from lack of action.[11]

During the 1830s anti-slavery organizations sent petitions to Congress that aggressively demanded a direct legislative response. The congressional inaction that greeted these new petitioners produced a more vocal outrage than the genial Friends 1790 petitions.[12] By 1833, Southern congressmen viewed anti-slavery pamphlet and petition campaigns as an area of increasing discomfort. The infamous "gag rule" of 1836 represents the climax of southern congressional efforts to restrain vocal anti-slavery appeals and to quell the possibility of legal emancipation for southern slaves. Henry L. Pickney, a southern congressman from South Carolina, successfully ushered through this bill which recommended that, "all petitions, memorials, resolutions, propositions, or papers relating in any way or to any extent whatever to the subject of slavery or the abolition of slavery shall, without being printed or referred, be laid upon the table, and that no further action whatever be taken thereon."[13] Northern anti-slavery newspapers reacted angrily with editorials that strongly condemned and critiqued the language of Pickney's provision, characterizing it as a startling threat to American civil liberties. *The Emancipator* voiced the sentiments of many anti-slavery publications when it called for a strong public backlash (and more petitions) to address the misuse of congressional power: "if congress can bury 10,000 names this year, let them have 20,000 next year, and 40,000 the next, and so on till at length some member is obliged, at least, to pronounce a decent funeral oration."[14]

In 1835 William Garrison was less interested in whether congress had overstepped its boundaries of authority (he believed, of course, that it had) than he was in a growing trend of northern violence towards anti-slavery advocates.[15] Southern success in congress led opponents of the anti-slavery movement to regard abolitionists as a dangerous threat to national security, to law-abiding citizens, and to social order. Groups of "concerned citizens" organized in the north and the south between 1834 and the summer of 1835 to suppress the influence of Garrisonian abolitionists. Business owners, bankers, lawyers, and men from other respected professions joined groups that protested the perceived public agitation that Garrison and his growing anti-slavery network caused throughout the region. These nameless grassroots groups lacked a coherent organizational structure, but remained united by a shared rhetorical interest in situating their crusade against abolitionists within a historic lineage of patriotic protest groups like The Sons of Liberty and the Minutemen.[16] One anti-abolitionist mob in Philadelphia even re-enacted the Boston Tea Party.[17] After stealing a significant number of abolitionist pamphlets and petitions, they dragged bags of them into the Delaware River, and then dumped them overboard.[18] Such symbolic populist dramatizations gained support from some members of the Northern press who viewed "patriotic protest" as a necessary counter-balance to the more extreme elements of the abolitionist movement that William Garrison embodied. The *New York Courier* and *Enquirer* offered support for symbolic gestures of dissent against abolitionists, while also preemptively rationalizing a justification for any real violence that might be directed against abolitionists in the future: "if they [abolitionists like Garrison are mentioned] openly and publicly promulgate doctrines which outrage public feeling, they have no right to demand protection from the people they insult."[19]

The northern press' dissemination of legal and philosophical justifications for mob violence against abolitionists coincided with an increase in real violence against anti-slavery groups between 1834 and

1837. William Garrison spent much of 1835 traveling through New York delivering sermons and lectures at the moment when New York became an epicenter of northern anti-abolitionist aggression, making him a frequent observer and sometimes victim of this trend. Throughout the summer of 1835 New York mobs destroyed the homes of abolitionists, burned down free black schools, and defaced local businesses that supported anti-slavery work.[20] These rampant displays of violence led Lydia Maria Child to write, "I have not ventured into the city ... so great is the excitement here ... 'tis like the times of the French Revolution, when no man dared to trust his neighbors."[21]

The public escalation of violence towards abolitionists parallels William Garrison's early rhetorical struggles to understand and to frame this violence within a broader narrative of Christian persecution and exemplary Christian suffering. An example of Garrison's early efforts to forge a new anti-slavery language is *The Liberator*'s public response to northern violence and the new perceived threat against Garrisonian abolitionist. Garrison responded by printing the first part of John Bunyan's famous Christian story, *Pilgrim's Progress* on the front page of the November 8, 1834, edition of his newspaper.[22] The first part of Bunyan's allegorical tale follows the characters Christian and Faithful on their journey to the Celestial City. They are pilgrims fleeing the worldly vices and the temptations of Vanity Fair in a search for God's "greater truth."[23] Their journey results in the physical abuse from atheists who are opposed to their quest and who ultimately jail Christian and execute Faithful for disturbing societal peace.

Garrison found much contemporary significance within Bunyun's older story, viewing it as a metaphorical rendering of "the case of the modern abolitionist in this country."[24] Garrison's response underlines his growing awareness and interest in the role of pain and violence within the Christian abolitionist narrative of redemption. As violence escalated in New England and New York, Garrison's theology placed an increasing degree of primacy on the abolitionist willingness to endure pain and suffering as a test from God. Like the pilgrims in Bunyun's tale the willingness to suffer separated true Christian abolitionists from heretical ones, demanding great sacrifices but promising even greater spiritual rewards. The same year that Garrison published Bunyan's *Pilgrim's Progress* on the front page of *The Liberator*, he also started an editorial column titled "Refuge of Oppression" that explicitly linked Garrisonian abolitionists to martyred figures within the early history of the Christian church.[25]

John Foxe's *Book of Martyrs* strongly influenced Garrison's understanding of the Christian martyr tradition and in letters to friends and associates he expressed admiration for the strength and steadfast faith that earlier Christians endured. Foxe's 16th century text contained accounts of religious persecution and stories of hundreds of English Protestants who were tortured and killed for their religious beliefs under the reign of Mary I between 1553–1558. John King's recent study of the relationship between the *Book of Martyrs* and the development of early modem print culture explains that Foxe's book was the most popular bestseller of its time and that by 1684 the eighth edition of the book still outsold most of its contemporaries.[26] He vividly describes the book's popularity by pointing out that it was more widely read and owned than the English Bible and the Book of Common Prayer.[27] Copies of the book were made available to all English citizens in public spaces so that those who could not afford to purchase a copy could still read it:

> Revered by Protestants as a "holy" book, it was frequently chained alongside the Bible for reading by ordinary people at many public places including cathedrals, churches, schools, libraries, guildhalls, and at least one inn.[28]

When English settlers arrived in Massachusetts in 1620 they continued this tradition by bringing this book with them and making it the most widely owned book in colonial New England.[29] Garrison grew up with this book and with a familiarity with its stories of the historical experiences of earlier Christians and he would draw upon the book's metanarratives of suffering and sacrifice as a way to frame his religious identity and antislavery work.

At this point, Garrison's own religious beliefs did not exclude the possibility of cultivating alliances with orthodox protestant denominations when such relationships were possible, but his calls for immediate emancipation often provoked hostile reactions from organized clergy that precluded such an arrangement. For instance, in June of 1834, the organization of New England Methodist Ministers formed an anti-slavery society and solicited Garrison's advice and support.[30] This invitation, which was extended by the group's leadership without consulting its member ministers, was met with outcry and protest from the decidedly anti–Garrisonian contingent from the New Hampshire association and was quickly rescinded.[31] In response, Garrison sent copies of *The Liberator* to every member of the New Hampshire organization, free of charge, for six months.[32] In the weeks that followed

Garrison used his paper to lambaste New England denominational structures of authority and blamed them for creating an atmosphere that proved to be remarkably conducive to pro-slavery sentiments.[33] This incident is representative of the growing popular consensus throughout 1835 that following Garrison threatened to bring individuals into conflict with traditional religious authorities. Garrison's steadfast confidence in the divine sanction of his antislavery work caused him to view the contemporary church as a source of persecution to be endured by himself and his followers. Such a belief placed his work and the hostility from traditional churches that greeted his efforts within a longer Christian narrative of righteous persecution.

The Christian martyr tradition and narrative form that Garrison looked to is rooted in the conviction that righteous, voluntary, persecution, suffering, and sacrifice has the ability to atone for the sins of others–it is a process of worldly sanctification with salvistic implications for the martyr. The martyr narrative traces back to the Bible and Jesus Christ's sacrificial example, but it became a central part of Christian identity during the early years of the church when writers like Tertullian and Origen stressed the importance of Christ's "voluntary" relinquishment of his deity in order to experience human pain and death.[34] These writings informed how early Christians read the Gospels, related to God, and understood the role of their persecution and suffering in the larger drama of salvation. The thematic focus in these stories is the regenerative and redemptive "work" of Christian persecution and pain. This is a genre that begins with Jesus Christ's narrative. James Tabor writes that early Christian martyrs transformed Christ's earthly suffering and death from proof of the failure of his mission into a moment of ultimate triumph over earthly mortality, persecution, and authority:

> [without the Resurrection] ... his death was a tragic failure. By the time we reach the Gospel accounts, written a generation or more after Jesus' death, a transformation has occurred. Jesus' death was not a mistake; his was not the execution of a failed apocalyptic prophet. On the contrary, it was precisely for this reason that Jesus came: to redeem the world from sin through his sacrificial death.[35]

The success of this narrative led early Christians to embrace suffering as a marker that distinguished them from the world and which allowed them to mirror Jesus Christ's narrative of victory. Ignatius of Antioch, an early Christian martyr who Garrison occasionally expresses admiration for in his personal correspondence, went so far as to suggest that meeting Christ through martyrdom was the Christian ideal-the epitome of the "noble death."[36] This idea suggests, "behind every act of martyrdom lay the self-sacrifice of Jesus himself."[37] In other words, the repetition and re-enactment of Christ's original narrative of suffering is a way in which one is brought closer to Christ-making one "Christ-like"-what early Christians described as "acquiring Christ."[38] Such a narrative places the martyr's suffering, whether in antiquity or in more contemporary history, within a lineage that exalts and glorifies self-sacrifice and understands such work to have a personal and public redemptive quality.

By invoking martyr images, languages, and narratives Garrison would map his understanding of the Christian past onto the debates over abolitionism taking place throughout Massachusetts. He created, in other words, a usable Christian past for his own contemporary Christian anti-slavery theology. Garrison constructed his Christian message through the model of texts like Foxe's *Book of Martyrs* and by remembering the legacy of the Christians in these stories he established a bond between the past and the present that emphasized the continuity between earlier traditions of Christian suffering and his own. To put it in terms that are concise but probably too simple: Garrison and his followers would construct their identities partly through the memory of past Christian suffering. Here it is instructive to remember Maurice Halbwach's observation in *The Social Frameworks of Memory* that Christianity offers the most complex example of collective memory because it claims to be both historical and eternal and timeless.[39] As Garrison would begin to look back to historical models of Christian sacrifice he would frame his movement as a "primitive" link to the past while simultaneously claiming that, unlike the more dominant organized forms of Christianity in New England, his beliefs were tied to a conception of an "eternal" and immutable church that was not influenced by the cultural and political debates of the time.[40] Yet, martyrdom and martyr discourses necessarily require an audience. In order for suffering to be seen as redemptive it must be narrated or interpreted for an audience whose assent and consumption gives it meaning. Garrison's immediate audiences (his family, friends and public lecture crowds) and his reading audience for *The Liberator*, therefore, participated in this process by witnessing and consuming the violent fantasies, ideals, and experiences that placed him and his followers in opposition to the dominant political, cultural, and religious norms of New England.

Garrison's desire to transform abolitionist suffering from a shameful display of lawlessness into a personal sacrifice with divine consequences is present in lesser degrees in his correspondence and public self-fashioning of the early 1830s, but fails to publicly solidify until 1834. As late as December 14, 1833, Garrison occasionally makes public appeals that intertwine the principles of the Declaration of Independence with "the truths of divine revelation."[41] In his "Declaration of the National Anti-Slavery Convention," he argues that all people, secular and religious, have an ethical responsibility to rid the country of slavery because such action is "prescribed in the Constitution of the United States."[42] There is an oscillation here between the religious appeal and the more broadly legal and humanistic political appeal that is missing from his later rhetoric. He claims that abolitionists are fighting for principles like "Justice, Liberty, and Humanity," but he also emphasizes that in order to achieve this goal abolitionists must be prepared to "perish ultimately as martyrs in this great, benevolent and holy cause."[43] As he struggled, however, to understand the symbolic and literal escalation of threats against his life, his religious beliefs, and his friends in New England between 1831 and 1834 he begins to see abolitionist suffering as a conduit that God might use in order to achieve the spiritual and political emancipation of American slaves.

Garrison's decision to print the first part of Bunyan's *Pilgrim's Progress* on the front page of *The Liberator* highlights the connections he makes around 1834 between witnessing, confrontation, and martyrdom. In Bunyan's tale, Faithful and Christian so anger authorities that they are pursued, vilified, beaten, arrested and finally executed. Bunyan's narrative makes Faithful's confrontation with "worldly" men and violent martyrdom a necessary part of his pilgrimage. This story dramatically and allegorically distills a tradition of Christian suffering—"suffering for Truth's sake"—that for Bunyan and other 17th century Christians was at the heart of protestant Christianity.[44] Bunyan imagined the Christian struggle, much like Garrison, as a contest between true and false churches. Bunyan's tale suggests that God appoints those who will suffer (the "saved" or the "faithful"), when and how they will be persecuted, and argues that embracing this suffering brings the believer closer to a Christ-like purity. This is violence as a form of sacred sanctification. Noted Bunyan scholar Richard Greaves argues that for Bunyan, "suffering is discipline imposed by God, and a means to spiritual growth."[45] In *Pilgrim's Progress* and other Bunyan texts, suffering is "inevitable for the godly" and each Christian should, "seek to understand its purpose."[46]

Garrison experienced tastes of injustice early in his anti-slavery evangelism during two separate brief imprisonments: for unauthorized preaching in the late 1820s and for libel in 1830.[47] His brush with the mob violence of 1835 led him to see true Christian faith as demanding the follower of Christ to act in ways that could not help but arouse hostility from the world. In a letter dated January 12, 1835, Garrison writes to his brother-in-law George Benson and grapples with the violent events taking place throughout Massachusetts and New York and attempts to clearly locate the role of Christian abolitionist suffering in this human drama. He begins by observing that "we [members of his anti-slavery group(s)] have had a share of the afflictions which are prevalent in our woe-stricken world; and happy will it be for us if we can learn to profit thereby, for time and eternity."[48] He describes his realization that sickness, pain, suffering, and death are "rough but useful admonishers."[49] And in a passage that is worth quoting at length he explains that he has come to view suffering as a condition that should not be lamented or avoided because such a wish stands in contrast to the Christian ideal of humble submission to Christ's divine design:

> When we write to those whom we love, we are too apt, perhaps, to hope that everything has gone smoothly with them; that they have had a cloudless sky, a bright sun, flowers without thorns in their path, and zephyrs playing around them; and that disease and adversity have not intruded upon their threshold ... [he then goes on to suggest that Christians should instead pray for "submission" and the strength to suffer with great humility] ... there is but one being in the universe, who sees the end from the beginning, and who can tell whether our friends need most to be chastised or prospered, to promote their eternal good.[50]

Garrison's private thoughts on suffering inform the way he crafts his new anti-slavery appeals that year. In this letter he acknowledges the importance that his thoughts on suffering will have in subsequent issues of his newspaper when he writes that, "I shall insert in the columns of *The Liberator* some of these extracts.[51] In the letter's conclusion Garrison links these reflections directly to his anti-slavery work, and abolitionist suffering to martyrdom: "we must bring back again the triumphant days of martyrdom. We must have a race of men who will be bold for God, and open-mouthed and trumpet-tongued for his truth, in the face of death."[52] What Garrison's private correspondence reveals is his new belief that true faith must prove itself through a willingness and even a desire to suffer, "unto blood," as Evangelist tells Christian and Faithful in *Pilgrim's Progress* about what to expect in

Vanity Fair, the corrupt and atheistic world in Bunyan's story. Faithful's martyrdom represents Garrison's ideal of heroic abolitionist suffering and foreshadows how he transforms this ideal into a literary form: the eye-witness pilgrimage that reports slave suffering and which uses this suffering to celebrate abolitionist spiritual and ethical valor.

Between January 1836 and the end of 1837 Garrison's correspondence explicitly links himself and his followers to a history of Christian persecution and suffering and claims their history as his own. In a January 17, 1836, letter to Samuel May, Garrison exhorts his friends at the Massachusetts Anti-Slavery Society to be "Bold for God."[53] This lengthy letter goes on to compare the abolitionist experience with persecution to that of Jews and Christians in Biblical texts like Exodus, Leviticus, 1 Samuel, Psalms, Matthew, Hebrews, Acts, and Revelation. Most striking is Garrison's correlation between himself and his followers and the twelve New Testament apostles who are given the task of preparing the world for Christ's second coming.[54] He even names William Jay, Arthur Tappan, Gerrit Smith, James Birney, Beriah Green, N.S.S. Berman, Isaac Knapp, Samuel May, Theodore Weld, and Angelina Grimke as worthy modem apostles who remain faithful in the tradition of older ones.[55] The inclusion of James Birney is particularly important because his conversion story, from slave owner to Garrisonian abolitionist by the 1830s, offered an important narrative testimony of the power and appeal of Garrison's message.[56]

The tone of Garrison's 1836 letter to May is urgent, with forceful appeals that they must "commence the work of converting the entire nation (so thoroughly has slavery corrupted it) beginning in Boston, as did the apostles in Jerusalem."[57] Here Garrison offers his belief that his anti-slavery work parallels that of the Biblical apostles, but he simultaneously expresses his understanding that this title must be earned through abolitionist blood and suffering, and that neither himself nor his followers had yet suffered enough to fully earn the title of "apostle."[58] As earlier mentioned, this martyr title is dependent on witnesses that attest to one's persecution and suffering. As a self-narrator, Garrison is particularly conscious during this period of the readership of his writings in *The Liberator* and by simultaneously stressing and rhetorically downplaying his own suffering he contributes to his own later memorialization. Later the next month, in a February 18, 1836, letter to Lewis Tappan, Garrison again laments the lack of "real" abolitionist suffering and voices his eager desire to experience the kind of suffering that would justly allow him to claim the title of "apostle" "without blushing."⁵⁹ Despite his public discussion in *The Liberator* about threats to his life, state ransoms, and near death brushes with violent mobs, he still viewed his "cross" to be "light, very light to bear ... which one of us has endured the hardships or run through the perils of the apostle Paul?⁶⁰ During these crucial years Garrison begins to associate persecution with righteousness and suffering with divine confirmation of the worthiness of the moral enterprise of the abolitionist cause. To "live a Christ-like life meant to suffer the same persecution as Christ, a process that ensured that an abolitionist's death at the hands of dissenters would, like Christ's own death, have redemptive ramifications for others: "we are always delivered unto death for Jesus' sake, that the life also of Jesus might be manifest in our mortal flesh."⁶¹

Openly seeking persecution was a radical religious belief even within the diverse Christian revivals of the 19th century religious marketplace. Garrison's Biblical readings led him to embrace physical suffering and to rhetorically perform the abolitionist's capacity to empathize with and experience spiritual pain through narratives of witnessing slave suffering in the pages of *The Liberator*. These stories allowed Garrison to use the paper as a medium by which to position himself and his followers as heirs of the early Church (i.e., the apostles) and, more importantly, to liken themselves with a martyr tradition and to martyr narratives that celebrated Christian persecution from "the world" and from the heretical Christian church.

Garrison's theology led him to see a strange kinship between the plight of the abolitionist and that of the slave. In an April 6, 1836, letter to James Birney he describes slaves as part of a "primitive" Christian tradition in need of leadership and action from other Christians who are in a better position to provide relief without violating Biblical directives.⁶² He writes that slave "infirmities, reproaches, and distresses" deeply trouble him and inspire him to action.⁶³ He "prays daily" that slaves will peacefully endure "the strange fiery trial" that they are currently undergoing and challenges them to "rejoice, inasmuch as ye are partakers in Christ's sufferings."⁶⁴ Garrison's language here is important and serves as an early indicator of his rhetorical tendency to dissolve the boundaries between real slave pain and abolitionist religious persecution by placing each within his narrative reading of Biblical suffering, which demands slave passivity and self-sacrificial abolitionist action. Suffering is privileged in both narratives as a conduit that draws slaves and abolitionists closer to Christ, but slave suffering remains meaningless and gratuitous without the redemptive suffering of abolitionists. Garrison views abolitionist suffering as essential, as part of Christ's work to "regenerate, and give rest to this troubled world."⁶⁵ Garrison describes the spiritual value of this suffering when he metaphorically characterizes it as providing "materials of holiness" that are "gathered to build up a spiritual house."⁶⁶ In this view, slave suffering is secondary to the cosmic significance of abolitionist pain, which occupies an ameliorator role in both redeeming slave suffering and regenerating the nation from the sinful blight of slavery.

Many prominent black abolitionist men like Nathaniel Paul and Charles Lenox Remond strongly objected to Garrison's religious views that emphasized abolitionist suffering and slave passivity in the effort to eradicate slavery. This sentiment is especially true of the tensions between Garrisonians and black male abolitionists between 1836 and 1841. For instance, Nathaniel Paul, the first pastor of the First African Baptist Church of Boston, devoted the final two years of his life to writing fiery letters to anti-slavery leaders throughout New England that described Garrison as "a religious infidel" whose beliefs threatened the spirit of their shared goal of emancipation.⁶⁷ Other black leaders, like Charles Lenox Remond, worried that the devotion that Garrison inspired amongst his followers had transformed what began as a Christian movement into something more nefarious: "I am of the Garrison party, but what was good, and noble, and Christian, and philanthropic, and antislavery in 1835, has become evil, mean, and heretical in 1841!"⁶⁸ For some black male abolitionists, Garrison's religious views, especially his calls for regenerative white suffering and black passivity, must have bore an uncomfortable resemblance to pro-slavery minstrel performative conventions that lampooned black men through feminized depictions. Black non-resistance seemed to encourage such stereotypes rather than dispel them. As black A.M.E. pastor Jabez Campbell would observe, "there was no account to defend oneself with Garrison."⁶⁹

The discomfort that some black male abolitionists voiced towards the paternalistic dimensions of Garrison's appeals were not shared by the majority of black women abolitionists, who remained a consistent bedrock of support for him during these same years. As early as 1832 Garrison wrote letters to female abolitionist groups and explicitly stated the importance of black women in his movement. In a March 5, 1832, letter to Sarah Douglass, the Secretary of the Female Literary Association in Philadelphia, he explained his belief that black women were essential to the success of his efforts: "my hopes for the elevation of your race are mainly centered upon you and others of your sex. You are committed, more than others, if not to the destinies of the present, certainly those of the rising generation."[70] He described the support of black women as "a new weapon into my hands to use against the southern oppressors."[71] Garrison's commitment to black women took many forms, from publishing the works of emerging writers or helping them to secure publishers to arguing the ecclesiastical equality between men and women. An example of the former is Garrison's association with Francis Harper, whom he helped to find a publisher for her collection, *Poems on Miscellaneous Subjects*, and even wrote the introduction for her first collection.[72]

Shirley J. Yee's *Black Women Abolitionists: A Study in Activism, 1828–1860* attributes the overwhelming support that Garrison received from black women to his grand and far-reaching vision of abolitionist work that assailed the government, the church, and other bedrock institutions for their complicity in the culture of slavery and gender inequality.[73] For these women, *how* Garrison made his argument was less important than the end result. Yee argues that Garrison's vision of societal change was so all encompassing that the alternatives offered by other contemporary white and black male abolitionists seemed "myopic" by comparison.[74] The support of black women abolitionists like Eunice Davis, Anna Logan, and Caroline F. Williams played an important role in eliminating some challenges from white women and black men that Garrison encountered. For instance, in 1839, on the eve of the infamous split within the American Anti-Slavery Society between Garrisonians and non-Garrisonians, a vocal group of black women worked together to remove Mary S. Parker, a critic of Garrison, and a prominent leader of the Female Anti-Slavery Society, from her leadership position when she sought to sever the society's financial support and public ties with Garrison. Yee recounts how seven black women were the first to register a protest to Parker's leadership and eventually found a way to remove her on procedural grounds.[75] Such instances of devout loyalty, however, in the minds of his detractors, further accentuated Garrison's ascension to a dangerous position of religious leadership and adoration.

Garrison's public and private ruminations on suffering and his strong religious language of martyrdom and apostolic lineage led readers of *The Liberator* to describe him in prophetic terms, as the leader of a new religious movement and sentiment. The January 16, 1836, edition of *The Liberator* features a poem titled "To William Garrison" that explicitly adopts and adheres to the language and narrative that Garrison crafts of himself and his followers as divinely inspired and distinct from other Christian anti-slavery abolitionists.[76] There is an explicit awareness of the power and the appeal of Garrison's narrative of Christianity and its role in the contemporary struggle against slavery. Reader appropriations of Garrison's language and his vision of the abolitionist anticipate the re-circulation of his ideal of exemplary anti-slavery protest in late 19th century eulogies by Wendell Phillips, Lucretia Newman, and Reverend William Yeocum; and in odes by Joseph Seaman Cotter in which Garrison's suffering is placed in the foreground of the history of American abolitionism.[77] It is clear from Garrison's correspondence and diaries that he enjoyed the complimentary remarks and narrative adherence that *Liberator* readers demonstrated in their letters, but he exercised strict editorial control of the paper's narratives of himself and his closest followers. He preferred that reader's depictions, no matter how flattering, be re-circulated and printed in the pages of other anti-slavery publications. In a January 26, 1836, letter to Henry Benson, he discusses the poem "To William Garrison" shortly after its publication in *The Liberator* and remarks that it is a "highly complimentary poem," but he wonders whether this poem and similar ones "might look very egotistical," before concluding that *The Liberator* should "be careful not to publish any more that may be communicated."[78] He advises Benson to instead forward similar reader submissions to either the *Emancipator* or the *Spectator* for publication.[79]

By 1837 friends, fellow New England abolitionists, clergy, and hostile southerners recognized William Garrison's particular anti-slavery theology as simply "Garrisonism."[80] The fact that Garrison's friends and detractors both comfortably used this vernacular label suggests the extent to which Garrison's beliefs were viewed as discernable and coherent, if not controversial, in the minds of many Americans. In a January 14, 1837, letter, Mary Benson, one of Garrison's sisters-in-laws, writes to him about a female anti-slavery meeting that she attended earlier that month in Boston that was "deeply and thoroughly saturated with Garrisonism."[81] It is hard to avoid hearing the strong cultic resonances in this language. Southern slaveholders linked "Garrisonism" with calls for the immediate legal emancipation of slaves, while northern clergy viewed "Garrisonism" as a radical protestant religious movement that differed from mainline churches in its understanding of humankind's relationship to God, doctrines of sanctification, ecclesiastical authority, and temperate contemplation.[82]

Garrison himself expressed awareness of the growing public association of his name with a religion that intertwined Christian theology with anti-slavery politics. In a February 4, 1837, letter to Anne Benson, another sister-in-law, he recounts that during his travels to various New England anti-slavery rallies his name alone could spark the crowd's emotions: "whenever my name was alluded to, a round of applause was surely to follow."[83] He believed that public reactions to his name, whether in the form of applause or disparaging remarks, bore little connection to his personage but did demonstrate a "powerful manifestation" of the religious ideas that his name was understood to signify to readers of *The Liberator*, to northern abolitionists, and to southern slaveholders and clergy.[84] In *Perfectionist Politics: Abolitionism and the Religious Tensions of American Democracy*, Douglass Strong similarly sees 1837 as an important year in the emergence of a clearly distinguishable Garrisonian religious language.[85] Strong emphasizes Garrison's 1837 encounter with antinomian perfectionist leader John Humphrey Noyes, a meeting that he argues results in the lucid development of "Garrisonian Perfectionism," a theology that viewed slavery as one component within "a larger panorama" of American sin that also extended to the government.[86] Strong's thesis builds on the abolitionist's belief in the centrality of their role in the eradication of sin, both from slavery and elsewhere, in American life.

The 1837 rise of "Garrisonism" resulted in contentious public denunciations of Garrison by New England clergy who accused him of usurping Christ's role by crafting a theology that placed him as the principal object of his follower's adoration. A series of public and private letters between Garrison and a New England minister named James T. Woodbury in 1837 are representative of the tensions between Garrisonian theology and contemporary mainline churches.[87] In a August 17, 1837, letter to the *New England Spectator*, titled "A Clerical Appeal," Woodbury directs his sharpest criticism towards Christians who now prefer to identify themselves as a "Garrison Man" or a "Garrisonite."[88] He characterizes a Garrisonite as a Christian who views Garrison as "abolition personified and incarnate."[89] Woodbury attacks the "blind infatuation" that Garrisonites offer to their leader and, in a passage worth quoting at length, he concisely details his objections to their extreme adoration:

> Mr. Garrison is the god of your idolatry. You live, and move, and have your being, in him alone. His thoughts are yours—his understanding and conscience yours—his ipse dixit yours. You have "swallowed" him—put him on—and he is as Christ unto you![90]

Woodbury's letter clearly expresses the belief of Garrison's contemporaries that his abolitionism was not only understood as an anti-slavery movement but also as a religious movement with a unique theology, a group of followers that looked to Garrison for religious leadership, and they argued that this movement posed some threat to traditional Christian beliefs and churches.

Garrison attempted to specifically define his "peculiar theology" in a response to Woodbury that he printed in the September 1, 1837, edition of *The Liberator*.[91] He begins his defense by stressing the interdenominational quality of his movement, namely that most of his followers retain their membership or association with traditional Christian churches.[92] Samuel May, he writes, maintained his membership with the Unitarians after becoming a "Garrison man," Amos Phelps remained a Trinitarian, and James Birney still identified himself as a member of the Society of Friends.[93] He argues that becoming a "follower of Garrison" involves "following the spirit of Truth," but since his anti-slavery work and his religious beliefs are guided by God's will, his theology shouldn't come into conflict with any "true" Christian church.[94] In a rather unique turn, Garrison then broadly distills his theology into a general religious appeal to 19th century Christian readers:

> I am as orthodox as was John Calvin; as to the Christian ministry, I hold a "royal priesthood"; as to the Christian ordinances, I believe in eating the flesh and drinking the blood of the Incarnate word, and being baptized into the death of the Son of God; as to the visible church, I believe that there is such a church, but visible only to those who are gifted with spiritual vision.[95]

Garrison counted himself amongst those gifted with "spiritual vision," and accordingly, "like an apostle," he didn't concern himself with popular opinion.[96] His denial of the visible church—at least as embodied in contemporary Massachusetts orthodox churches—demonstrates the extent to which devotion to his understanding of Christianity necessarily differentiated its enthusiasts from other Christian activists.

During the early and mid–19th century the popular press compared William Garrison to Joseph Smith and other controversial and maligned religious leaders, viewing unorthodox religious fanaticism and political treason as inseparably related. Mormons, Millerites, and other "fringe" religious sects espoused egalitarian and communal doctrines that northern and southern clergy and readers perceived as a threat to American ideals of individualism and orthodox Protestantism.

To many, the theology of Garrisonian abolitionism maintained the same degree of socially un–American, religiously heretical, and more generally violent tendencies as the Mormon movement. The editor of the *Democratic Review* wrote in 1850 against Garrisonian efforts to wage, "direct, inveterate warfare against the Constitution and the Union."[97] He criticized the prophetic adoration that Garrisonians gave to their spokesman, arguing that, "the first and most effectual step in subjugating mankind ... is that degree of enthusiasm, which amounts to fanaticism ... represented by men like Joseph Smith and William Lloyd Garrison."[98] Both men he goes on to write "proposed stupendous doctrines ... to which they arrogate the sanction of heaven."[99]

Those living in Massachusetts and New York in the early 19th century would have been familiar with the exploits and trajectories of both men since their stories do, in many ways, run parallel and the implications of the *Democratic Review's* comparison should not be ignored. Garrison achieved his first major public visibility and notoriety as he feverishly wrote stories of his unjust incarceration from his Baltimore jail cell beginning on April 17, 1830. Eleven days earlier, on April 6, 1830, Joseph Smith similarly entered public consciousness when he published his controversial *Book of Mormon* that began with an explanation of his divine mandate to restore the full gospel of the true Christian church. During this time, both men rejected the authority and practices of the dominant orthodox Christian churches; Smith went even further by not only producing a new work of scripture in the *Book of Mormon* but also by completing his own "uncorrupted" version of the King James Version of the New Testament in June of 1830.[100]

A year later in 1831 Garrison started *The Liberator*, which became his primary vehicle for spreading his religious and political message. That same year Smith began devising his own paper, which would eventually become the *Nauvoo Expositor*.[101] Garrison's writings incited violent displays against him and on October 21, 1835, an angry mob attacked him in Boston. Smith's writings produced similar levels of outrage. On March 24, 1832, a mob attacked him in Kirtland, Ohio and badly beat him, tarred and feathered him, and attempted to castrate him.[102] According to famed Mormon historian Richard Lyman Bushman, the visions of Smith and Garrison, "clashed with the legendary optimism of Jacksonian America ... and were equally pessimistic about a society rotting at the core, ready to be hewn down and cast into the fire."[103] Garrison's religious beliefs led him to describe the constitution as a "covenant with death."[104] Smith shared these sentiments but opted

## 1. The Construction and Evolution of Narratives 43

to try and restructure the American government by running for President on the 1844 ballot. Amongst his campaign promises was the immediate abolition of slavery.[105] Smith's *Doctrine and Covenants*, one of the three holy books of the Latter-Day Saint faith, even prophesized that an organized revolt of black slaves would occur in America that would restructure society and hasten the apocalypse: "and it shall comes to pass, after many days, slaves shall rise up against masters, who shall be marshaled and disciplined for war."[106] Smith's controversial religious and political beliefs led to his murder on June 27, 1844. And so, when the *Democratic Review* draws comparisons between Smith and Garrison, six years after Smith's murder, it is more than a casual reference. It is also a threat of violence against Garrison and it speaks to the significant degree of public animosity towards him and the perceived threat he posed to American political and religious institutions.

Comparing Garrison with the prophetic-centered Smith provides insight into the orthodox Northern clergy's fears that Garrison's brand of Christianity provided a hostile challenge to "universally recognized doctrines of Christianity" and that this challenge, in turn, posed a danger to the Constitution, the sanctity of marriage, gender roles, and the divinity of Christ.[107] According to Sarah Barringer Gordon, the relationship between religious authority and social order was not merely a cultural phenomenon debated in newspapers or between clergy, but also a legal principle.[108] She points out that to judges like James Kent of New York the "Christian religion" was synonymous with "the principles of virtue, which helps to bind society together."[109] Within this framework, Garrisonian abolitionism posed a threat to social order and Orthodox Protestantism, demonstrating that American religious liberty possessed limits.

Apostolic language, martyr rhetoric, and prophetic comparisons in *The Liberator* framed Garrisonians as mediators between God's divine plan and slave suffering. Garrisonians advocated pacifistic resistance to slavery and discouraged southern slaves from partaking in violent uprisings.[110] For Garrison, his "selfhood" and identity emerged from his willingness to sacrifice his physical body. Enduring suffering and the desire to witness suffering are the beginnings of his antislavery discourse. *The Liberator* advocated "patience" and "endurance" on the part of the slave, while suffering and martyrdom were required of the abolitionist. Garrison argued that if slaves were strict and patient in their adherence to this plan they would "hasten the day of their peaceful deliverance from the yoke of bondage."[111] Garrison stressed the centrality of the abolitionist sacrifice and the importance of slave passivity in a published letter to the editor of the *Boston Courier* (that was also subsequently reprinted in *The Liberator*).[112] He reasoned that God would "continue to raise up friends and advocates to plead the cause, and the power of TRUTH will make them free indeed; whereas by violent and bloody measures, they will prolong their servitude, and expose themselves to destruction."[113] The only appropriate shedding of blood in the Garrisonian drama of salvation was that of the abolitionist, whose acceptance of death and violence, unlike the slave death, served a sacred, divinely ordained purpose. Abolitionist pain held the capacity to function in proxy of slave pain. Within this theology and rhetorical strategy, Garrisonians invoked slave pain in an effort to demonstrate their own capacity to empathize with slave suffering and by doing so they were brought into a closer proximity with God since they viewed pain as a necessary condition for true discipleship.

These 1837 ideas provide the ideological foundations of Garrisonian narratives of spectacular slave executions and abolitionist eyewitness fantasies of death and martyrdom. The Garrisonian focus on a religious language that celebrated abolitionist spiritual and physical suffering in *The Liberator*, what people called "Garrisonism," attracted the criticism of many prominent intellectuals in the northern states. Boston Unitarian minister William Ellery Channing, for instance, expressed discomfort with Garrison's "undirected moral energy."[114] Channing publicly described Garrisonians as "pious fools with violent impulses."[115] Here Channing is referring to *The Liberator's* penchant for focusing on stories that describe violence against slaves by southerners; accounts of slave acts of resistance; and for Garrison's inflammatory tone, which he believed escalated sectional tensions.[116] Far from being an easy anti-slavery advocate, Channing's comments nevertheless appropriately indicate some of the popular northern discomfort with the Garrisonian interest in violence and abolitionist pain in their theology and anti-slavery appeals.

Garrison's theological emphasis on the abolitionist capacity to empathize with slaves (as primitive Christians) and his aggressive desire to experience persecution and suffering on their behalf manifested in *The Liberator* in narratives that appropriated and re-staged pro-slavery accounts of slave lynchings through the narrative presence and spiritual anguish of a Garrisonian eye-witness/narrator. Garrison highlights this rhetorical strategy in a September 5, 1835, letter to George Benson when he formulates ways that pro-slavery speeches and violence might serve the anti-slavery cause.[117] He understands that in their original context pro-slavery accounts of violence are written to "strengthen the feeble hands and comfort the desponding hearts of southern taskmasters," but he also believes that if these stories are carefully re-told from a Christian perspective they might "prove of more benefit to our cause than forty anti-slavery lectures ... thus the God of the oppressed sustain his veracity: he maketh the wrath of man to praise him."[118]

This rhetorical philosophy is remarkably consistent with Garrison's understanding of suffering: that God uses pain and persecution for redemptive divine purposes. This Biblical perspective is one that looks to the way that the God found within the Gospel narratives transforms Jesus' earthly persecution, suffering, and death into a moment of ultimate triumph and the beginning of the Christian church. The narratives of early Christian martyrs recalled and re-enacted Christ's original triumph, transforming persecution and suffering from an act of punishment to a sacred act that brought the martyr closer to God. In each case narrative repetition and re-telling is crucial because it not only invokes the power and the redemptive ending of the original, but the telling of the story itself becomes a "miracle" that can be retold and invoked by others in a self-perpetuating cycle. Garrisonian narratives relocate the abolitionist to a position of narrative authority to discern the slave's suffering, and more significantly, to contextualize his or her own suffering in relation to the slaves. By re-staging pro-slavery acts of violence Garrison was able, like the Gospels and earlier Christian martyrs, to literally imbue violent southern spectacles with spiritual significance: the slave's death could be understood as wrongful persecution to be empathized with, while Garrison assumed a God-like position as the story's author, framing how slave suffering should be read and stressing the abolitionist's duty to witness it. The debasing of the slave body paradoxically signifies the purity of the abolitionist witness. By symbolically traversing the physical terrain of the south, the Garrisonian witness defines himself against the world's authority and in doing so imitates Christ's original example of self-effacement.

Re-printing and rewriting newspaper articles from other regions remained a common practice in the 19th century America. Lacking contemporary copyright laws, there was a system of "newspaper exchanges" in which papers procured articles from other parts of the country and reprinted the content at no cost.[119] This exchange system gave readers a greater awareness of events taking place in distant locations, and allowed small papers the ability to economically broaden the scope of their inquiries. Editors simply clipped articles from other papers and published them as written or with modifications, sometimes not giving credit to the original author.[120]

By the winter of 1836 William Garrison's letters already discuss ways to re-imagine horrific accounts of slave violence that appear in Southern newspapers. A significant amount of his correspondence on this subject occurred with his brother-in-law George Benson, who traveled through Virginia that same year and who maintained acquaintances with southern abolitionist-sympathizers.[121] Garrison asked Benson to locate and then forward southern newspapers to him in large bundles to his residences in Boston and New York. In one letter, dated January 11, 1836, Garrison implores Benson not to waste time and to quickly send him a new bundle of papers "immediately, to Boston, for possible insertion in the *Liberator*."[122] Garrison believed that, if framed correctly, these stories would produce "all kinds of emotions in the minds of the people—rage, astonishment, alarm" but also offer hope and confidence.[123] Similarly, in a February 28, 1836, letter to Isaac Knapp, Garrison sends sentiments of gratitude for the "huge bundle of newspapers" that arrived in the mail a few days before.[124] He writes that he stayed up until 2 a.m. "devouring the contents of the whole mess, and went to bed without feeling any fatigue," ready the next morning to "drive my editorial quill somewhat freely."[125] This practice of re-scripting freed Garrison to construct his own narratives for public consumption and abolitionist self-fashioning. Despite his lifelong pacifist views and his abhorrence to violence, these southern accounts also gave Garrison the ability to aggressively invoke violence through the presence of a witness/narrator that recounts his horror and spiritual anguish, while simultaneously preaching endurance and righteousness through the physical pain of the slave and the spectatorial pain of the abolitionist.

The narrator in Garrison's newspaper accounts offers the reader access to a hellish landscape of inexplicable pain, suffering, and torture. The spectacular displays of slave punishment and suffering in these reports mimic those of Biblical martyrs and serve to illuminate abolitionist spiritual torment and to outline the work of Christian spectatorship. The identities of the slaves who are subjected to these violent acts are secondary to the repetition of the form, a form that gives meaning to slave suffering by placing it within a larger Christian lineage. These strategies, however, produce a static slave pain while venerating the personal pain of the narrators who must witness the act. The spectacular chaos and bloodshed in southern newspapers transforms into an act of Christian martyrdom and an idealized system of meaning for Garrisonian abolitionists. This theology and its widespread dissemination throughout New England is essential to the construction of the more generalized popular memory of Garrison in the late 19th century. It is a process by which the heightened expressions of abolitionist interiority are performed for an imagined, implied, and idealized reading audience.

Responding to practices of oppression and violent torture, *The Liberator* constructed a world in which abolitionists were imagined as exemplary sufferers through their participation in witnessing slave pain. Drawing from the language of spectacles of suffering that were common in southern newspapers, *The Liberator* reframed, through the presence of a narrator-eyewitness, the meaning of the act, transforming it from an act of senselessness violence to a heroic and selfless redemptive act with a larger religious purpose. The problems that such a strategy might present for contemporary readers paralleled the concerns voiced by Garrison's contemporaries, like Frederick Douglass, who accused him of literally controlling the discourses of former slaves, their voices, and their texts.[126] *The Liberator's* stories of slave suffering and torture are fundamentally similar in structure and description in different issues of the paper: therein lay much of their strength. Such a tendency, however, highlights a paradoxical tension within these narrative structures and representations: by placing slaves within allegorical martyr narratives, the individual slave is lost in a favor of more general figures. While such a strategy does re-script, memorialize, and promote reader empathy for slave suffering, the Christian narrative lineage, its corresponding images, and its metaphors simultaneously place limits on their power. Garrison's theology, at worst, co-opted slave pain in order to venerate abolitionist suffering, placing Garrisonian spectatorial struggles within a larger Christian discourse that lay at the heart of their righteous identity. A closer examination of this complex discourse helps to more carefully reveal and unravel the racialized power dynamics between slaves, abolitionists, and mass-produced representations.

The southern *Daily South Carolinian's* October 24, 1856, report of the execution of a slave named "William" and *The Liberator's* January 23, 1857, re-staging of this drama exemplify the abolitionist paper's strategies of evoking slave empathy via a language of Garrisonian sacrifice. According to the paper, a slave named William masterminded a conspiracy to start a slave insurrection. Despite the more than 20 years since violent events like the Denmark-Vessey Affair and Nat Turner's rebellion, southern newspapers and southern audiences remained sensitive to the day-to-day potential of violent slave resistance. Turner's rebellion resulted in the deaths of around sixty people, including women and children, and his ability to elude capture for close to two months terrified southern audiences. Yet, as Kenneth Greenberg argues, the fear caused by Turner's revolt also stemmed from the slave's decision to name himself "Nat Turner," which asserted his autonomy and constructed the parameters by which southerners could even talk about him.[127] For newspaper readers in predominantly slave-populated states like South Carolina and Georgia, reports of slave trials and executions offered the promise of rhetorical control and the illusion of stability for a situation that was anything but stable.[128] Southerners viewed William Garrison, in particular, as a dangerous instigator of these slave insurrections despite his repeated denunciations of insurrectionary slave violence.[129] Pro-slavery papers argued, therefore, that violent slave resistance should be treated as a threat to their livelihood and asked the courts to suppress it harshly and quickly.[130] The newspaper coverage of the slave William's arrest, subsequent escape, and final arrest and trial—he apparently evaded authorities for about a month, during which time the governor offered a reward for his capture—provided a necessary antidote to the unsettling prospect of slave disorder and rebellion. William received a speedy trial that climaxed with a death sentence common for African Americans in the south: execution by burning. The newspaper reports that thousands, young and old, arrived to witness the spectacle that became William's public execution. The article quotes one visiting family from a nearby town that awoke "to the bustling noises of the neighborhood people" who busily prepared for the communal gathering that they interpreted as an affirmation of law and order.[131]

The paper's pro-slavery narrative notes the public's clamor to attend the execution, but the overriding tone is one of reasoned resignation. The author writes that while the spectacle of the burning delighted some, he views this particular execution method as, "a mode of punishment [that] ... will soon itself become obsolete."[132] To be clear, the author firmly believes that William should be executed, but questions whether "burning" is the most suitable form of capital punishment. He particularly laments that northern audiences view "burning" as an unnecessarily cruel method of execution, which leads him to speculate that if the method of execution were different, perhaps the event would be read as a triumph of social order and the legal due process.[133] For the *Daily South Carolinian's* southern audience, the event is read as a victory of American democratic principles.

In a January 23, 1857, article titled "A Slave Whipped and Burned to Death" *The Liberator* re-scripts the *Daily South Carolinian's* narrative of law and order through a language and imagery of Christian martyrdom that celebrates abolitionist spectatorial pain. In this narrative, the author-eyewitness describes a scene that "would have made the bloodthirsty Nero tremble."[134] The story he goes on to relay recounts the major facts, often verbatim, from the pro-slavery account: William is accused by his master of plotting an uprising and of plotting to kill the master's family. Following the arrest and trial of the alleged conspirators, *The Liberator's* account focuses on William's denial of the charges against him and then carefully and explicitly details the actual process of his torture through the eyes of the Garrisonian witness:

> It was deemed necessary to torture this miserable creature before their eyes. Accordingly, he was stripped—the weather being cold—and then he received 200 lashes on the bare back ... not yet satisfied, these inhuman monsters, excited as it were by the blood they had already drawn, proceeded to tie him up to a stake, with the intention of burning him. When told he was next to be burned, the screams of the poor creature were indeed terrific and heart-rendering; but, despite his entreaties and cries, a pile of wood was heaped around him and again he was told if he would not confess, he would be burned to a crisp; still he refused, when the pile was lighted, and soon began to blaze around the victim.[135]

The emphasis on torture in this story parallels narratives of Christian martyrdom that similarly view unwarranted physical suffering as a consequence and marker of Christian identity. In the Roman criminal process against Christians, for instance, torture was practiced in the process of interrogation. Behind the terror of the act was the belief that only torture could ultimately guarantee truth.[136] Early Christians and 19th century Garrisonians adopted a rhetoric that stressed the willingness to suffer for truth. Accordingly, *The Liberator's* stories of slave suffering featured highly theatrical and spectacular displays of slave disfigurement and pain. The lengths that abolitionists went to "render the horrors of slavery," a horror that was inevitably intended to shock the reader is characterized by Saidiya Hartman as a genre concerned with "the minutest detail of macabre acts of violence, embellished by his own fantasy of slavery's bloodstained gate."[137] In Hartman's view, abolitionist stories of slave torture are designed to promote empathy in the reader, which is achieved through an evacuation of the black body within the narrative and a substitution of the white reader's imagined presence. This is the black body as an empty vessel. The empathy the reader feels becomes less about the violence inflicted on the slave than the white reader's internal imagining of such pain inflicted on himself or his family. Empathy becomes a violent response within this critical framework. Such a theory, in regard to martyr narratives, however, does not fully account for the power dynamic that is played out in religious stories.

Garrison's narratives are not just about the reader and they should be approached with an awareness that they are part of a Christian textual tradition that understands spectatorship as an act of self-sacrifice that defiles the conscience of the one who watches. Early Christian texts like St. Augustine's *Confessions* argue that the mere act of watching violence poses a very real spiritual threat to the Christian.[138] Augustine recounts the story of his friend Alypius' trip to Rome and his reluctant participation in watching a violent spectacle with a large Roman crowd.[139] The story implies that part of Alypius' self is irretrievably lost once his eyes are exposed to this violence. In Garrison's stories it is important to realize that this spectatorial victimization also produces the desirable ecstasy of being brought into closer union with God since it looks back to and mimics Christ's voluntary sacrifice.

In *The Liberator's* article, "A Slave Whipped and Burned to Death," the evacuation of the slave's body does not merely elicit white sympathy, but also constructs and transfers martyr status from the slave to the white Garrisonian witness. The Garrisonian witnesses' personal discomfort and pain in the story escalates in intensity as William's actual pain grows. Eventually the witnesses' pain parallels and then surpasses that of the slave. Descriptions of the slave's "terrific" and "heart-rending" entireties are discarded in favor of the abolitionist's spiritual pain when his outward protests to end the torture are met with dismissals such as "mind your own business," from those who are carrying out the execution.[140] The narrator finally tells the reader that he was "unable longer to witness such unexampled cruelty," and rides away on his horse before the final execution is completed.[141] The narrator writes that locals later informed him that the slave did die that night. By leaving before the execution is completed, however, the pain of the slave is temporarily obscured and mediated, while the personal pain of the witness remains vivid. When the author-witness does report the death of the slave it is filtered through his personal ruminations and is only capable of evoking a more general sympathy. The slave's pain is physically distanced through the act of riding away and the memory of the slave's pain is emotionally replaced by an increased awareness of the Garrisonian witnesses' own spiritual torment. The author ends the article by arguing that such horrific scenes are ignored by northern newspapers and audiences and that if the "glorious undertaking" of the "liberation of the human race" is to occur, then these scenes must be told by "humane passerbys" who witness them.[142] Martyr status, therefore, is temporarily bestowed upon the slave through the eyewitness' descriptions, but this status is transferred to the actual "humane" eyewitness who is forced to experience, record, and live with the vivid knowledge of southern evil and northern compliance. The Garrisonian narrator becomes a heroic tourist in the trafficking of the pain of others.

Garrisonian narratives of slave suffering in the 1840s and 1850s emerge from a 1830s theology that is built around passive slave suffering active abolitionist spectatorship and witnessing. A June 1, 1849, narrative that appeared in *The Liberator*, titled "The Execution of Washington Goode" is a prime example of the complex relationship between voyeuristic and moralistic tensions within Garrisonian religious stories of slave and abolitionist suffering.[143] The article offers little information about the personage of Washington Goode, giving him the aura of an abstraction rather than a real person, but the article does go to great lengths to describe the three days leading up to his execution and the horrifying spectacle of it being carried out. The story recounts how Goode unsuccessfully attempted to commit suicide twice during the days preceding his execution. In one of these attempts he shoved wads of tobacco, paper, and blankets down his throat in an effort to suffocate himself. The details are remarkable: the noises the jailer heard that first attracted his attention (various types of "gurgling"), the race to save Goode's life, and Goode's periodic bouts of sleep and vomiting during the rest of the night.

On the day of the execution, the Garrisonian narrator shifts the emphasis to his own pain and anguish as he walks through crowds of southerners with, "expressions of the most diabolical nature [that] were constantly put forth by the vulgar and profane, of which the crowd was mostly composed."[144] The narrator heroically maneuvers around groups of slaveholders and eavesdrops, whenever possible, reporting short snippets of conversation like, "God d-n it, don't the scriptures say that the d-d black scoundrel ought to be hung?"[145] In each case, the narrator points out that the grounds for supporting the execution are voiced by the lower, uneducated, "vulgar classes" who misread the scriptures.¹⁴⁶ The narrator's adventures through these barbarous and bloodthirsty crowds and his discomfort with the entire scene align the pain and persecution of slaves with that of abolitionists. The "diabolical nature" of the crowd is stressed when the crowd shouts to the executioners to "tear down the wall, and let us see his d-black face."¹⁴⁷

Washington Goode's literal and narrative unmasking on the scaffolding parallels the Garrisonian narrator's fear of being discovered by those in the crowd. The narrator perceives that his righteousness makes him stand out amongst the crowd. But despite such danger he nevertheless evangelizes and wins over a member of the bloodthirsty pro-slavery spectators. This pivotal "conversion" event reclaims the meaning of the execution and inverts it from a spectacle of southern law and order to a victory of abolitionist bravery and piety in hostile terrain. This transformation occurs through a local shopkeeper who arrives at the execution with expectations of pleasure and enjoyment (he is described earlier by the narrator as a man "cursing" and "joking"), but after hearing the Garrisonian message from the narrator he departs from the scene unfulfilled and, presumably, changed.¹⁴⁸ The narrator boasts that the shopkeeper returned to his business that same day only to close early, leaving a sign that proclaims to all that, "a brother was hung today, and that he should do no business during the day."¹⁴⁹ The power of the Garrisonian within the narrative is the same as Christ's power in the gospels: to transform earthly punishment into a triumph of cosmic significance.

Pro-slavery advocates recognized Garrison's rhetorical strategy as a form of abolitionism that remained distinct from typical Massachusetts appeals. On July 12, 1848, roughly seven months into his tenure as the new junior senator from Mississippi, Jefferson Davis, the future president of the Confederate States of America, described Garrisonian abolitionism as "a new form of the monster."¹⁵⁰ He found this new form particularly disturbing because within Garrison's appeals and circles, "duty, fraternity, faith, give way, and masses worship with a type of fanaticism that only might excuse the apostasy. With them, what argument can prevail?"¹⁵¹

*The Liberator's* distinct narratives of southern violence towards slaves and the spiritual anguish that such journeys inflict on the Garrisonian narrator/eyewitness does, however, foreground a paradox in Garrisonian martyr-centered Christian anti-slavery appeals: Garrison's belief in the necessity of abolitionist sacrifice as an essential and sacred act and the reality that no prominent member of his own anti-slavery circle was actually martyred for the anti-slavery cause. By 1857, perhaps aware of this contradiction, Garrison clarifies the spiritual role of the abolitionist and goes on to craft what I describe as a theology of "living martyrdom." Garrison consistently proclaims this new and evolved version of his anti-slavery theology through the 1860 start of the Civil War. This new theology clearly asserts that the physical well being of the abolitionist must be preserved at all costs. It concedes that *actual* travel through the south would put the abolitionist's life in real and unnecessary danger, which could potentially disrupt God's divine plan for the eradication of slavery.

Garrison wrote to Nathan Johnson in 1860 on the eve of the Civil War to reiterate to the chair of the Vermont Anti-Slavery Convention that this theology simply reiterated what "prophets and apostles uttered ages ago, and for which Jesus offered up his life on Calvary."[152] He encourages Johnson to continue his evangelism despite persecution, arguing that without worthy abolitionist sacrifices, "there is no hope of human redemption, and Christ will have died in vain."[153] Garrison still frames witnessing slave pain (the word "martyr," after all, means "to witness") through narratives in *The Liberator* as a form of evangelizing that consistently remind readers of Christ's ultimate triumph. These narratives firmly situate the abolitionist as the building block for the new nation that will regenerate once slavery is finally abolished. Until the time that slavery is abandoned the role of the abolitionist is to continue to preach despite persecution and rejection by the outside world, to empathize with the slave, to bear witness to slave suffering, and to sublimely embrace spiritual pain and martyrdom as a testimony of Christ's grace to non-believers and to the larger nation. Jesus Christ's apostles built the early Christian church on the repetition of his narrative of persecution, suffering, death, and triumphal redemption. Garrisonian anti-slavery appeals, like other historical Christian movements, found ways to recall Christ's original pain and sacrifice in order to perform its victory in their own historical and cultural moment. This belief system re-read slave suffering and the desire for abolitionist martyrdom as the ultimate remedy to spiritually and legally purge this institution for God's greater glory, not as a consequence or extension of the vitriolic slavery debates that tore apart 19th century America.

During the years of Garrison's anti-slavery activism, from 1830 up to the passage of the Thirteenth amendment in 1865, the central and least discussed aspect of his antislavery religious beliefs and his newspaper's abolitionist appeals remains its interests in the problem of how to properly understand and endure suffering. The paper became a space for Garrison and his followers to imagine the spiritual regeneration of the nation through their sacrifices for the anti-slavery cause and, in the tradition of Bunyan's *Pilgrim's Progress*, it exists as a spiritual autobiography of the Garrisonian theology of suffering and protest. Garrisonian persecution and righteousness were so central to their conception of the abolitionist mission that this ideology evolved into a prescribed way for them to witness their faith. Garrison's private correspondence reveals his approach to the Bible as a dramatic narrative with archetypes with which he could readily identify within the tumultuous and widespread violence of the 1830s. The clarity of his theology of suffering evolved and further developed through his public rhetorical battles with northern clergy, each instance of which reinforced Garrison's portrait of himself and his followers as an embattled community of Christians experiencing persecution for what they understood as the true faith. By the 1850s, *The Liberator's* narratives shift to prisons and to the spectacles of slave executions, where patient slave suffering rather than resistance becomes the new form of "boldly speaking" for Christ. The presence of the Garrisonian eye-witness narrator and the new story this observer tells is one in which the abolitionist and the slave defeat the intent of southern punishment. By accepting and facing death (for the slave) and by demonstrating joy in suffering and persecution (the abolitionist) the new narrative that emerges highlights the limitations of southern power. The slave and the abolitionist desire to righteously endure affliction and punishment becomes proof of God's presence and power.

Garrison's complex and shifting relationship to suffering in the pages of *The Liberator* defies the most influential academic writing on punishment and pain. Michel Foucault's important writing on punishment, for instance, offers little help in unraveling the dynamic I describe. Foucault's analysis of the spectacle of public executions in France as a political ritual in which state authority is inscribed on the body of the victim, affirming state sovereignty, fails to account for the Christian narrative of spiritual triumph over physical punishment. Foucault rejects the idea of the "soul" in Christian theology in favor of the "historical reality" of a soul "born ... *out* of methods of punishment, supervision, and constraint."[154] Such a theory allows little room to understand a Garrisonian theology that seeks *out* persecution and pain as an ideal, a belief system in which suffering refines the spirit.[155] Perhaps a more fruitful alternative is to remember Elaine Scarry's argument about pain and torture and the ways that torture brings the torturer into being.[156] This idea is applicable to understanding Garrison's own understanding of abolitionism because his (and his followers) redemptive sacrifices, like all Christian martyr narratives, are dependent upon an audience and in Garrison's stories it is only through witnessing slave violence and willfully subjecting oneself to persecution and torment that the abolitionist comes into being. Pain becomes the wellspring of enhanced spiritual power. This belief and the power of this narrative shaped a lasting historical ideal of Garrisonian abolitionist heroism. By re-enacting a drama of suffering learned from the Bible and the martyr narratives of the early Christian church, Garrisonian theology produced the foundation for a new American mythic drama of white anti-slavery subversion, it lay the foundations for the historical memory of Massachusetts's morally exemplary activism during the antebellum years, and it constructed a model of progressive resistance narratives organized around black passivity and white persecution, initiative, and spectatorship.

# 2

# Commemorating Garrison

*Origins of the Garrison Revival in Post-Bellum American Memory, 1867–1910*

On May 19, 2010, Republican Senate candidate Rand Paul, fresh off a victory in his party's Kentucky primary, conjured the image of William Garrison and New England abolitionism on MSNBC's *The Rachel Maddow Show* to combat allegations of racism following his controversial critique of the Civil Rights Act of 1965.[1] Just days earlier Paul's libertarian political philosophy led him to characterize aspects of the Civil Rights Act of 1965 as unconstitutional, particularly as this law relates to the regulation of private businesses. He expressed tentative support for the legislation's original intent, at least in theory, but argued that such laws should only apply to public government-affiliated institutions. During the first 24 hours after Paul's remarks charges of racism followed from diverse sources like the *New York Times'* Frank Rich and the Republican National Committee's chairman Michael Steele.[2] Over the three days that followed Paul repeatedly evoked the historical memory of William Garrison to fight these accusations and to ameliorate the strong public backlash. He claimed Garrison as one of his "favorite American heroes" and described him as "a champion and abolitionist who wrote about freeing slaves back in the l810s, '20s, and '30s."[3] Most significant is Paul's circulation of Garrison's antislavery rhetoric of abolitionist persecution and sacrifice. Paul went on to explain that he admires Garrison because he fought for a righteous cause despite being, "flogged, put in jails."[4] Garrison is important in American history because, "he was with Frederick Douglass being thrown off trains.[5]

Paul's invocation of Garrison is a testimony to the endurance of the historical memory of Garrisonian abolitionism as an ideal narrative of anti-slavery protest, sacrifice, and righteous suffering. Paul's language participates in an American tradition that developed during the latter part of the 19th century in which Garrison's life is mapped onto larger narratives that are not only about the historical fight over slavery, but are equally invested in the transcending and redemptive effects of his suffering. Paul's comments support historian John Stauffer's recent observation that despite advancements in the scholarship of antebellum anti-slavery rhetoric, William Garrison's movement and his rhetorical discourses still dominate and more broadly characterize popular narratives of the American abolitionist movement.[6] Garrison is viewed as the "principal inspiration" for American abolitionism, leading Stauffer to humorously describe him as the "dean" of American abolitionism.[7] In *Beyond Garrison: Antislavery and Social Reform*, Bruce Laurie similarly laments what he views as the "persistent desire of each generation of Americans ... to rediscover Garrison."[8] Laurie points out that during the past 30 years at least 24 major historical biographies of Garrison have been published, along with countless numbers of journal articles, all of which, testifies to America's "enduring fascination with Garrison, a fascination that leaves the antislavery movement in his shadow."[9]

This chapter examines the post-bellum social, political, and cultural forces that converged to perpetuate Garrisonian narratives of abolitionist suffering and sacrifice between 1865 and 1910 throughout New England and America. It tells the tangled and remarkable story of the popular culture transformation of William Lloyd Garrison and his form of abolitionist activism from a fringe antebellum religious movement into a representative example of New England's antislavery legacy that emphasized Garrison's selfless sacrifices on behalf of the slave and the union. In the late 19th and the early 20th century those who intimately knew Garrison, like Samuel May and Parker Pillsbury, as well as novelists, poets, and ministers who were born after his 1879 death, like the poet Henrietta Ray, perpetuated stories of heroic abolitionist self-sacrifice that retrospectively imagined Garrison as the founder and leader of a unified antebellum New England abolitionist movement and framed his efforts as giving birth to the modern American republic. Newspapers, memoirs, eulogies, poems, and novels published between 1865 and 1910 adopted this language, and in doing so participated in a cultural moment that I alternately describe as a "Garrison revival" or a "culture of commemoration." This revival should be understood as a period in which Garrison's self-mythologizing, the work of his closest followers, and the needs and desires of a variety of different groups coalesced around the historical memory of the suffering and self-sacrificial Garrison as a means to articulate their region and the nation's past struggles with slavery and to optimistically imagine a more peaceful future.

As Americans living in a post-bellum era fought over the legacy and meaning of the Civil War it was the celebration of Garrison's narrative of noble suffering and redemptive sacrifice that provided Massachusetts and New England audiences with a means to emphasize the region's long tradition of national moral leadership through its unique commitment to progressive societal reform. Dating back to colonial America there is a literary history of New England poets and novelists who romanticized the region as a moral example for the nation and the world. Works like the Reverend Timothy Dwight's 1794 poem "Greenfield Hill" are part of a longer New England literary tradition that stresses the region's exceptional qualities.[10] The seven-part epic poem "Greenfield Hill," for instance, describes New England as the pinnacle of the evolution of Christian civilization.[11] Such works perpetuated a regional mythology that sentimentally situated New England as a unique symbol of the best aspects of American character. Robert G. Deamer claims in his book, *The Importance of Place in the American Literature of Hawthorne, Thoreau, Crane, Adams, and Faulkner*, that New England mythology occupies an important role in the consciousness of the citizens of this region and in how Americans conceptualize their national identity: "the New England place-myth, of all the American myths of place is the most richly complex ... in the stance it takes towards the world and the American dream."[12] As late 19th century New England writers, politicians, and artists increasingly invoked Garrison's narrative as *the* story of New England abolitionism and of their own participation in the Civil War the tendency of these stories to focus on Garrison's suffering offered a vehicle by which to express the region's sacrifices for the anti-slavery cause. By the turn-of-the century Garrison's story of uncompromising protest and sacrifice would become synonymous with the "New England narrative" of the war and it would be continuously re-invented in poetry and fiction for a wider national audience. As the literary trope of the "suffering abolitionist" that appeared in these popular stories of Garrison's suffering and of antebellum abolitionist efforts was adapted, transformed, and disseminated to regions outside of New England these narratives also became a way for Americans struggling to come to terms with the Civil War to replace the war's legacy of racial injustice with tales of abolitionist heroics, moral fortitude, and paternalistic guidance.

The abolition of slavery and the spiritual regeneration of America stood as *The Liberator's* principal theological and political purpose, aligning the formal end of slavery with the end of Garrisonian proselytizing. That end came on February 1, 1865, when Congress unveiled the Thirteenth Amendment, which prohibited human slavery in the United States. Three days later Garrison delivered a speech titled, "The Death of Slavery" at a Grand Jubilee Meeting in Boston. *The Liberator* reprinted this speech six days later in the February 10, 1865, edition.[13] "The Death of Slavery" marks the first of Garrison's final major public speeches that address the end of the institution of slavery. Filled with a celebratory tone, it announces the end of American slavery, the end of *The Liberator,* and it argues that Garrisonian suffering and righteousness played a central role in the legal abolition of slavery and in convincing the American public to embrace the anti-slavery cause. This address, along with Garrison's "Valedictory Address" in the final issue of *The Liberator* provide the salvistic climax to the Christian antislavery narrative that Garrison began writing of himself and his followers in the 1830s.

"The Death of Slavery" is a remarkably condensed version of Garrison's antislavery religious beliefs, but it also begins the work of significantly expanding the definition of Garrisonian abolitionism to more broadly signify American abolitionism. Garrison begins with a nod to his antebellum narratives that emphasize the trials and tribulations of such reform work: he reminds his audience that he and his followers endured "suffering, bereavement, and lamentation" for the anti-slavery cause.[14] He succinctly describes the Garrisonian experience as one characterized by "years of conflict and persecution" during which time he and his followers were "misrepresented, misunderstood, ridiculed and anathematized from one end of the country to the other."[15] He interprets the passage of the Thirteenth Amendment as a triumph of his religious beliefs, as proof of the effectiveness of his moral appeals, and as the ultimate response to his detractors and critics. He claims the Thirteenth Amendment as a personal triumph: "friends and strangers stop me in the streets, daily, to congratulate me."[16] He also directly addresses northern and southern clergy who repeatedly labeled him a dangerous religious zealot and fanatic and proclaims that even these harshest critics must now admit that he is not "a madman, fanatic, incendiary, or traitor, but have at all times been of sound mind."[17]

Garrison's speech rehearses the major points of his antebellum anti-slavery appeals but it is equally self-consciously concerned with posterity and imbued with language that underscores his intent to carefully frame the historic legacy of Garrisonian abolitionism. In the wake of the Thirteenth Amendment he passionately argues that "impartial" critics must now concede that, "only RADICAL ABOLITIONISM [the label used by northern and southern critics to describe his religious appeals] is, at this trial-hour, LOYALTY, JUSTICE, IMPARTIAL FREEDOM, NATIONAL SALVATION."[18] His narrative here effectively lays the foundation for a new American mythology that seeks to use the "miracle" of the Thirteenth Amendment and the "national salvation" that it inaugurates as a means to shift Garrisonian abolitionism away from its wholly religious associations and to characterize this movement as a more general representation of American abolitionism. Garrison ahistorically stresses the inclusive rather than exclusive nature of his religious appeals in order to argue that by the start of the Civil War his ideas became "the dominant sentiment of the land."[19] He interprets the legal abolition of slavery and the Union's military victory as the fulfillment of his desire to purge this national sin from American life.[20] He views this outcome as a victory that all Americans who *now* oppose slavery can also partly claim and in doing so he rhetorically and retrospectively transforms all Americans into Garrisonians: "it may now be comprehensively declared, we are all abolitionists, we are all loyalists, to the backbone."[21] This is Garrisonism as Americanism and it turns Garrisonian sacrifice from a marker of exclusivity into a component of American character by describing the fight against slavery as a shared national experience.

The final issue of *The Liberator* is appropriately titled, "Valedictory: The Last Number of *The Liberator*" and, like "The Death of Slavery," it establishes the historic role of the paper in the legal abolition of slavery and it commemorates Garrisonian suffering as an essential part of this progress. The final issue's December 29, 1865, publication date coincided with Secretary of State William H. Seward's announcement that the necessary number of states had ratified the Thirteenth Amendment. The "Valedictory" issue includes a reprint of the paper's original January 1, 1831, statement of intention and this inclusion frames the historic movement towards emancipation through the paper's work. Garrison's personal correspondence suggests that this presentational choice also emerged from his desire to find closure and to respond to those members of his circle, like Wendell Phillips, who viewed his choice to close the paper as an unnecessarily premature response to the Thirteenth Amendment.[22] Regardless, the layout and content of the final issue reflects its founder's desire to bring symbolic, if not real, narrative closure to the issue of slavery and to declare Garrisonian antebellum work an unprecedented success. He publicly declares victory in this final issue and argues that his abolitionist work is now complete: "hail, redeemed, regenerated America! Hail the future, with its pregnant hopes, its glorious promises, its illimitable powers of expansion and development."[23]

Garrison begins his final editorial address by filtering the history of the American abolition struggle against slavery through his paper's history of persecution. He writes of *The Liberator's* struggles against "southern slaveholding villainy on the one hand, and Northern proslavery malice on the other," and points out that both groups denounced the paper as un–Christian and unpatriotic.[24] He characterizes the level of oppression and resistance that *The Liberator* faced to be unprecedented in American history: "never had a journal to look such opposition in the face—never was one so constantly belied and caricatured."[25] Garrison argues that the paper continued to fight for its existence in order to vindicate "the sacred claims of the oppressed" despite the fact that it "could not have been more vehemently denounced or more indignantly repudiated."[26] This language of noble sacrifice mirrors the rhetoric circulated in the paper's pages between 1831 and 1857 that told stories of heroic abolitionist suffering in the wake of staunch opposition. But the narrative here is richer and more coherent and it is more explicitly concerned with historical posterity. A clear timeline of events, beginning with Garrison's first job with the *Free Press* in Newburyport in 1826 and ending with the abolition of slavery, fold the history of anti-slavery thought and American abolitionism into the history of public Garrisonian activism. Garrison's last editorial speaks of the paper's many conversions (changing readers' "character and lives") and, more importantly, it singles out the paper as the only vessel that "vindicated primitive Christianity in its spirit and purpose."[27]

The final issue of *The Liberator* imagines American abolitionism as a unified movement and positions William Garrison as its principle founder and leader. Garrison himself argues that such a title is warranted and that his struggles, persecution, and example remain unmatched by any other American anti-slavery advocate. He survived "such a struggle as has never been paralleled in duration in the life of any reformer, and for nearly forty years been target at which all poisonous and deadly missiles have been hurled."[28] He encourages readers to remember that the end of slavery was only "gloriously consummated" through his suffering, the suffering of his followers, and through the paper's struggles.[29] The passage of the Thirteenth Amendment gives Garrison rhetorical space to transform the religious critiques levied against him during the antebellum years into a marker of his righteousness:

> better to be always in a minority of one with God—branded as a madman, incendiary, fanatic, heretic, infidel—frowned upon by "the powers that be," and mobbed by the populace—or consigned ignominiously to the gallows ... burnt to ashes at the stake like Wickliffe, or nailed to the cross like him who "gave himself for the world."[30]

He closes with a reminder to his readers that a great deal of injustice remains in the world and offers his own life and efforts as evidence that suffering assumed for the greater glory of God will always result in victory. It is this broad narrative that is re-circulated in cultural artifacts throughout the latter portion of the 19th century that will increasingly associate anti-slavery work with Garrisonism.

During the weeks leading up to *The Liberator's* final issue Garrison wrote a significant number of letters to friends and supporters in which he asked them to produce congratulatory tributes that would attest to his account of the paper's struggles and also offer eyewitness testimonials of his personal sacrifices. Oliver Johnson was the recipient of two such letters in late-December of 1865. In one letter dated December 23, 1865, Garrison asks Johnson to "send me a congratulatory and farewell letter for insertion next week."[31] Garrison reminds him that he "must receive it by Wednesday morning, at the latest—Tuesday morning would be more convenient still."[32] Johnson's brief letter did, of course, arrive in time and it appears in the last issue of the paper. His letter strongly praises Garrison's work and voices support for his decision to close *The Liberator*, proclaiming the paper's mission to be accomplished.[33] In another letter to Theodore Tilton, Garrison requests that if Tilton "feels moved by the spirit" he would greatly appreciate a brief letter that offers a testimony of his and the paper's persecution and endurance.[34] Garrison laments that he "cannot find room for a long letter, of course, for I shall be crowded for room; but one half a column in length will do."[35] As requested, Tilton wrote a short letter that arrived in time for publication. The published version of his letter praises the paper and describes Garrison as a "prophet and apostle."[36] At least twelve similar letters were sent out to prospective writers between November and December of 1865. In each case Garrison requested that the prospective writer either discuss *The Liberator's* role in the abolition of slavery or provide eyewitness testimony of his persecution and suffering.[37] In other words, even before the press began commemorating Garrison's work, his last public writings and speeches in 1865 made substantial efforts to preserve his narrative of personal suffering and his history of the American abolition movement.

As Garrisonian abolitionists celebrated the passage of the Thirteenth Amendment as a personal victory, the northern press aligned with Garrisonians in an attempt to claim part of the perceived abolitionist political victory as their own. This shift marked a drastic change in the northern press' attitudes towards William Garrison and his followers and signaled the beginning of the popular movement that would transform the most controversial and reviled Christian anti-slavery advocate (who was frequently described as a "religious fanatic" and "madman") of his day into the most visible and representative symbol of the region's antislavery efforts. This cultural moment of commemoration proved to be contagious. Some prominent northerners who once rallied against the emancipation movement now came forward to express public support for the cause and did so through a religious language and narrative of "conversion" that stressed their new receptivity to and appreciation for Garrison's efforts. In New York, Morgan Dix, the son of General John Dix, a Union military commander who was decidedly anti–Garrisonian, wrote a public letter expressing "humble gratitude" to "Almighty God" for Garrison and members of his New England anti-slavery circles.[38] Dix explains in his letter that he anticipates shocked responses from those familiar with his family and with his old politics and he tries to temper such reactions with a humorous and frank assessment of his "conversion": "how strange the change of times! Four years ago I was an out and out ultra-Southern and pro-slavery man."[39] Dix's conversion story, along with others that offered similar testimonies, became a part of a burgeoning popular culture interest in William Garrison and in the narrative of his life and work. These stories elevated Garrison and validated his own self-narration that stressed the power of his suffering. Such testimonies are consistent with a long-standing convention of Christian martyr stories in which an individual who witnesses an act of Christian sacrifice undergoes a conversion and spiritual awakening that the martyr's voluntary suffering inspires.[40] The conversion story, within the broader literary narrative, has the effect of bolstering the martyr's righteousness and highlights the "miracle" of redemptive sacrifice: that good emerges from evil.

The northern press celebrated and recited Garrison's pronouncement that with the passage of the Thirteenth Amendment, the Constitution, which he once regarded as a "covenant with death" now became a "covenant with life."[41] *Harper's Weekly* echoed these sentiments in their February 18, 1865, edition with large images and stories of the House of Representatives in the midst of an uproarious celebration on the floor of their chambers following the final congressional vote.[42] Noticeably absent from these paper's accounts and from *Harper's* popular visual representation of bustling politicians happily embracing and waving handkerchiefs in celebration is the reaction or even the presence of African Americans. The celebrations of Garrisonian abolitionists and the public elation over the triumph of the 13th Amendment threatened to erase a long history of black resistance by obscuring the visibility of black anti-slavery work in the movement towards emancipation. Even at this early stage, what remains is a commemoration of abolitionist heroism and democratic politics that looks to the victory of legal emancipation as a more general signifier of white northern ethics of determination.

The northern press' wide resuscitation of Garrison's image and its celebration and dissemination of his narrative of abolitionist suffering continued throughout 1867. *Harper's Weekly*, for instance, publishes four brief profiles of Garrison between 1867 and 1868.[43] During this period the paper describes him as a "moral inspiration" to northern readers, it details his "heroics" in the wake of great persecution, and it concedes that in retrospect Garrison was "entirely correct."[44] In 1867 *Harper's Weekly* even proclaims that African American advocacy groups are no longer necessary because Garrison and his followers made "the whole country an anti-slavery society."[45] George Curtis, *Harper's Weekly's* editor during this era, and the author of these articles, rhetorically realigns the north with Garrison and Garrison with all New England abolitionism in order to extend the reach and impact of Garrisonian abolitionist thought to Union soldiers. Curtis reasons that since the northern region is now "anti-slavery," Union soldiers should be celebrated as abolitionists who fought for a "holy cause."[46] This logic is as an important indicator of the extent to which commemorations of Garrison by northern papers facilitated northern attempts to differentiate themselves and their role in the Civil War from their Southern counterparts. Remembering and celebrating Garrison aided in the demarcation of these regional distinctions. While Union soldiers are depicted as abolitionists fighting a "holy cause," Confederate soldiers are represented as men who turned their back on

God and fought for an immoral and unjust way of life. As Curtis writes, future generations of Southerners "will never be proud that ancestors of theirs fought heroically to perpetuate slavery."[47]

Northern papers praised Garrison's decision to end *The Liberator* and also supported his call to end the American Anti-Slavery Society and the New England Anti-Slavery Society. The *New York Times* went further than most papers in its enthusiastic support of the end of organized abolition societies when it wrote that, "an anti-slavery society has no more business to be stirring now-a-days than a dead man to be walking about his coffin."[48] As the *Times* praised Garrison and his antislavery movement, northern states became, in essence, retrospective Garrisonians, making future civil rights advocacy unnecessary. Just as Garrison declared "mission accomplished" with the passage of the Thirteenth Amendment, the northern press simultaneously declared military victory with the defeat of the confederacy and retrospectively aligned themselves ideologically with abolitionists like Garrison in an effort to strengthen and ennoble the memory of the Union cause. This observation supports Alice Fah's recent argument that an understudied aspect of Civil War history is the unique ways that military and cultural histories of the war are frequently linked in 19th century discourses.[49] They are, indeed, far from distinct and here remembering Garrison becomes a way to elevate the cause and legacy of the military conflict from a regional disagreement over states rights into a debate over the meaning of freedom and a fight for racial equality.

The Garrisonian rhetoric of sacred abolitionist persecution, suffering, and heroics provided a perfect narrative vehicle for Union states to explain the cause and meaning of the unprecedented bloodshed and horror of the Civil War.[50] This is not to suggest, however, that the beginning of the popular northern commemoration of Garrisonian persecution took place without any objections or criticism. The African American newspaper *The Brooklyn Eagle* printed scathing assessments of William Garrison, Wendell Phillips, and the northern eagerness to embrace the abolitionist-centered narrative of slave emancipation: "it would be interesting if somebody clever at figures would estimate how much abolitionist agitators have contributed to the accomplishment of the work that society felicitates itself ... what is the amount in which the negro is indebted for his emancipations?"[51] The paper sarcastically dismisses Garrisonian accounts of their enduring Christian commitments and selfless sacrifices and instead characterizes their "persecution" as "little more than ill-natured remarks."[52]

The *Brooklyn Eagle's* objections are representative of a lingering frustration within the minds of some African Americans over the perceived sovereignty that Garrison and his antislavery work had assumed within the popular culture. Dating back to 1827, a large contingent of black abolitionists, led by northern free black ministers like Nathaniel Paul, believed that the abolition of slavery would be an act of God's liberating power on behalf of the slaves. Nathaniel Paul, Daniel Payne, and other black Christian abolitionists espoused antislavery appeals that expressed a confident belief that God would vindicate and exalt the suffering that blacks endured under the southern institution of slavery. As Payne told a New York congregation in the 1830s: "but then there came in my mind those solemn words: with God one day is as a thousand years and a thousand years as one day. Trust in him, and he will bring slavery and all its outrages to an end."[53] The widespread celebration of Garrison was interpreted as an affront to the longstanding beliefs of postwar African Americans who subscribed to Paul and Payne's vision of emancipation. Nevertheless, major publications adopted and disseminated Garrison's narrative of heroic suffering, endurance, and victory despite the quiet efforts of some African Americans to provide a more palpable counter-narrative. The historical memory of Garrison's legacy was quickly taking shape and those who objected were overwhelmed by the decidedly more vociferous voices of neo-Garrisonians. Newly minted Pro-Garrisonian papers encouraged readers to celebrate Garrison's sacrifices and pledged to former abolitionists that they would work to ensure that the northern public, "will not forget; they will diligently remember."[54]

Garrison's commemoration began in the northern press, but it was also widely perpetuated by the early memoirs of former Garrisonian abolitionists. These memoirs lacked the literary value of earlier tributes, like John Greenleaf Whittier's 1832 poem "To William Garrison," but what they lacked in style they compensated for in their close adherance to Garrison's antebellum narratives that emphasized abolitionist suffering and sacrifices.[55] Samuel May's *Some Personal Recollections of Our Antislavery Conflict* (1869) and Parker Pillsbury's *Acts of the Anti-Slavery Apostles* (1883) exist as two of the most prominent Garrisonian memoirs produced during the latter half of the 19th century. Both May and Pillsbury were privileged members of Garrison's inner circle (his self-described "apostles") and both of their memoirs were published during periods in which other abolitionists questioned the centrality of Garrison's story in the developing postwar narrative of America's historical anti-slavery struggle. May's early memoir appears in 1869 during the beginning of the country's celebration of abolitionist efforts. The book's publication coincided with a strong demand for stories about abolitionist leaders and more general historical narratives about New England anti-slavery efforts and their mediating role in the transformation of a divided nation into a reunited republic. He sets out to write the history of American abolitionism and in it he cites Garrisonian abolitionism as the unifying force behind American anti-slavery activities. In doing so he re-makes the history of American abolitionism into the history of Garrison and Garrisonian abolitionism. The book's 1869 publication date distinguishes it as the first major book-length postwar abolitionist memoir and history of the conflict.

Efforts to commemorate Garrison were already well underway in 1869 and May's memoir helped to solidify the connection within the public consciousness between Garrison and New England abolitionism. Parker Pillsbury's 1883 memoir similarly emerged during a time when some of Garrison's former friends and associates published books and articles in which they downplayed their former leader's role in the anti-slavery movement and elevated their own efforts.[56] Pillsbury's memoir, therefore, served a practical function as a counter-narrative to the stories circulated by writers who denigrated or dismissed the role of Garrison's persecution and sacrifice in the eradication of slavery: "everybody now is an abolitionist, so son, or grandson of an antislavery parentage, and so all seem to claim equal honor."[57] His book, he boasts, stands as a corrective to popular "misrepresentations."[58] Collectively, these two memoirs perpetuate the Garrison narrative in the wake of their leader's inability to write his own story despite many lucrative book offers and his acceptance of a $5,000 advance.[59] It is both ironic and strangely fitting that despite the meticulous editorial control that Garrison maintained over his own image and narrative in *The Liberator* that in the postwar period it is his closest friends who fought hardest to preserve it and to publicly disseminate it.

Samuel May's *Some Personal Recollections of Our Antislavery Conflict* is the earliest postwar memoir that argues that Garrison's role in the abolition of slavery should be preserved for future generations. The desire to record the personal stories of abolitionist heroes for posterity was a widely held sentiment in 1869. That same year, for instance, the *Philadelphia Press* argued that the current generation's efforts to remember and honor abolitionist work in print would "prove more permanent than a marble monument."⁶⁰ These early stories, therefore, were understood to play an important role in how future audiences imagined the language, personage, and historical narrative of antislavery reformers. In May's memoir, Garrison's presence is felt throughout. His first historical chapter, "The Rise of Abolitionism" links the beginning of the movement with Garrison's rise to prominence and recounts the author's first introduction to Garrison following a public lecture. May's memoir introduces Garrison as a man ordained by God to carry out "a great purpose and a sacred mission."⁶¹ It is a spiritual autobiography, not of May's conversion to the antislavery cause, since his antislavery stance predated his meeting with Garrison, but instead of his "conversion" to Garrisonian abolitionism. He recalls intimately sensing Garrison's "Christ-like" humanity and his uncanny ability to empathize with slave pain at their first meeting. "He only," May writes, "had his eyes so anointed that he could see outrages perpetuated upon Africans."⁶² Garrison, amongst all others, taught the nation to "hear the cries of enslaved black men and women."⁶³ May is so intrigued with Garrison at this first meeting that he can only describe him through a Biblical language that enthusiastically proclaims him to be a martyr for Christ and a divinely sanctioned representative of Christ on Earth. He remembers hearing Garrison speak for the first time and cites this as an important moment that led him to see Garrison as "a prophet" of the nation.⁶⁴ He maintains a tone of religious awe as he recalls the first time he touched Garrison's hand. He ecstatically claims that his life changed at that moment: "my soul was baptized in his spirit, and ever since I have been a disciple of William Lloyd Garrison."⁶⁵

May's autobiography carefully characterizes American abolitionism as a unified movement and argues that Garrison served as the leader of it. He reasons that Garrison's ascendancy to the leadership role must have been part of a larger providential design since no man would willingly choose to endure the persecution that Garrison experienced during the antebellum period. Garrison, in May's narrative, "found himself left and impelled to become the leader of the great antislavery reform."⁶⁶ He argues that the scope of Garrison's magnanimous goal to make the republic whole again (both literally and spiritually) ensured his persecution and necessarily demanded that he would be set apart from every man except Jesus Christ. He quotes lines from Alexander Pope's poem *Essay on Man* to valorize Garrison's persistence during the long years of persecution, misrepresentation, and physical violence: "truths would you teach to save a sinking land? All fear, none aid you, and few understand."⁶⁷ Here and elsewhere May compares Garrison to Christ and correlates the sacrifice of Garrison and his followers with the legal abolition of slavery and the "softening" of the nation's heart.⁶⁸ He ardently proclaims, "never since the days of our savior, have these lines of Pope been more fully verified than in the experience of Mr. Garrison."⁶⁹ He testifies that his time with Garrison led him to conclude that the founder of *The Liberator* was a man "not of this world" and that he instead grew to see him as a messenger charged by God to lead an anti-slavery cause that would denounce northerners, southerners, and all other guilty parties of perpetuating the systematic practice of slavery, "as Jesus had to denounce the scribes, Pharisees, and priests of Judea."⁷⁰

*Some Personal Recollections of Our Antislavery Conflict* became the first major abolitionist memoir to find success in the new literary marketplace of the late 1860s. The book found a prestigious publisher in Fields & Osgood in 1869, which also issued Harriet Beecher Stowe's *Oldtown Folks* and printed the poetry of John Greenleaf Whittier.⁷¹ The book's critical and financial success bolstered public awareness of Garrisonian narratives and re-circulated the Garrisonian history of the anti-slavery movement to a wider American audience who were now more sympathetic to this view of the war. The abolitionist Lydia Maria Child reviewed the book for the *National Antislavery Standard* and described it as "very interesting, partly consisting of history, but mainly of the author's own memories."⁷² The *New York Times* praised the book's insight and described Mayas "one of the few persons able to tell the antislavery story" due to his close proximity to Garrison and other "prominent persons" in the movement.⁷³ In addition, the city of Boston co-sponsored a National Anti-Slavery Festival just months after the publication of May's memoir to honor "the moral grandeur and heroism" of William Lloyd Garrison and other Massachusetts abolitionists.⁷⁴

May satiated the public's desire for popular stories of abolitionist heroism by offering William Garrison as the ideal model of Christian piety and suffering in order to position him as the national leader of a unified antislavery movement. He paints a history of Garrisonian persecution and suffering for slave liberty through Biblical comparisons that place his activism firmly within a tradition that celebrates abolitionist sacrifices as part of a national atonement for the sin of slavery that saved the union. In May's story the entire country is tied to Garrison and the memoir's title, *Our Antislavery Conflict,* echoes this belief with its refusal to categorize Garrisonian abolitionist work as activism carried out by a religious minority and to instead historicize it as part of an American debate ("our" conflict) in which Garrison is the redeeming savior.

Parker Pillsbury's memoir *Acts of the Anti-Slavery Apostles* (1883) presents an ardent defense of William Garrison and Garrisonian abolitionism four years after the founder of *The Liberator's* death. Pillsbury's introduction laments that the "present generation knows little of the terrible mysteries and meanings of slavery or anti-slavery."[75] Of particular concern to Pillsbury was the growing trend throughout the 1880s of former Garrisonians publicly emphasizing their own efforts in the antislavery cause and doing so by downplaying Garrison's sacrifices. He interprets this posturing as a dangerous revision of history. Even more disturbing to Pillsbury, however, is the potential influence of this narrative on younger generations who were born after the Emancipation Proclamation. The counter-narrative that most perturbs Pillsbury is the one voiced by a small minority who describe Garrison as a historical obstacle to the speedy resolution of the debate over slavery.[76] This charge would surface again in the 1930s when Gilbert H. Barnes published a modified version of this thesis in his book *The Antislavery Impulse, 1830–1844*.[77] Such groups claim, Pillsbury writes, "that it could have been sooner and more easily done, had Garrison and his small, but motley following been out of their way!"[78] Pillsbury's anger is further compounded by the belief that the rhetorical lineage of these criticisms is the antebellum accusations and vitriolic charges of religious heresy espoused by northern clergy in the 1830s and 1840s. In 1883 Pillsbury remained one of the few Garrisonians still alive and in relatively good health, which put pressure on him to produce a record of the antislavery movement that, in his own words, adhered to "strict truth, exact justice."[79]

*Acts of the Anti-Slavery Apostles*, like the Biblical *Acts of the Apostles* that its title references, is principally interested in the eye-witness testimony of the works and words of Garrison and the abolitionist movement that Pillsbury observed first-hand.[80] The Biblical *Acts of the Apostles* contains stories of the earliest years of the newly formed Christian church's ministry. It follows Peter and Paul as they gather the apostles together following Christ's resurrection and ascension and then begin the work of building a faith based on their personal experiences and eye-witness testimonies. *Acts of the Apostles*, for instance, offers the testimonies of those who physically touched and observed

Christ during the 40 days of ministry that he engaged in following his resurrection and the text argues that those who saw him during this period were inspired to set up religious communities, to endure persecution, and to die for their new faith.[81] Pillsbury's memoir borrows this basic structure to remember the early years of organized antislavery efforts and the story he tells locates the beginning of this reform movement and religious "ministry" with the emergence and rise of William Garrison. Like Samuel May, Pillsbury includes his personal "conversion" to "true" antislavery activism and links his change of heart with his first encounter with Garrison. He describes this meeting as one that changed his faith and his "earthly mission."[82] As one of the "very few surviving associates" of Garrison he explains that the "modest" goal of his book is to offer his "abundant testimony" of the work that ultimately led to the eradication of sin and slavery from American life.[83] In doing so, he hopes to preserve the heroic deeds of Garrison and Garrisonians who, against popular sentiment, "went everywhere preaching the word."[84] Pillsbury is writing a book for posterity and his detailed accounts of the sacrifices of Garrisonian abolitionists are directed to an audience largely composed of the first generation of Americans who were born into a post–Emancipation culture. Just as early church leaders countered narratives that disparaged Christ with stories that emphasized their own triumphs, martyrdom, and spiritual victories, so does Pillsbury's account rebuke contemporary narratives that criticize Garrison with a story of the centrality of Garrison and Garrisonian heroics as the essential way to remember American abolitionist activity.

Pillsbury's memoir locates the genesis of the abolition movement with the 1831 publication of Garrison's paper *The Liberator* and cites the publication of the first issue of the paper as the origin of authentic Christian abolitionist protest. He laments that he did not get involved in the abolitionist struggle, or meet Garrison, until the movement was roughly ten years old.[85] With Garrison and *The Liberator* as a reference point, the history of the abolitionist movement begins with a chapter that is economically titled, "William Lloyd Garrison."[86] What is fascinating is the extent to which Pillsbury's account of the first ten years of the abolitionist movement—which are years that admittedly predate his own time with Garrison—are addressed through a personal biography or "boyhood history" of Garrison.[87] Early on he concedes that his book "may not be the place to speak" about Garrison's early life but he assumes this task anyway as a necessary burden that is part of any serious attempt to understand the origin of "true abolitionism."[88] For example, in his account of Garrison's early disagreements with Benjamin Lundy over the immediate emancipation of slaves he draws an important distinction that is central to his historical understanding of abolitionism: that it is possible to be an "anti-slavery man, though hardly a pronounced abolitionist."[89] The difference is important to Pillsbury and it echoes his careful demarcation of the impermeable boundaries between what he perceives to be "authentic" forms of antislavery protest and the secular/humanistic arguments made by other organizations that were, as he concedes, filled with "brave and true-hearted" antislavery advocates, but they remained splintered from Garrisonians and they consequently lacked the spiritual authority or divine sanction to fully carry out this grand task.[90] Such a distinction allows Pillsbury to consider the true historical abolition movement to have existed and worked under a wholly unified front that was founded, organized, and led to victory by William Garrison. He makes this claim early on in two different ways: 1) when he writes that the entire American abolitionist movement was organized around "the philosophy and method of Mr. Garrison"; and 2) when he stresses that all "real" abolitionists understood Garrison to be the "acknowledged leader of the movement."[91]

Pillsbury's memoir remembers the Garrisonian movement through the vivid revolutionary religious language of righteous suffering that he and his follower circulated during the days of *The Liberator*. His book explains how Garrison was "divinely constituted" and charged by God to carry out "the sublimest movement in behalf of liberty and humanity for future generations."[92] Garrison's "vision was anointed" for this cause and this divine calling provided him with a greater capacity for Christian empathy for slave suffering than other northern clergy and abolitionist movements possessed. Pillsbury details Garrison's core theological convictions and teachings by quoting from a sonnet Garrison wrote in the 1830s titled, "Sonnet to the Bible." Even though he is writing in the 1880s his book resurrects and answers past charges levied by Garrison's antebellum critics concerning the alleged heretical and cultic nature of his religious faith. He offers his eyewitness testimony that in his personal life, in his formal teaching, and throughout his years in the pulpit and in lecture halls, "I surely have seen few the peer, none the superior of William Lloyd Garrison."[93]

Pillsbury utilizes part of his book as a space to re-create the atmosphere and debates of the 1830s and 1840s and through these debates he solidifies and reinforces the memory of Garrison's heroism, his prophetic role, and the redemptive work of his suffering. Pillsbury's careful recollections of the antebellum debates between Garrison and other New England antislavery groups is a narrative strategy indebted to a Christian literary tradition that places a primacy on the retelling of stories of believers who chose the path of suffering and persecution. His story's climax, which is the passage of the 13th Amendment, offers proof and vindication of the rewards that come from faithfully enduring pain. The victory here is the ability to live up to Christ's call in Mark 8: 34–35: "if any man would come after me, let him deny himself and take up his cross and follow me."[94] Robin Lane Fox points out that Christian stories of believers who endure persecution are revered because they signify the believer's ability to access tremendous amounts of power.[95] The bold willingness to surrender one's body "effaces all sin after baptism" and it possesses the ability to make one "pure and spotless."[96] By re-enacting these debates in narrative form Pillsbury skillfully leads the reader to understand the conflict as one between good and evil. Accordingly, he discusses Garrison's Christianity at length and favorably differentiates it from the antagonistic role that he reserves for mainstream northern Christian churches. It was Garrison, Pillsbury emphasizes, who prophetically warned the nation about the true cost of the sin of slavery, while northern churches and clergy demonstrated more interest in obstructing Garrisonian meetings, lectures, and ministering.

Pillsbury's aggressive tone towards orthodox northern churches in 1883 should also be understood as a reaction to the efforts by some of Garrison's historically vocal critics to publicly resuscitate their own image by retrospectively aligning themselves with his movement. Pillsbury wrote to Frederick Douglass in 1883 and cited this trend as a principle reason for his memoir: "I was compelled into *Acts* in consequence of some of the clergy and discipleship who now claim ... that they or their fathers abolished slavery!"[97] Pillsbury' would spend the rest of his life reminding readers of Garrison's persecution by re-creating in print the contentious atmosphere of antebellum New England. For example, shortly after publishing *Acts of the Anti-Slavery Apostles* in 1883 he reprinted, at his own expense, copies of 1840s Garrisonian anti-clerical pamphlets that highlighted the moral and spiritual corruption that Garrison and his followers saw in contemporary pulpits.[98] These pamphlets were originally circulated at the height of the slavery debates and now he offered them again as proof of the singular righteousness of Garrisonian abolitionism. *The Church as It Is; or, The Forlorn Hope of Slavery, Brotherhood of Thieves, or, A True Picture of the American Church and Clergy,* and *The American Churches: The Bulwarks of American Slavery* are all pamphlets that Pillsbury used to re-create for younger generations the staunch opposition that Garrisonian abolitionists encountered during his life.[99]

*The Acts of the Anti-Slavery Apostles* sought to replace the image in the public's mind of the ethical and virtuous antebellum New England clergyman with an image of Garrison as a savior with "a life pure and spotless as the white plumage of angels."[100] Garrison's whole character is "beyond reproach" and Pillsbury writes that those who came in contact with him were "spiritually blessed."[101] He reassures that Garrison's life observed the "sacred requirement" of selfless sacrifice that he "preached in his journal, *The Liberator,* and preached everywhere.[102] Informed by *The Liberator's* antebellum narratives of suffering, Pillsbury's memoir conjures and performs Garrison's stoical endurance in the wake of "years of violent opposition and persecution" and it is this steadfastness that he ultimately credits with restoring both the nation and the American church.[103] His ardent defense recirculates the narrative that Garrison told of his own life and it highlights the power of written narratives in defining American history and broader mythologies of national character. Pillsbury's account is a product of a "culture of letters" and a late 19th century public fascination with biographical sketches that circulate stories of historical figures as a way to impart ethical lessons and to understand the causes and consequences of the Civil War.[104] His memoir, when read alongside Samuel May's reminisces, offers one avenue through which Garrisonian narratives were perpetuated, transformed, and absorbed during the period of national commemoration that celebrated the triumph of heroic Garrisonian individualism and allowed a broad array of Americans to partake in the celebration of Garrison's life and victory.

The visibility of sentimental commemorations of Garrison's life steadily increased following his death on May 24, 1879, and the language of these tributes were all informed to some degree by Wendell Phillips' moving funeral eulogy that imagined Garrison as the embodiment of the newly reunited republic's best attributes. Phillips delivered his eulogy in Boston on May 28, 1879, and shortly afterwards it was widely circulated to members of Congress and to the general public in printed form.[105] Phillips' funeral eulogy, like Pillsbury's later memoir, is directed towards "young listeners who did not see that marvelous career," and so it attempts to convey to this new generation "why on both sides of the ocean, the news of his death is a matter of interest to every lover of race."[106] What follows is a prototype of the narrative that will dominate national historic memory of Garrison and American abolitionism over the next century. Phillips begins by representing Garrison's message as providentially instilled. He compares him, for instance, to great revolutionary Christian leaders like Martin Luther and to Christian intellectuals like Pascal.[107] However, Phillips' argues that Garrison's accomplishments eclipse both of these men when one takes into account that he was only 21 years old when his work began ("he confronted a nation in the very bloom of youth") compared to Luther's 24 years.[108] The abolitionist sacralization of American liberty is one of Phillips' key themes and Garrison is imagined within this language as the patriarch of this "holy cause."[109] He depicts him as "the first man to begin a movement to annihilate slavery," and he did this "alone, utterly alone," until he was able to marshal the entire nation together.[110] Phillips' messianic language is religious and political: Garrison is the object of Christian spiritual emulation and nationalistic patriotic adoration.

Phillips' funeral eulogy anticipates a common theme among Garrison's eulogists: the notion that God intentionally fashioned the abolitionist to suffer to fulfill his purposes. Phillips writes that Garrison suffered greatly. He "starved on bread and water," wherever he traveled "mobs assaulted him in every city," his life was "often in deadly peril," and financially he was "often in great need."[111] He experienced persecution of the worst kind from politicians and from northern and southern churches. So great was this torment, Phillips exclaims, that it reached a level that "no American has ever endured."[112] Garrison's willingness to endure this pain set his vision of progress apart from others and, in both his earthbound example and in his lasting legacy of reform, he views Garrison as a reflection of America's best national characteristics. All future social reform movements from the next generation that advocate liberty and equality for all races are described as standing "on the platform that Garrison built."[113] The transformation of Garrisonian abolitionism in this eulogy is remarkable: Garrison morphs from a fringe religious zealot with a penchant for political agitation and self-righteousness into a sacred symbol of America's divine origins and an instrument used by providence to forge national unity and reconciliation. The act of mourning Garrison, then, becomes the site of a complex exchange of Christian history and Christian symbols of death, resurrection, and redemption with an American patriotic market that consumes, celebrates, and canonizes a national iconography of great leaders and heroes. Phillips delivered this eulogy in a post-bellum period of regional instability and division and the cultural work of his representation of the historic and symbolic Garrison is one with designs that extend far beyond their New England origins as Phillips offers Garrison as a more general symbol of abolitionist righteousness and national belonging.

Wendell Phillips' eloquent eulogy and the strong public support that encouraged and consumed this burgeoning Garrisonian culture of commemoration infuriated groups that were the target of Garrison's harshest criticisms during the antebellum period. The Unitarian Church, one such group, responded to these Garrison hagiographies with highly critical articles written as a "counterpart" to the "undiscriminating eulogies, "which have lately prevailed."[114] *The Unitarian Review and Religious Magazine* discounted, rather than celebrated, Garrison's anti-slavery rhetoric, especially its focus on "violent language" and concluded that Garrison's emotional tactics only proved "the mediocrity of his intellect."[115] The magazine also attacks the notion that Garrison's suffering and example led to the abolition of slavery and instead describes his life as a "continual history of opportunities wasted, influence forfeited, and faithful friends and benefactors alienated."[116] The article describes Garrison's rhetorical focus on Christian suffering and violence as "sickening" and it criticizes the attempts Garrison made during his own life to label the anti-slavery cause as uniquely his own.[117] Yet even this article demonstrates the extent to which Garrisonian memory and the mythology of abolitionist suffering permeated much of the late 19th century popular discourses concerning the historical legacy of anti-slavery activism. Whether supporting or attacking Garrison's legacy in the popular culture the historical meaning and memory of his work became a hotly contested space.

While some African Americans took exception with the language used to commemorate Garrison it is important to recognize that African American ministers, poets, artists, and newspapers also played an important role in protecting Garrison's memory from groups that challenged his legacy after his death. The history of African American participation in this new Garrisonian culture of commemoration traces back to 1840 during the early years of Garrison's work at *The Liberator*. Celebrated African American luminaries, from Frederick Douglass to James Forten, praised Garrison during these years in terms indistinguishable from those of their postwar white counterparts.[118] Garrison's antebellum popularity in the African American community remained so high in the 1840s that it was not a surprise when African American newspapers like *The North Star* reported that James Forten's last death bed utterances proclaimed his love and devotion to William Garrison.[119] Garrison's image and presence, as well as Forten's "debt" to him, remained part of the story that preceded Forten's funeral, which became an event that attracted thousands of attendees.[120] Such reporting underscored the perceived centrality amongst many African Americans of Garrison's work in the eventual emancipation of slaves.[121] He was affably referred to as "Father Garrison" by many black abolitionist periodicals and this nickname provides a revealing glimpse into his popularity amongst a segment of African Americans who were so moved by his uncompromising commitment to immediate abolition that they ignored (and perhaps even embraced) the paternalistic nature of his rhetorical appeals.[122]

Following his 1879 death, numerous African American writers and papers eulogized the personal dimension of Garrison's selfless sacrifice for the slave's welfare and would continue to be ardent transmitters of this narrative throughout the late 19th and early 20th century. Frederick Douglass, for instance, fondly remembered hearing Garrison speak for the first time when he was less than a year out of slavery: "[he] complied with Emerson's idea of a true reformer. It was not the utterance, but the man behind it that gave dignity, weight and effect to his speech."[123] Douglass goes on to call Garrison "the chief apostle of abolitionism" and he explains that despite their disagreements and their famous split he saw, in Garrison, the nation's hope of a better future: "in him I saw the resurrection and the life of the dead and buried hope of my long enslaved people."[124] Douglass eulogy to Garrison concluded with the poignant call for African American to guard and protect Garrison's memory: "let us guard his memory as a precious inheritance, let us teach our children the story of his life, let us try to imitate his virtues, and endeavor as he did to leave the world freer, nobler and better than we found it."[125]

Other African American eulogies quickly followed Douglass' stirring funeral oration and similarly called on former slaves to remember and honor Garrison's life and legacy. One June 3, 1879, African American eulogy stressed the abolition of slavery as the singular focus of Garrison's entire life. Garrison's intelligence, station and oratorical skills are emphasized in order to point out the dreams and possibilities that Garrison gave up in order to devote all of his talents to the abolition of slavery:

> He was not ambitious for office. He did not labor in any professional capacity. He did not devote himself in any remarkable degree to literary pursuits. From the beginning of his long career, he had but a single purpose, and that was the abolition of slavery.[126]

This eulogy goes on to interpret Garrison's life as a symbolic representation of the "half century struggle against slavery" and it characterized this struggle as one that he alone could finally claim as "a complete triumph."[127] Two years later Reverend William H. Yeocum, writing in the African American newspaper *The Christian Recorder*, remembers Garrison in a eulogy titled "The Mind That Was in Christ."[128] Yeocum's tribute enthusiastically described Garrison in Christian language as an "animated apostle."[129] The minister counts Garrison as an equal to John Wesley and the apostle Paul, each of whom, like him, "labored, suffered and died."[130] Yeocum's eulogy reminds of the Apostle Paul's words to Timothy concerning the rewards for righteous suffering as a way to praise and honor the lasting value of Garrison's struggles and pain.[131] Even the title of the eulogy itself, which references Paul's admonition to imitate Christ's example, links Garrison's work and suffering with a divinely ordained plan for America. The apostle Paul correlated suffering and the willingness to suffer persecution with a greater degree of intimacy with God: "let this mind be in you which was also in Christ Jesus."[132] He offers Garrison's disposition, feelings and opinions and sentiments" as an example of Christ-like perfection in man and as a paradigm that others should strive to emulate.[133] In Yeocum's view, only Sumner and Lincoln begin to approach his greatness and this leads him to conclude that studying and understanding Garrison's thoughts and feelings on slavery becomes a way to begin to approach those of God.[134] The African American community's fondness for Garrison resulted a few years later in their broad support for a public monument to him in Boston.[135] In the monument, Garrison sits paternalistically in a comfortable, elevated, armchair and observes the surrounding city. Papers described the tribute as "a colossal statue of bronze, nine feet high," a size and material deemed appropriately grand enough to convey the work of Garrison's life.[136]

African American newspapers paid tribute to Garrison throughout the late 19th century and into the early 20th through a modified version of the traditional Garrisonian language that emphasized the religious nature of the historical conflict over slavery, the national and spiritual consequences that this debate posed, and the abolitionist willingness to endure suffering to eradicate this sin. They routinely discussed slavery and emancipation through stories of Garrisonian heroism and the abolitionist willingness to face "the most fearful odds" in a way that exhibited "that rarest form of bravery."[137] While these stories would have been familiar to most readers by 1884 they were perpetually retold for a new generation of African Americans born after the end of slavery. Garrison's greatest feat, such articles claimed, was his ardent pursuit of emancipation despite threats of great physical suffering from northern and southern audiences. The fact that he excelled within such a harsh environment becomes proof of the divine nature of his call: "the hissing of the crowd made thy colossal form more magnetic, thine eagle eye more searching, thine oratory more eloquent and sublime."[138] One article goes on to boldly claim that Garrison's sacrifice brought African Americans into a moment of political-secular salvation that bound them together as a free people ("thou hast made us a people," is the exact phrase) through the power of his extreme act of grace, which leads the author to conclude that all future generations should remember Garrison as "the unrivalled friend of the negro."[139] The narrative within this and other African American eulogies is that Garrisonian abolitionism was: (1) a divinely inspired movement; (2) that Christ carried out his will through Garrisonian abolitionists in a particular historical and cultural moment in a way that necessitated abolitionist suffering and which led to abolitionist persecution; and (3) that their political work and spiritual pain led to the emancipation of African Americans and the redemption of the newly united union. The relationship between emancipator and slave in these eulogies parallels the stories told in *The Liberator* during the antebellum period and also those within the post-bellum culture of abolitionist commemoration as imagined by Samuel May and Parker Pillsbury.

By early December 1905, African American newspapers continued to retell Garrison's story in anticipation of the 1th of December, which marked the 101st anniversary of the founder of *The Liberator's* birth. The December 9, 1905, edition of the *Afro-American*, for instance, emphatically encourages its African American readership to remember Garrison's sacrifice "as something of more value than gold."[140] The history of the abolitionist movement is told through Garrison's biography and through anecdotes that compare him to religious figures like John the Baptist.[141] These parallels confer upon his character a supernatural quality that is grand enough to approach his call to fight the institution of slavery "single handed and alone."[142] Despite repeated references to "the story of his great life of suffering and sacrifice," however, early 20th century white and African American narratives feature less of an emphasis on the strong religious dimensions of Garrison's suffering than the 1860s and 1870s accounts and, as a result, his heroics remain more generalized. One author even claims that the details of Garrison's legacy of suffering are not necessary because they are, "too well known to be rehearsed."[143]

Religious comparisons still appear and stories of Garrison's bravery remain but it is significant that abolitionist pain in the early 20th century is acknowledged and honored but the social and national meaning of Garrisonian work is more strongly emphasized. As writers tone down the religious language the Garrison story begins to move out of New England and becomes a national narrative. The cultural definition of Garrisonian abolitionism expanded in the post-bellum years to become a synonym for all Massachusetts and New England abolitionist movements and as the nation crept towards the beginning of the 20th century New England abolitionism slowly became part of a national narrative of sacrifice for democratic ideal and political participation.

Late 19th and early 20th century poetry about Garrison illustrates the profound ways in which remembering Garrison and New England abolitionism increasingly evolved into a site for broad patriotic national self-definition in which the history of the nation's experience with slavery was replaced with a narrative of progress and sacrifice. The poems written during this era use the symbol of Garrison's life and work to project a renewal of national civic life.

The poems of Joseph Seaman Cotter and Henrietta Cordelia Ray illustrate this trans formative shift from religious language to tributes that imagine Garrison as a symbol of American civic responsibility. In Joseph Seaman Cotter, Sr.'s 1895 poem "William Lloyd Garrison" Garrison is a patriotic savior and redeemer of the nation.[144] Cotter's tribute to Garrison interweaves religious symbols with sentimental language to position him as the origin of the social movement towards racial unity and national reunion. Cotter's poem imagines Garrison as a divine figure who paternalistically and pantheistically gazes, sadly but resolutely, upon the nation during the years of slavery. He alone, the poem tells us, knew that slavery "held God partner in the hellish stain, And saw Christ dying on a racial cross."[145] Garrison's first appearance in Cotter's poem inspires awe and nostalgia by transforming him into a larger-than-life hero who embodies the nation's divine providence, goodness, and permanence:

> A man stood God-like and his voice rang true.
> His soul was sentry to the dallying throng, his thought.
> Was watchword to the gallant few.
> He saw not as his fellow being saw;
> He would not misname greed expediency.
> He found no color in the nation's law, And scorned to
>   meet it in its liberty.[146]

If Ben Franklin is the American Adam, Garrison, in this poem, is its Jesus.[147] In death, the poem asserts that Garrison continues to look down upon the union as its "savior" and the author find peace and comfort in his gaze. Garrison "died that he [the slave] might rise up strong and free—A creature subject to the highest laws. And master of a God-like destiny."[148] Here Garrison is the workman-creator of a new union [he helped to "purge their laws and make them first for God"] that he helped to realize through a selfless supernatural Christian altruism and capacity for empathy.

In contrast, Henrietta Cordelia Ray's 1905 poem "William Lloyd Garrison" offers a very different vision of Garrison's life and legacy ten years later in a work originally written for the Garrison centenary.[149] Ray's poem, as much as Cotter's 1895 work, invests in romantic tones that affectionately and nostalgically look back to the days of Garrison's triumphs. Her poem still contains traces of the ecstatic religious language of divine vocation and power found in mid–19th century religious tributes: "thou heardest the divine voice," is the magnanimous opening line of Ray's brief sketch of Garrison's life.[150] Yet Ray's poem prefers to remember the practical civic lessons that a close study of Garrison's life teaches. Praise for Garrison's conscientious public service develops into its own form of veneration, however, and evokes a nonreligious awe that situates the realization of social and racial justice as the secular equivalent to spiritual salvation. It is Garrison's zeal for social and legal justice that the author praises most ardently: "so to thee who hast climbed heroic heights, and led the way to where chaste justice reigns."[151] Ray lauds Garrison less for the atoning implications of his suffering than for his political and civic contributions and even these are removed from the context of traditional Christian martyr narrative conventions. To be clear, he is still "called" by God in this poem and he is also divinely supported in his worthy endeavors but it is the historical, social, and political results that the poem finds most worthy of praise. In a key passage from the poem it is Garrison's unwaveringly humanistic beliefs in the dignity of all people that takes precedent to the spiritual outcomes of his work and it is this legacy that inspires the author's most hyperbolic language: "An anthem—tears and gratitude and praise,/Its swelling chords,—uprises and invites/A nation e'en to join the jubilant strains, which celebrate thy consecrated days."[152]

Ray's poem is representative of the beginning of a 20th century national celebration of Garrison's legacy that represents his anti-slavery work as an example of the patriotic virtues of an active and ethical life. His life and its various retellings, in non-fiction and fictional forms, becomes a barometer by which Americans are encouraged to measure their own progress. Ray's poem is also significant because it demonstrates the extent to which early 20th century versions of Garrisonian narratives begin to depart from the prescribed patterns of their 19th century predecessors. Absent here is the distinct Garrisonian Christian theology present in the accounts of Garrison's followers, the New England popular press, and early post-bellum Massachusetts tributes that embraced Garrison's religious difference as a marker of their distinct regional identity. In other words, how Garrison's rhetoric, life, and image are remembered is necessarily linked to particular cultural and historical contexts. Early post-bellum 19th century narratives of Garrisonian suffering and persecution offered a way for New Englanders to broadly imagine their region as abolitionist and to emphasize the key role that the region's sacrifices played in the union's victory. The early 20th century marks the beginning of a narrative that views Garrisonian abolitionism as an exemplary example of American heroics, privilege, responsibility, ethical conscience, and civic duty.

The influence of the shift towards a national and more general narrative of Garrisonian abolitionism is observable in the explosion of early 20th century novels that depict abolitionists as the embodiment of moral resoluteness and domestic stability. This fiction allegorically narrates the history of abolitionist protest in antebellum America by focusing on harmonizing images that stress the national historic purpose of antislavery activism. This fiction places less emphasis on historically accurate attempts to differentiate the immediatist religious doctrines of Garrisonian abolitionism from other forms of anti-slavery thought and instead conceives a common, only nominally religious, ideology as the representative example of all anti-slavery protest.

William E. Barton's 1900 novel *Pine Knot* is an example of a fictional work that frames immediatist religious abolitionism as American abolitionism and which also represents the abolitionist figure as a broad paternalistic instrument of national reunion.[153] Barton's fictional story concerns the daughter of an immediatist abolitionist teacher who, through a series of narrative twists, falls in love with a confederate officer from Kentucky. In choosing to pursue a romantic relationship with the confederate soldier she abandons a potential (and presumably more obviously desirable) marriage with a Union Army chaplain who also desires her romantic attention. The novel is a prototypical work of sentimental fiction, which is a genre with an extensive and well-documented history of scholarly debates by literary critics and cultural historians like Ann Douglas and Jane Tompkins.[154] However, of most significance to this study is the representation of "Buzbee," the father who remains in the background of much of Barton's narrative. Despite his status as a minor character in a few key moments he nevertheless helps his daughter become aware of the need for personal reconciliation and forgiveness, which serves as an allusion to national peace, harmony, and sectional reconciliation.[155] 'Liberty,' he tells his daughter, is the "catechism" of the national creed.[156] As he supports his daughter's proposed nuptials, his character and the novel, justify this union through a language of harmony that is not explicitly religious, but is instead about America becoming conscious, once again, of itself as a nation. As he joins his daughter in a marriage with a confederate soldier, the abolitionist is framed as the catalyst of American solidarity and the symbol of an American voice that ameliorates fears of instability and division. In fiction, Garrison's vision of the abolitionist who righteously projects the power of scripture is transferred into a representative archetype for American abolitionism as a mythically harmonizing patriotic and paternal voice.

Fictional narratives of abolitionist heroism that equate the virtues of anti-slavery protest with sectional reconciliation persist throughout the early 1900s. Elizabeth Meriwether's 1910 novel *The Sowing of the Swords* demonstrates that southerners also adopted variations of this narrative in their fictional attempts to reconcile the celebratory myths of the newly reunited America with their past efforts to fracture the union.[157] Meriwether's gothic tale of rape, geographical destitution, and regeneration is told through the eyes of a New England abolitionist's daughter who helps to spiritually regenerate the inhabitants of a dilapidated and largely abandoned Louisiana plantation. Hannah, the story's main protagonist, assumes the task of confronting and purging the demons that both literally and figuratively haunt Meriwether's plantation. They are the ghosts of the plantation's former inhabitants and reminders of the region's participation in the slave trade.[158] The novel's commingling of birth and death imagery [Hannah leaving home for the first time and making her first solo adult voyages contrasts with the traces of the plantation's violent history and physical demise] suggests that Hannah, an extension of her New England father's ideology is metaphorically "giving birth" to a new nation that is capable of moving forward by looking back and remembering abolitionist values and warnings. This new union is one that progresses by acknowledging that all Americans, even New England citizens, are historically and ethically tied to the sin of slavery. Hannah makes this revelatory remark in the book's second chapter while she takes a moment to think about her father:

> father had always been a ferverent abolition preacher. It has been said that from hating the sin of slavery New England abolitionists came to hate the men who owned slaves. This is not true. New England history shows that we of New England disliked the people of the south even while we engaged in the slave traffic.[159]

The story's paternalistic abolitionist father figure, like the one in Barton's story, remains an undeveloped but formidable presence who serves as the story's moral bridge and who analogizes the nation's rebirth with the white male abolitionist as the natural historical parent of this new society. My point is that without the abolitionist in this story there is no hope of renewal or birth and past wrongs, both spiritually and morally, promise only death. That southern novelists, even ones like Meriwether who notoriously romanticized the demise of the antebellum plantation culture, would circulate traces of the Garrisonian narrative only further demonstrates its cultural power.[160]

The allusion to the abolitionist "father" figure remained a persistent motif during the early 20th century that rhetorically conflated abolitionist paternalism with the "natural" birth of the union. Katherine Holland Brown's 1928 novel *The Father* makes the connection between abolitionist proselytizing and the remaking or "conversion" of American culture to an anti-slavery viewpoint more explicitly than others of this era.[161] Her novel tells the story of a young abolitionist newspaper writer whose fiery editorial calls for immediate emancipation attract public outrage and invite persecution from his detractors but his views eventually win converts and change the course of American history.[162] Abraham Lincoln makes a brief appearance in Brown's story just before his 1860 presidential election. He befriends Henry, the story's abolitionist, who persuades him to adopt an anti-slavery stance based on the moral arguments of his controversial and emotionally driven anti-slavery newspaper articles. The point of the whole novel is that it is this conversion that leads to Lincoln's refusal to compromise with the south, which plunges the nation into Civil War and which, in the end, leads to a transforming moment of national renewal following the confederacy's military defeat. The novel's young protagonist is overtly modeled after Garrison's own likeness: he is "tall and lanky," he wears spectacles, and he is prematurely going bald.[163] He possesses an uncommon pious and gentle quality but he is also capable of a "fiery temper" when confronted with the issue of racial injustice and violence.[164] His righteousness and heroism are the driving moral force behind the national changes that take place during the book, which culminate in the election of Lincoln. The book's ambiguous title *The Father,* an affectionate paternalistic title that some African American periodicals used to describe William Lloyd Garrison and some northern periodicals used to describe Abraham Lincoln, suggests the unheralded role of the abolitionist in the preservation of the union and American liberty.[165]

Just like the literal father in Barton and Meriwether's novels the abolitionist in this story is a supernatural guardian over the nation and speaks through and influences those who hold actual positions of governance. These fictional narratives diverge from the 1870s focus on the overtly religious dimension of abolitionist pain and suffering but they do continue to emphasize a central outcome of these early stories: the way abolitionist suffering and guidance freed America to be itself. Paternal abolitionist oversight in these stories enables continuity in American republican life. This continuity, however, also produces the same problematic outcome as Garrison's theology of abolitionist suffering and his rhetorical appeals for the abolition of slavery: the history of slave suffering is obscured, the memory of black anti-slavery protest is forgotten, and both of these ideas are replaced with the celebration of white abolitionist activism as the symbol of national reunion and the best of hope for the maintenance of future societal virtue and stability.

The late 19th and early 20th century explosion of non-fiction and fictional commemorative narratives of abolitionist suffering and heroism obscured the hardships experienced by African Americans during Reconstruction and the reality of Jim Crow. With the passage of the Thirteenth Amendment Garrisonians believed that their role came to a definable end. Antebellum Garrisonian rhetorical appeals in *The Lib-*

*erator* castigated northern and southern complicity in the sin of slavery, empathized with slave suffering, and celebrated Garrisonian sacrifices and triumphs through a unique religious language, iconography, and martyr-centered narrative. With the passage of the Thirteenth Amendment, however, Garrisonian narratives were re-read and re-circulated by a variety of groups and peoples outside of Garrison's circle in an attempt to understand the cause and meaning of the Civil War. New England publications drew on Garrisonian narratives to construct an idealized memory of their region's antebellum protest to the institution of slavery. Other publications like *Harper's* revisited their negative antebellum assessments of Garrison and were "born again" in a manner that allowed them (and their readers) to retrospectively imagine all northern opposition to slavery as Garrisonian.

The 19th century memoirs of Garrisonians like Samuel May and Parker Pillsbury aided in the construction of the memory of a nationally unified, Garrison-led, anti-slavery movement. These early memoirs, along with the post-bellum New England desire to explain their region's participation in the war and to explain the war's favorable outcome, produced a culture of commemoration that celebrated William Garrison and Garrisonian conceptions of abolitionism through their own self-mythologizing language of suffering, witnessing, and heroism. Garrison's 1879 death only intensified the preponderance of these stories. By the late 19th century the production of eulogies, poems, and physical monuments that drew from this sacrificial language made the Garrisonian narrative the dominant way of remembering American anti-slavery protest.

Contemporary historians like James McPherson, for instance, go to great lengths to critique, "the prevailing assumption that most abolitionists abandoned the battle for Negro rights after 1870."[166] This "assumption," of course, only makes sense through a definition of abolitionism that is limited to Garrisonian reform rhetoric and history That the Garrisonian narrative still maintains such a powerful influence on contemporary historians and public political figures is a testimony to the strong social and cultural currents and needs that widely propelled Garrisonian abolitionism into the American consciousness between 1865 and 1910. Early 20th century novelists used this template to create a genre of Civil War fiction that derived from and reproduced the omniscient paternalism so important to the rhetoric of Garrisonian abolitionism. Explicit Garrisonian theology fell by the wayside in these and later novels but the centrality of abolitionist sacrifice and moral suasion (whether for secular or religious ideals) remained (and remains) present. It is these early stories, both in fiction and non-fiction, that inform early 20th century audience understandings and, to a lesser degree, our contemporary understandings of Civil War–era America. It is important to remember that this narrative, with its rush to commemorate and celebrate abolitionism heroism is equally invested in forgetting past slave suffering and in displacing serious attempts to address current racial inequality.

# 3

# "For Future Generations"
## Garrison's Children, Massachusetts Educational Reform and the Institutionalization of the Garrison Narrative in Boston Schools, 1880–1922

The Garrison revival of the late 19th century pressed upon a new generation of Americans an imaginative sensibility that framed William Garrison and the historical anti-slavery struggle as an epic narrative of abolitionist suffering and sacrifice that guided the nation's progressive movement toward the eradication of slavery. Harrowing stories of Garrison's activism appeared in popular fictional and non-fictional texts that celebrated his passionate and unwavering demand for racial equality and encouraged audiences to think about the eradication of slavery as an extension of his personal sacrifices. In the previous chapter I discussed the major texts of this popular culture phenomenon and the people and forces that helped this commemorative movement maintain a high degree of visibility throughout the postwar years. However, an equally important regional component of the Garrison revival operated on a more subtle institutional level: the development of the modern New England educational system and its efforts to widely disseminate Garrison's story of suffering as an essential component of the region's anti-slavery history to children in Boston's public schools.

This chapter tells the story of the emergence and implementation of the Garrison narrative within the standardized curriculum of Boston schools between 1905 and 1922. It interweaves the history of the efforts made by Garrison's sons Wendell and Francis ("Frank") Garrison in the late 19th century, and those by his first daughter Helen Francis Garrison ("Fanny") in the early 20th century, to preserve and promote their father's place in New England antislavery history with Massachusetts's movement towards standardized curriculum and its increasing interest in educational reform and the textbook as a site for widely disseminating regional narratives of the Civil War. I show that these discourses were interrelated and indicative of a cultural moment in which states began the arduous process of finding ways to narrate the history of the recent Civil War by deciding who and what new generations of children should remember. In doing so, this chapter reveals the discourses that helped to transform Garrison's narrative of redemptive abolitionist suffering into an "official" institutionally sanctioned memory in turn-of-the-century Boston.

This chapter begins with Garrison's children because following their father's 1879 death, they assumed the responsibility to publicly espouse and protect his story and their family name in Boston. Despite the political gulf that developed in the postwar period between Garrison and his children, they nevertheless used his memory and life as a symbol to legitimate, promote, and frame their own reform work and to narrate Massachusetts's antislavery history. Between 1885 and 1889 Wendell and Frank, in particular, achieved public prominence through the publication of a massive four volume biography of their father and the New England abolitionist movement titled, *William Lloyd Garrison, 1805–1879: The Story of His Life Told by His Children*.[1] Through the book they re-introduced a story of their father's life and the antislavery movement that he popularized through his own self-mythologizing in the 1830s and the 1850s to a new generation of Americans born after the passage of the Thirteenth Amendment. Their book and their public efforts to convey their father's story were so well-received and documented by the northern press that their approval and input on city-sponsored Garrison tributes was sought by Boston legislators and public officials during this era of national commemoration in which poems, eulogies, abolitionist memoirs, and fictional representations of their father were abundant and each emphasized, in different ways, the scope, power, and meaning of his reform work. The critical and financial success of their book, for instance, led Boston officials to appoint the two Garrison brothers to city commissions that were charged with the very task of deciding how to best commemorate their father in the city that was the setting of his greatest reform work.

Such efforts to commemorate and remember Garrison in Boston, however, occurred within a vibrant postwar Massachusetts culture in which public officials viewed school children and educational curriculum as a key site in their efforts to construct a coherent regional identity that depicted New England as a stabilizing and unifying moral force for the nation during the Civil War. And so, in Massachusetts, during the period between 1880 and 1922, regional celebrations of William Garrison's place in state history were conjured against a backdrop of Massachusetts educational reform debates that viewed the production of new textbooks and school curriculum as key sites for expressing concerns over children's welfare and for transmitting clear narratives about the state's past. Wendell and Frank Garrison's personal interests in producing a definitive history of their father and the antislavery movement similarly intersected with their burgeoning investment in new reform movements, educational pedagogy, and children's literature. Analyzing these familial efforts, city remembrances, and educational debates together shows the diverse forces that transformed—or at least facilitated—the Boston educational system's transformation into a vehicle for the transmission, perpetuation, and institutionalization of narratives and images of William Garrison's suffering, reform work, and his role in national emancipation. This chapter shows that as part of a new standardized curriculum, generations of Boston residents would learn of abolitionism through the Garrisonian narrative, which linked anti-slavery advocacy with abolitionist suffering and suffering as the cornerstone of their own identity and that of their region.

Wendell Phillips Garrison, the third child and second son of William Lloyd Garrison and Helen Eliza Benson, became an unlikely protector of his father's memory and narrative in late 19th century Boston. He was born in Boston in 1840, nine years after his father published the first issue of *The Liberator*, and into the chaotic environment that marked the historical height of the city's anti–Garrisonian protests. Wendell's early life and upbringing bore a startlingly resemblance to the career trajectory followed by his father. He was a product of Boston culture and strongly attached to the region: he attended Boston Latin School, he went to Harvard, and he spent much of his youth as a speaker on the Boston abolitionist lecture circuit. His birth name came from Wendell Phillips, the so-called "golden trumpet of abolitionism," who was also his godfather. Wendell, like his father, even became involved in writing about reform and civil rights as the co-founder of his own periodical, *The Nation*. He started the paper in 1865 during the last days of the Civil War at the moment his father prepared to permanently close his own paper, *The Liberator*.

These cursory resemblances, however, masked the strong political differences and frustrations that manifested privately, and sometimes publicly, between Wendell, his father, and other surviving Garrisonian abolitionists. The same year that Wendell began writing *The Nation* he became so frustrated with his father and his circle of abolitionists that he relocated from Boston to Orange, New Jersey, where he would keep a permanent residence for the remainder of his life.[2] He and his father exchanged hostile private letters between 1865 and 1877. Wendell's staunch editorial support for President Andrew Johnson in *The Nation* throughout 1867, for instance, conflicted with his father's public calls for a congressional impeachment. In personal correspondence, the elder Garrison critiqued his son's support for the "rampant corruption" that he believed Johnson's violation of the Tenure of Office Act of 1867 represented.[3] In a letter to his father, dated April 4, 1868, Wendell took exception with such criticism and used this disagreement as an opportunity to harshly dismiss the widespread public flattery given to Garrisonian abolitionists and to instead argue that the disproportionate attention to their past protests only discouraged new work from the next generation of reformers: "latter-day abolition saints and martyrs like yourself will never change their minds and step aside for the next generation."[4]

The clear frustration that Wendell expresses in this April letter occurred during a month in which commemorative events for his father were held throughout the city of Boston. William Cooper Nell, a black Boston abolitionist, who authored *The Colored Patriots of the American Revolution* (1855), organized one of these tributes on April 26th and as part of the festivities former black Boston abolitionists offered personal testimonials of William Lloyd Garrison's struggles and then presented him with an elaborate bronze clock that represented "history teaching by example."[5] The proceedings were followed afterwards by "cake, ice cream, and lemonade" for all in attendance.[6] Nell wrote to Garrison earlier that month to propose such an event and Garrison quickly accepted. In one of several letters that Garrison penned to Nell following his invitation he wrote:

> I have no doubt that I am indebted to your strong friendship and warm appreciation of my anti-slavery labors for the presentation that will be made on that occasion. It will be all the more valued on that account; though I shall feel none the less obliged to everyone contributing to the testimonial.[7]

The tensions caused by the elder Garrison's public prominence and adoration and his continued desire to weigh-in on public matters, even when they brought him into personal conflict with his son, persisted throughout 1867. In a December 18, 1867, letter to Wendell, Garrison wrote to explain his anticipated absence at Christmas and his desire to avoid any potential conflict during the holiday: "I would like to be home, but I hardly feel reconciled to be making you such a hurried visit."[8]

By 1875 Wendell's disagreements with the elder Garrison became public when his father attacked him in an editorial printed in the pages of Boston's *The Independent*.[9]

Their disagreement this time centered on the role of slavery and emancipation in American historical memory. Garrison believed that the nation should be continuously reminded of the sin of slavery and of the suffering and pain that reformers endured for its abolition.[10] He criticized his son's effusive support of reconstruction efforts that he believed were badly mismanaged and would only result in a national deepening of white racism.[11] In "glorifying" attempts to mend old wrongs, Garrison accused his son of supporting sentiments that overlooked the "criminality" and severity of past historical sins.[12] The unspoken implication of Garrison's public rebuke was that Wendell had abandoned the family work and was possibly tarnishing his (and their) association with the leadership of the national project of abolition. Such accusations weighed heavily on Wendell and in a February 7, 1875, letter to his father he expressed frustration with his continued postwar obsession with race and the legacy of his abolitionist activities: "it is useless for you and me to exchange arguments on this matter. You see in every issue a race issue. I do not."[13]

Three years passed between Wendell's 1875 letter-the climax of their private and public debates—and the death of William Garrison and during these years father and son slowly reconnected with one another. Perhaps the 1877 death of Wendell's wife Luck McKim brought him closer to his father. Or perhaps his father's declining health tempered the severity of past arguments. What is clear is that a few months before his father's 1879 death Wendell decided to begin work on a definitive biography of his father that would narrate his antislavery work and commemorate his lasting impact on the nation. By April 1878, he was earnestly collecting and transcribing materials about the abolitionist movement that he received from his father and his closest followers. Wendell penned a letter to his father on April 2, 1878, in which he enthusiastically described his research progress and his hope to produce a book in which "every item of antislavery interest is discussed."[14] However, his letter also expresses his growing awareness of the daunting scope of the project that he proposed. He explained that in one writing session he copied over 40 of his father's letters, which proved to be an insignificant number compared to the formidable number remaining.[15] Nevertheless, he remained determined to continue with such an approach: "at first I intended to copy only the most important things, but so far, I have included everything, disliking to omit even the trivialities."[16] Shortly after, Francis Jackson Garrison or "Frank," Garrison's seventh child and Wendell's youngest brother, joined Wendell in working on his father's biography.

Wendell and Frank Garrison set out to formally write the definitive biography of their father and the history of American abolitionism and to link the two as inseparable. Perhaps their father's inability to write his much anticipated history of abolitionism in 1866 inspired them to undertake this enormous task.[17] Or perhaps they believed that despite the plethora of biographical sketches and writings that emerged during the Garrison revival that someone from the family should assume some public responsibility for telling their father's story.[18] Whatever their motivation, what remains clear is that in the years following their father's death, Wendell and Frank continued to feverishly collect and transcribe their father's letters, issues of *The Liberator*, and repeatedly consulted his old friends and the family members who knew him best. This research resulted in the 1885 publication of the first two volumes of an intentionally grand, undeniably verbose, and formidably voluminous history of William Garrison and New England abolitionist efforts: *William Lloyd Garrison, 1805–1879: The Story of His Life Told by His Children*.[19] In this work the two sons explicitly link the history of New England abolitionism with their father's single movement. The magnanimously describe their book as "the archives of the abolition cause" and credit it alone with capturing "the spirit of the age on the great subject of slavery."[20] Yet the book also expresses its objective in deceptively simpler language: "here, in all sincerity, we must plead our simple intention to produce a biography."[21] In other words, their father's history is inseparable from the history of abolitionism and the history of abolitionism is their father's biography.

The portrait the Wendell and Frank construct of their father in the first two volume's roughly 2,000 pages is a distilled version of his own antebellum self-mythologizing that emphasizes Garrisonian witnessing and suffering as playing a major part in the nation's redemption. For instance, they celebrate their father's religious beliefs as separate and distinct from his contemporaries who also claimed to be abolitionist: "the so-called Christian contemporaries of Mr. Garrison judged him and his 'isms' not by the Bible to which he constantly referred them, but by temporary considerations, of personal advantage and public welfare, which have always prevailed with the human race above abstract professions, however sacred."[22] They also differentiate between their father and other "imposters" by situating his form of anti-slavery activism as the only authentic form of protest and certainly the only one worthy of historical remembrance.[23]

The 1885 publication of these first two volumes occurred within the tumultuous era of Massachusetts's educational reform debates as lawmakers and activists debated how tot properly teach the history of Massachusetts and its role in the Civil War to children. This burgeoning popular interest in teaching Civil War history occurred in an era in which a plethora of Civil War amusements were routinely marketed towards children. Between 1880 and 1890 children accounted for more than a third of the American population and, as James Marten shows, few elements of northern children's lives were left untouched by "the vibrant post-war culture" that encouraged them to participate in rituals of remembrance that commemorated Union military victory.[24] Civil War entertainments like battle paintings, commemorative music, plays, public reenactments and panoramas dominated the landscape of northern post-war popular culture and relied on spectacle to re-create the war for a generation who did not live through it.[25] It is undeniable that popular culture played an important role in shaping northern children's attitudes about the Civil War, but focusing exclusively on these texts ignores the fact that the late 19th century was also the major era of Massachusetts educational reform and that the New England schoolhouse, as a real and symbolic image, became just as important a site for disseminating northern Civil War narratives as the popular amusements that children routinely participated in and consumed. The story of the Garrison revival, then, is also one about overlapping cultural discourses centered around education and children: the post-bellum born child as an optimistic symbol of national reunion and the Massachusetts focus on educational reform, textbooks, and young children as an important way to transmit regional narratives and perpetuate ideas about the moral implications of William Garrison and Massachusetts antislavery protest during the Civil War.

Both Wendell and Frank were keenly aware of the educational debates happening around them and they explicitly cite a concern with education and the accuracy of the historical curriculum in Massachusetts's schools as a strong impetus for writing their book. In their 1885 preface they tackle the same problem that faced Garrison during his own lifetime; namely, how to tell the story of abolitionism to those children born after the Thirteenth Amendment. They position their book as an excellent resource for historical instruction:

> The growing but still small number of anti-slavery memoirs afford hardly a glimpse of the inner workings of the movement which it was Mr. Garrison's destiny to create and to direct. In the following pages we are brought face to face with a world which will appear wholly new and strange to the generation now upon the scene. The school histories of the United States, with scarcely an exception, ignore it altogether; it barely comes within the horizon of the manuals of American history.[26]

Such rhetoric fit nicely with the dominant Boston cultural sentiment surrounding Garrison in the post-war period. The magnanimous conclusion that Garrison was, in fact, abolitionism personified did not seem to bother his sons or their potential readers. Wendell and Frank were savvy enough, however, to recognize that their familial ties might offer critics an avenue by which to question their ability to objectively render the movement. They address this point directly in the book's preface when they concede that they are far removed from the supposedly indifferent, unbiased, historians who normally author such texts, but they simultaneously assure the reader that their relationship did not unduly impact their conclusions: "writing not without bias, surely, but in a spirit emulous of the absolutely fairness which distinguished our father, we have done little more than coordinate materials to serve posterity in forming that judgment of him which we have no desire to forestall."[27]

In 1886, a year after the publication of the first two volumes of their planned four-volume biography, Wendell and Frank were invited to serve in an advisory capacity on Boston committees charged with the task of deciding how the city could properly memorialize their father and publicly tell his story.[28] This appointment consisted of two primary tasks: the first involved giving input and final (e.g. public) approval to the design and construction of a proposed monument to their father by Olin L. Warner that would be placed on Boston's Commonwealth Avenue.[29] The second involved examining how their father's story might be used to help make school children "literate, educated, and moral."[30] The city believed, in other words, that Garrison's life might serve a practical educational and instructional purpose. In letters written between February and April of 1886 Wendell and Frank exchanged correspondence about how to proceed with the task of best advising members of the city educational committee. Frank stayed in Boston to work directly with the committee, while Wendell remained in New Jersey, and together they decided to select stories from their biographical research that might provide worthwhile lessons in "Christian morality" while also teaching children about the region's history.[31] Wendell, in particular, viewed education as a greater and more permanent tribute to their father than statues and sculptures.[32] In fact, despite signing off on the Olin L. Warner's design for the city's monument to his father, he secretly confided to Frank that he found it "too crass to be art."[33]

Wendell Phillips Garrison, even more than his brother Frank, developed a genuine interest in educational reform, pedagogy, and children's literature while serving on these memorial committees. In 1887, while working as an advisor to the Massachusetts school systems he made his first of several forays into writing children's literature with a book handled through a Boston publisher, titled, *Bedside Poetry: A Parent's Assistant in Moral Discipline*.[34] He filled it with poems by abolitionist writers like John Greenleaf Whittier and imagined it, as the title implies, as a book that parents would read to their children at bedtime.[35] During these same years, he actively worked to promote and protect his father's memory in his official capacity for the city of Boston and through his contacts with other publishers. For instance, in a June 15, 1887, letter to the literary critic George E. Woodberry, he praised Woodbury for featuring excerpts from his father's letters and poems in a volume of the *Advocate*, but also lamented that he "was far from being represented by his best pieces."[36] He instead suggested some alternate speeches that could be found in *The Liberator* [speeches which he and Frank also reprinted in their biography] as better examples of his father's work.[37] Such instances illustrate the way the favorable 1887 reception that greeted the first two volumes of Wendell's biography of his father and the early years of the abolitionist movement led him to assume a great deal of responsibility for how this story was told publicly. Wendell divided his days between managing and writing for *The Nation* and working on the second half of his biography of his father, and devoted his evenings to writing children's literature.[38]

By 1897, Wendell Garrison's passion for education led him to write and publish books and guides focused on issues of early childhood education and, in particular, his interest in pedagogical approaches to teaching history. His 1897 book *Parables for Home and School* is a representative example of his interest in children's texts and education.[39] In it, he writes that all lessons, regardless of their specific subject, should be taught with an awareness of advancing a lesson in "applied morals."[40] He argues that a common fault in children's texts is their tendency to "condescend to children."[41] To avoid this tendency he advises educators to choose texts and adopt an approach to teaching that is not restrained by a fear to "soar above their [the children's] intelligence. The aim is to broaden their outlook and stimulate their thought."[42] These conclusions, he explains, are the result of his own careful pedagogical studies that were based in the classroom: "I tested them severally in the school-room, obtaining, with the help of ready teachers, satisfactory evidence of the amount of attention secured ... hundreds of their written abstracts confirm, I can but think, of the general utility of my plan."[43] Having students memorize the biographies of important historical figures, along with "a little science" and "a little geography," account for a significant part of Wendell's plan to teach important moral lessons through historical illustrations.[44] Wendell's book, perhaps even more than its content, reminds of the ways that personal identity, historical memory, a concern for children, and an avid interest in school textbooks intersected in the minds of Garrison's children and other city officials during the period between 1880 and 1897.

Wendell's developing views on education in *Parables for Home and School* (1897) were published during a period of unprecedented urban growth in Boston and were encouraged by the emergence of new educational theories that viewed the textbook, and not the teacher, as the most important site of knowledge transmission. By the late 19th century, the school textbook and the "curriculum model" of education reform claimed that texts represented the singular most important mediating force between the private domestic values of the home and regional and national values. In 1892, Harvard University president and National Education Association chairman Charles W. Eliot's work to eliminate curricular distinctions between those New England students who were preparing for college and those who were "preparing for life" exemplified this trend.[45] Eliot's educational reform appeals stressed the social benefits of maintaining a strong uniform curriculum within each American region.[46]

Wendell's complimentary interests in children's literature and in promoting his father's memory as the leader of American abolitionist efforts during this period should also be understood as expressing a common impulse throughout American history that links children to national and regional identity. As Caroline F. Lavender posits in *Cradle of Liberty: Race, the Child, and National Belonging from Thomas Jefferson to W.E.B. Du Bois*, "the child" has historically been an important site of "the mutually enforcing alliance ... between self and nation state."[47] An American interest in futurity made symbolic representations of the child and discourses organized around a concern for school children a popular way to express late 19th century hopes and anxieties. Even in the antebellum period, fictional and non-fictional works, especially collections of fables like *Book of Fables for the Amusement and Instruction of Children*, were marketed to parents as a valuable tool to teach simple lessons about the importance of strong individual morality.[48] Other books, like *Charles Ashton, the Boy That Would Be a Soldier*, prepared children to grow into citizens who could protect and perpetuate American democratic ideals through patriotic service and the military defense of the country.[49] Children's stories of this era, both implicitly and explicitly, placed the private virtuous citizen as the sustaining strength behind American democratic institutions.[50] And so, the rise of post–Civil War stories of historical figures like Garrison were readily embraced by those interested in textbooks as a tool to provide children with moral lessons on how to live a virtuous life.

This new educational emphasis on the centrality of the textbook in the 1890s is representative of a longer Massachusetts interest in school as a prominent site for constructing and protecting their region's history. Throughout the 19th century, Massachusetts passed more educational laws than any other state and in doing so the region led efforts to link education with fostering a coherent regional and national identity. In 1837 Massachusetts became one of the first American states to formally establish school systems that monitored and taught a standard curriculum to all students.[51] Other states such as Pennsylvania, in 1843, Vermont in 1850, and Indiana in 1851, quickly followed this example.[52] By 1852 Massachusetts went even further when it became the first state to unanimously pass compulsory school attendance laws.[53] Uniform curriculum worked to solidify regional identity. As Benedict Anderson persuasively argues in *Imagined Communities: Reflections on the Origin and Spread of Nationalism*, print culture and nationalism played a vital role in the ability of Americans to "imagine" themselves as part of a larger cohesive community and to differentiate themselves from others.[54]

The 1852 passage of Massachusetts's compulsory attendance laws should be understood as a manifestation of the importance that the state placed on education to instill a sense of civic duty that would be rooted in a common understanding of the region's past. This is not to ignore, however, the racial, class, and religious tensions that provided a formidable challenge to legislative efforts to produce a common morality and history through its textbook curriculum. Between 1850 and 1910, the proportion of Americans living in urban areas expanded from around 20 percent to well over 50 percent.[55] A significant proportion of these new urban dwellers were immigrants, Native Americans, and former slaves and many settled in Boston.[56] The visibility of the children of these "non-white" parents challenged the lofty ideals of the Boston School Committee and other government agencies that aspired to one day implement a uniform curriculum that could cultivate a consistent vision of the upstanding Massachusetts and American citizen. In 1850, for instance, the Boston School Committee directly addressed the formidable challenge of racial, economic, and cultural diversity in their city school system: "taking children at random who are undisciplined, uninstructed, often with inveterate forwardness and obstinacy, and with the inherited stupidity of centuries of ignorant ancestors; forming them from animals into intellectual beings, and ... from intellectual into spiritual beings."[57] Religious conflicts also existed within the Boston educational system: Catholic communities, for instance, protested the decidedly protestant language and focus of public school curriculum.[58] These conflicts never escalated to the extent that they did in other cities like New York and Chicago during this same period, but during the 1850s Catholic leaders in Boston did propose a separate Catholic network of schools that would receive public funds and use a slightly modified version of the general city curriculum that was originally designed for the allegedly "protestant-focused" public schools.[59]

Massachusetts state lawmakers began a concerted push towards implementing a standardized curriculum in their school systems during the ten years preceding the Civil War and their legislative preoccupation with solidifying their state's regional identity occurred as the stability of American national identity was increasingly being called into question. Legislators like Horace Mann pushed the state government to create a uniform curriculum that provided equal opportunity and he equated the failure to do so with a kind of moral "infanticide." In an 1848 speech filled with hyperbolic language, Mann forcefully pleaded with lawmakers by appealing to a desire to cultivate a common morality: "every state is morally bound to establish a system of free schools," and if it failed to do so it might as well "enact a code of laws legalizing and enforcing infanticide."[60] Mann's vision involved creating a state government regulated school system and a standardized curriculum that would promote social equality, a common history, dialect, and speech, and common values. The legislative implementation of Mann's vision was radical but his ideas were not entirely new. In the 18th century Noah Webster's texts for teachers and educators attempted to implement a similar program on a national level. Webster called for a uniform American grammar and dialect system and a clear narrative of American history. Webster was especially fond of stories that mythologized "great" American heroes. Webster viewed a regimented commitment to this program as a vital part of producing a robust and unified understanding of American history: "Begin with the infant in his cradle ... let the first words he lisps be WASHINGTON."[61] Nevertheless, Mann's Massachusetts program contained more paternalistic overtones and the reformer saw the state Board of Education as an entity that should be able to "step in and fill the parent's place."[62] Still, his advocacy for a common understanding of history and language became the regional fulfillment of Webster's dream of nourishing a distinct character through education.

Boston-born Winslow Homer and other late 19th century artists like Charles Frederick Bosworth transformed Mann's aspirations for standardized curriculum and his vision of the idyllic New England schoolhouse into a widely recognizable regional and national emblem.[63] In 1873, for instance, as Massachusetts post–Civil War educational debates raged, Winslow Homer completed a series of paintings in Massachusetts titled *Country School* that mythologize the classroom as a place of order and enlightenment.[64] Homer's painting depicts the interior of a brightly colored, airy, and open classroom with a teacher standing, with a large textbook in hand, between two groups of students who sit attentively at their desks opposite one another. Light streams in from large windows and fills the entire classroom, suggesting growth and knowledge. The classroom's high rounded ceilings accentuate the large space between the seated students and the ceiling and reminds the viewer of how much knowledge these children lack-that they need instruction. Such a composition visually captures the way that educational debates of this era stressed the impressionable quality of a child's mind. Mann argued that children need intellectual "sustenance, shelter, and care" in order to grow into responsible citizens.⁶⁵ Here education promises to fill that void with useful moral and educational lessons.

Homer's composition places the teacher and the large textbook that she holds between the two groups of students and, most importantly, between the classroom's large windows that allow outside to stream in an illuminate its interior. Light here is symbolic of knowledge and the teacher and the textbook are elevated through this spatial arrangement as the dispenser of knowledge and the arbiter of region's egalitarian values (i.e., the classroom is balanced and ordered). Collectively, the painting's composition and its thematic emphasis on the image of the studious child conveys the New England classroom's order (i.e., the teacher is at the center of the classroom) but, more importantly, the arrangement of the children (who sit across from one another on a level plane) suggests the egalitarian, self-disciplined principles that were essential to the Garrison narrative of the region's protest to slavery and remind of the state's unique national moral leadership on the issue of the legal abolition of slavery.

I view the push to create a Massachusetts "standardized curriculum" and the prominence of nostalgic artistic representations of the New England schoolhouse during the post–Civil War period as a language related to the impulse behind the late 19th century Garrison revival and the New England desire to engage north-south disagreements about how to interpret the Union's military victory. After all, the 1865 military conclusion of the war did not answer the question of the mechanics of reunion. There were many in Massachusetts that viewed the post-war New England educational system as an ideal image of the nation's best virtues and hypothesized that their model might be adopted by other states to promote national political unity. In 1870 one newspaper columnist went so far as to describe the Massachusetts interest and investment in its public school system as offering the greatest possible guide for national reconciliation: "schools are as vital to our political system as air to the human frame."⁶⁶

The decision to prominently feature Homer's *Country School* series as a representative sample of American art at the 1878 Paris Exposition further underscores the way American identity during this era intersected with distinctly New England images and narratives.⁶⁷ Showcasing the success of the American educational system at the 1878 Paris exposition became a way for Americans to symbolically use the New England schoolhouse and classroom to stress the harmony between individual Americans (embodied in the students) and structures of authority (the teacher). The 1861 secession of southern states and the formation of the Confederate States of America produced a regional schism that pointed to a larger ideological crisis over the relationship between "democratic" federal governance and the overarching power of centralized authority. For at least four years southern leaders maintained their own government, their own currency, and their own military. And as Drew Gilpin Faust's studies of Confederate nationalism show, the Confederacy went to great lengths to extensively plan for a national future outside of the United States of America.[68] Therefore, the wide cultural interest in the New England schoolhouse is representative of a developing national tendency during this era of "reconciliation" to look to Boston as a space capable of resolving old tensions by promoting a shared history that nostalgically overlooks past injustices by celebrating New England values and heroes as American values and sacrifices.[69]

Homer's 1873 *Country School* series and its celebration of New England images overlapped with the first centennial of the American Revolution in 1876 and a renewed cultural interest in the production of patriotic messages for children that commemorated a time of American greatness and suggested a bright future for the newly reunited nation. Children's books published in the context of this anniversary, like Will Carleton's *Young Folks Centennial Rhymes* (1876) and *The Centennial Frog and Other Stories (1877)*, taught children patriotic songs and used fiction to celebrate the commonality between all Americans-encouraging them to look back upon the days of the American Revolution with great pride.[70] Homer's images similarly emphasize the nation's restoration to a state of harmony. The leisure order depicted in his paintings provided a stark counter-narrative to the heated debates taking place between the northern popular press and southern thinkers over the role of slavery as the cause of the war and whether abolitionist valor was the most important lasting legacy of the conflict.[71]

Massachusetts's interest in producing a standard, teachable, historical narrative and a burgeoning national interest in the symbolic space of the New England schoolhouse helped to transform Wendell and Frank's celebrated biography of their father and the abolitionist movement into an important cultural event. Readers, critics, and historians lauded the Garrison sons for their "objective" rendering of the movement in 1889 when they completed the final two volumes of their four book series. *The New York Tribune* praised the book's handling of the history of the American anti-slavery movement by writing that, "no reader who cares for the subject at all will wish to leave it unfinished."[72] *The Philadelphia Ledger* admiringly described the work as a landmark book that remained almost entirely free of "defects."[73] *The Boston Daily Advertiser* summed up the overwhelmingly positive sentiments that the popular press expressed towards the book by crowning it a "masterpiece of modern historical biography."[74]

The 1889 completion and positive critical reception of the Garrison son's four volume series coincided with the 10-year anniversary of William Lloyd Garrison's death and the height of the popular resuscitation of his story and each helped to further reinforce this narrative of the anti-slavery movement as historical fact. While the anti-slavery memoirs of Samuel May (1869) and Parker Pillsbury (1883) accomplished much of the same narrative work, neither was afforded the same degree of prestige that greeted Wendell and Frank's opus. Their book sold so well that five years after the publication of the original completed manuscript, Houghton, Mifflin, and Company purchased the rights to the book from Century Company and issued a handsome leather-bound edition that would be appropriate for a major library's archive.[75] The prominence that the Garrison brothers' re-issued memoir received led them to donate copies of it to public schools throughout Massachusetts and to major libraries, like the Boston Public Library.[76] They also donated copies to the Library of Congress, The New York Public Library, and even to the British Museum in London.[77] These leather-bound volumes bore the inscription "Valediction" on their spine, a reference to the last issue of *The Liberator* and a gesture that signaled their belief that their biographical work should stand alone as the last word on American abolitionist history.

Frank and Wendell's wildly popular book and their public work to remember their father's sacrifices greatly impacted how Boston, in particular, and Massachusetts, more generally, thought about him and it should come as no surprise that this new revival paralleled his emergence in public school textbooks. Garrison first appears in Boston standardized curriculum around 1905, amidst this period of intense interest in celebrating his legacy. In an early 1905 edition of Melvin Hix's blandly titled, *Approved Selections for Supplementary Reading and Memorizing* William Garrison appears in a section titled "Patriotic Selections for all Grades."[78] Different grade levels received lessons with widely varying, age appropriate, degrees of nuance. In this book, Garrison's short biography appears in a section populated by other important American historical figures like Paul Revere and Benjamin Franklin. Anonymously excerpted selections from a hymn by the abolitionist poet John Greenleaf Whittier are juxtaposed on the adjacent page to Garrison's biography: "Thou friend and helper of the poor,/Who suffered for our sake,/To open every prison door,/and every yoke to break."[79] The textbook makes no mention of the fact that these lines are the second verse of Whittier's "Oh None In All The World Before," which was a popular liturgical hymn written about the birth of Christ for protestant Christmas services.[80]

Hix's juxtaposition fits neatly into narratives of abolitionist sacrifice and redemptive suffering that came out of the Garrison revival. The placement of a song that celebrates the birth of a savior whose mission is to suffer and to ultimately atone for humanity's sin alongside Garrison's biography asks the reader to make the connection between Christ's mission to redeem mankind and Garrison's mission to redeem the nation and the slaves. Whittier's hymn eagerly anticipates the work of Christ: "Look down, O Savior sweet! And smile,/And help us sing and pray;/The hands that blessed the little child/Upon our foreheads lay."[81] The language here is an exhortation that stresses the penitent's helplessness and utter dependence on Christ's salvation. The Jesus portrayed in this song is still a child, yet his name is already honored, praised, and beseeched for intersession. Compare these calls with the appeals made towards the end of Hix's description of Garrison's place in history: "We must place his honored name in the forefront of our ranks ... which great evidences of respect will but poorly repay."[82] First, Boston students are encouraged to place Garrison in the "forefront of our ranks." To whom the ambiguous "our" in this appeal refers is not clarified. It seems to refer to the more common rhetorical claiming of Garrisonian abolitionism as New England abolitionism and New England abolitionism as the dominant sentiment of the land during the war. Garrison's history becomes the region's past and part of a student's education is intertwined with claiming Garrison's work as part of their individual experience and shared understanding of the war. Students are taught that revering Garrison's memory and paying their respects is the least they can do, while the text's biographical sketch also reminds them that this respect "will but poorly repay" the sacrifices that he made.[83]

The same year that Garrison first appears in Boston standardized textbooks—roughly eleven years after the final re-issue of *William Garrison, 1805–1879: The Story of His Life Told by His Children*—the city of Boston organized the Garrison Centennial, a major state holiday that devoted two days to festivities and commemorative events that encouraged citizens to remember Garrison's anti-slavery work and his important place in Massachusetts state history. Frank and Wendell wrote another book in honor of this occasion titled *The Words of Garrison: A Centenary Selection* (1805–1905) that introduced Garrison's narrative of suffering and sacrifice to a new generation of readers through a collection that included a 20 page biography, articles from *The Liberator*, fiery anecdotes and quips attributed to their father, and fond sentiments from Garrison admirers.[84] Most interesting, however, is a quote featured prominently in the book's first page that is attributed to "Testimonies of People of Color."[85] Many notable African Americans like Mary Church Terrell did playa vital role in the organization of the Garrison Centenary, but this testimony's perfect conformity to Garrison's own narration of his life both raises questions about its authorship and, more importantly, demonstrates the widespread use of suffering and redemptive language in memorial tributes to Boston abolitionists.[86] The anonymous "People of Color" lament the hardships that Garrison experienced during his life, but celebrate his persecution as the source of the nation's ultimate deliverance:

> We feel fully persuaded that the day cannot be far distant when you will be acknowledged—by the very lips of those who now denounce, revile, and persecute you as the vilest and basest of men, the uprooter of all order, the destroyer of our country's peace, prosperity, and happiness— to be its firm reliance, its deliverer, the very pillar of its future grandeur.[87]

This tribute has the effect of elevating Garrison's suffering, while erasing the presence of slave pain. The fact that an anonymous, and presumably collective, "people of color," praise Garrison's pain only reinforces the Centennial's suggestion that the lasting legacy of the war and the greatest sacrifice worth remembering is Garrison's social, political, and religious activism.

The 1905 Garrison Centennial's vision of the war challenged other contemporary narratives, particularly those that stressed the shared combat experience, valor, and sacrifice of the common foot soldier. President Woodrow Wilson's July 4, 1913, address at Gettysburg is an event that historians like David Blight cite as a representative climax of a longer cultural movement towards disowning slavery from American histories of the Civil War.[88] In both the Wilson and Garrison visions one can see a movement towards white supremacy ideologies, but while the Blue-Gray reunion sought to erase the history of slavery, the Garrison narrative emphasized the nation's experience with slavery as the cause of the war and the fight to eradicate it as the central ideological conflict between the north and the south.

Forgetting slavery, after all, meant forgetting Garrison and forgetting Garrison offered the unacceptable alternative of ignoring Massachusetts's history of heroic abolitionist activism. As a result, it is not surprising that the abolitionist narrative of the war drew supporters from a wide range of groups with differing interests, from white politicians to former Garrisonians to contemporary African American civil rights advocacy organizations. Garrison remained a powerful symbol and his influence informed debates of the early 20th century in sometimes surprising ways. It's important to remember, for instance, that the children of former Garrisonians ran several major African American advocacy groups like the NAACP. In *The Abolitionist Legacy: From Reconstruction to the NAACP,* historian James McPherson describes the leadership rosters of the NAACP during the early 20th century as reading "like a membership list of the old New England Anti-Slavery Society."[89] To be clear, McPherson's observation is no exaggeration. Frank Garrison served as president of the Boston branch of the organization and gave the national keynote address by the time of the 1911 National NAACP Convention in Boston. Amongst the other members in attendance were Albert Pillsbury, the son of Parker Pillsbury, Garrison's longtime friend and advocate who penned *Acts of the Anti-Slavery Apostles* in 1883.[90] The younger Pillsbury himself described the atmosphere of the convention as appearing "like an old-fashioned anti-slavery meeting."[91] McPherson points out that 14 children of Garrisonian abolitionists played a prominent role in the early years of the NAACP and took public leadership roles on a variety of important issues like the Federal Elections Bill of 1890.[92]

By 1910, William Garrison's appearance within Massachusetts's standardized curriculum also reflected the efforts of his daughter Helen Francis Garrison to continually re-circulate and publicly assert her father's role in New England and American history. Helen Francis Garrison, who friends and public officials affectionately refer to in letters as simply "Fanny" was Garrison's fifth child with Helen Eliza Benson and in the early 20th century she became, like Wendell and Frank, an important protector of her father's memory. In 1886, eight years after her father's death, Fanny married Northern Pacific Railway railroad tycoon and *New York Evening Post* co-owner Henry Villard and together they carried on her father's legacy by involving themselves in a variety of activist projects, ranging from women's suffrage to the formation of the NAACP. When her husband died in 1900 she became equally concerned with promoting and recounting the history of the Garrison family's altruistic work. A series of legal challenges to Henry Villard's will by their daughter Helen and son Oswald, both of whom believed they did not receive enough of their father's considerable estate, only furthered her desire to speak of her father's selfless nature. Her family's disagreements quickly led to a scandalous public feud that northern newspapers eagerly reported and which posed a threat to the Garrison family's heralded reputation.[93]

Like her brothers, Fanny began her quest to publicly revive her family name by writing an extended two-volume memoir of her husband that Houghton, Mifflin, and Company published in 1904. Her book appeared under the title, *The Memoirs of Henry Villard: Journalist and Financier, 1835–1900*.[94] Her narration of her husband's life and professional work provided an alternative to the image of the ruthless businessman that filled the tabloid-hungry pages of turn of the century newspapers.[95] In doing so she dissented with those who negatively compared her husband's work (and specifically his wealth) with her father's comparative poverty and singularly determined commitment to abolishing slavery. She instead worked to link her father's name and his highly regarded reputation with altruistic work being carried out by the current generation of Garrisons. In the preface to the book she portrays her husband as a kind and gentle man who did not desire public praise or attention for his social work. "His philanthropy," she writes, "is only faintly portrayed by his own hand; of its full extent he alone was aware."[96] Later that same year Fanny formed the William Lloyd Garrison Equal Rights Club, which sought to build on her father's reform legacy. The organization's name kept her family's past anti-slavery legacy aligned with her charitable pursuits, the burgeoning women's movement, and civil rights movements taking place in Massachusetts during her own time. Fanny used her family name to promote her social activism and her link to her father's symbolic power gave her access to government officials. Legislators and political hopefuls gave Fanny their undivided attention because she reminded them of a bygone era in Massachusetts history when the state was viewed as taking the national lead on moral issues such as slavery.[97] For her part, Fanny took advantage of every opportunity to remind the public of her father's anti-slavery work and the important ties between contemporary reform efforts and those of antebellum abolitionists.

As late as February 10,1910 she still invoked her father's legacy in speeches as a way to frame her own activism and in doing so she reinforced ties in the public imagination between contemporary New England reform movements and the name William Lloyd Garrison. Her speech on this date is indicative of others she gave during this era: "my father, William Lloyd Garrison, and my brother of the same name have successively pleaded this cause before Committees of the Massachusetts legislature. I feel it all the more a privilege and a duty, now that their voices are still, to renew the appeal."[98] These public efforts offered brief glimpses of a more private campaign that Fanny waged throughout turn of the century Massachusetts and New York. Early on, for instance, she limited leadership positions in her organizations to former Garrisonians who she trusted would loyally protect her father's legacy. She appointed a Garrisonian named Abby Hopper Gibbons to serve as president of a series of "diet kitchens"—organizations meant to put low income families in touch with physicians and to provide low cost (or free) milk, barley, and rice-that in 1902 were spread out in Massachusetts and New York.[99] Towards the end of her life, shortly after she turned 80 years old, she still tirelessly promoted her father's legacy by authoring a book on him titled, *William Lloyd Garrison on Non-Resistance Together with a Personal Sketch by his Daughter, Fanny Garrison Villard*.[100] This collection of personal memories of her father and of her childhood as a Garrison was clearly meant for posterity since she died within a year of its publication.

The work of Garrison's children, former Garrisonians, and the efforts of Boston officials to claim and memorialize Garrison's story in Boston public monuments and standardized school curriculum framed the way contemporary Civil Rights reformers located the genealogy of their work. When W.E.B. Du Bois called for a "New Abolition Movement" in 1912 his very choice of words references the dominant model of progressive activism and the specific language of reform that nostalgically tied his calls for racial equality to past Massachusetts antislavery culture. Du Bois would also praise the work of Garrison's children in his own writing by calling them "worthy of their father."[101] Du Bois, along with other contemporary African American civil rights activists, protected Garrison's memory by reminding his reading audience of the risks that some white reformers of the past willingly assumed for the benefit of African Americans. Garrison and those who worked with him on *The Liberator* were never too far from his thoughts or the pages of the magazines he edited. Between 1910 and 1934 he wrote a number of major articles that linked contemporary reformers to William Lloyd Garrison.[102] Even comparatively "minor" 19th century abolitionists like Charles L. Mitchell, who worked with Garrison on *The Liberator* in 1853 and who later served in the Massachusetts state legislature, were commemorated in Du Bois' recurring column titled "Men of the Month" in his magazine *Crisis*.[103]

As Massachusetts politicians, "neo-abolitionists," prominent black intellectuals and others in the early 20th century invoked Garrison's legacy and stressed the centrality of his sacrificial work, new Boston educational texts continued to disseminate and expand on this narrative in greater detail through curriculum selections that were annually adopted for city schools. Prominent African American abolitionists like Frederick Douglass continued to be remembered and admired, but Douglass' contentious split with Garrison in 1851 and his public denunciation of him as a "mean-spirited and despotic person" did not fit well with the early 20th century vision of Garrison and New England abolitionism.[104] The rhetorical transformation of Garrison's personal narrative of suffering in the early 19th century to a regionally celebrated occasion for commemoration in the late 19th century to an institutionally sanctioned narrative in the early 20th century is remarkable. By stressing Garrison's narrative of redemptive suffering, early 20th century Boston children were encouraged to adopt Garrison's legacy as their own and in doing so Garrison became a conduit by which to broadly claim the region's greatest virtues during an era of extreme duress. The visible public presence and reform work of Garrison's children and the children of other Garrisonian abolitionists provided historical continuity with the region's abolitionist past and a reminder of the way actual children, and not just the symbol of the child, maintained and perpetuated regional and national patriotic ideals. Discourses that utilized the symbol of the child, educational texts directed at real children, and the public example of the children of former Garrisonian abolitionists all transformed New England history into a special place-the "city upon a hill" for the rest of America. Du Bois most elegantly expressed this idea in 1922 when he fondly pondered New England's role in the movement towards greater social equality: "New England has learned, albeit hardly, to let these prophets and rebels speak. And this is the glory and hope of New England and of America."[105]

Du Bois' warm sentiments towards Garrison and his praise for his "prophetic voice" are only equaled by the language of the history lessons found in textbooks like *The Boys and Girls Fifth History Reader*, which Boston area schools used in early 1922.[106] The book's structure is a curious mixture of Greek mythology, a broad history of western civilization (which appears under the label "History from Foreign Lands"), and American history. The third section of the book, which is entirely devoted to American history, is titled "Our Country-Past and Present."[107] The short chapters in this section chart the progression of America from "Columbus Crosses the Unknown Sea" (the title of the first chapter) to a final chapter titled "What the Flag Stands For" that relates the details of a speech given by Henry Cabot Lodge on April 6, 1917.[108] Only two chapters from the book's American history section deal with Civil War. The first of these chapters is simply titled "The Abolitionists" and it deals with the story of William Garrison and his work in Boston.[109] The second chapter is entirely devoted to Abraham Lincoln and is curiously titled "Training for the Presidency."[110] The relationship between Lincoln and Garrison in the text's structure looks back to a tradition that began in late 19th century works of popular culture that linked the two men. In chapter 2, for instance, I noted the way that Lincoln becomes associated with Garrisonian abolitionism during the post-war period of commemoration in novels like *The Father*.[111] Fictional dramatizations of encounters between Garrison and President Lincoln in such popular fiction credited the President's late conversion to anti-slavery convictions with the moral suasion espoused by William Garrison.[112] Other influential mid–20th century novels like *Raintree County* would continue to feature meetings between abolitionist protagonists and President Lincoln, in this case in a battlefield hospital, as a way of accentuating the lasting impact of the suffering of the former.[113]

While this particular history textbook does not explicitly discuss Lincoln and Garrison together (they each, in fact, have their own chapters that tell different narratives), it is significant that their stories are juxtaposed together and that they are the only ones used to teach the story of Massachusetts during the Civil War. This is especially curious given Lincoln's historically strong ties to Illinois culture.[114] "The Abolitionists" chapter has a broad title but a specific focus, which speaks to the degree to which Garrison had become so associated with abolitionism that it wasn't even necessary to name the chapter specifically after him. Further, by placing the Lincoln-centered "Training for the Presidency" chapter directly after "The Abolitionists" chapter of the book the author suggests a discernable historical progression from

Garrison to Lincoln. "Official" history here adopts the narrative strategies of postwar abolitionist themed fiction, which depicted abolitionism and the emancipationist impulse to be a product of Garrison and Massachusetts anti-slavery culture. The book describes Lincoln's presidential administration and Civil War legacy in two brief but revealing sentences: "When he was fifty years old he was made President of the United States at a crisis in our history. He freed the slaves and became one of the most influential men that ever lived in America."[115] Again, reading the end of this chapter, within the context of the one immediately preceding it, implies a link between the two ideas. Though anachronistic, and certainly not historical, Lincoln becomes a by-product of Massachusetts anti-slavery culture through this narrative. This makes "Lincoln's story," as the book calls it, inseparable from Garrison's story and from the region itself. Garrison symbolically *authenticates* Lincoln's ties to New England history and places Massachusetts at the center of an important era of change and growth within American culture. This is an emancipationist narrative of the war that foregrounds the region's moral clarity, its prophetic voice (to borrow Du Bois' language), and its relentless activism as the most important marker for this period of history.

The book frames Lincoln's presidency and his rise to cultural prominence through a language of education, honesty, wisdom, and persistence, while the chapter titled "The Abolitionists" draws on a Garrisonian language of suffering and sacrifice. This chapter begins with a promise to tell the history of American abolitionism, which it describes as a Massachusetts movement. Other men, like Wendell Phillips, appear but William Garrison remains the center of this history. The book defends this approach by arguing that "anyone interested in history" should know of the "determination" of Garrison and his paper *The Liberator*.[116] The book describes Garrison's willingness to suffer by citing rhetorical anecdotes made within the pages of *The Liberator*. The reader is told that

Garrison promised in the very first issue of his newspaper that he would "sustain it *as long as could live on bread and water*" and that he "practiced what he so nobly resolved."[117] This strong resolve, the book argues, is part of Garrison's greatness but the author also concedes that it is this quality that made him controversial during his lifetime. The book describes him as a "pioneer" and later as a "great man" whose character was "misunderstood."[118] Garrison's resolve in the wake of public controversies leads the book to observe that some of his contemporaries compared him to "the Apostle Paul when he stood before the Roman Governor."[119] This comparison is important because the Biblical story it references—Paul's appearance before the Roman governor Felix in the book of *Acts-recounts* how Paul's steadfast devotion to God and his unrelenting willingness to sacrifice his own life to obediently maintain divine directives frightens the young governor and ultimately leads to his release and victory:

> And as he reasoned of righteousness, temperance, and judgment to come, Felix trembled, and answered, Go thy way for this time; when I have a convenient season, I will call for thee.[120]

The reference to Paul's imprisonment forces one to recall the language that Garrison and his admirers used to describe his own time in prison for remarks made against Francis Todd of Newburyport in the *Genius of Universal Emancipation* in 1830.[121] Between April 17, 1830, and June 5, 1830, Garrison wrote daily letters from his jail cell in Baltimore that stoically embraced his punishment and that promised righteous retribution. For example, in a letter to Henry Thompson, the prominent Baltimore merchant who financially supported Francis Todd, that is dated May 13, 1830, Garrison draws on a language of retributive justice that is indicative of the type of stoic patience and trust in divine authority that Paul's story in Acts highlights:

> If the severe, pointed, thundering rebuke from my Counsel, before a listening Court, failed to make any impression upon your ample countenance, what condemnation of mine can make it yield? Yet I do not wholly despair. Even Bronze is susceptible of change.
>
> The pleasure you derive from my incarceration, I do not grudge. It is a small reward for your disinterested and unremitting exertions in behalf of your employer. I shall charitably give a donation. Be patient. Every day adds compound interest to the principal.[122]

Indeed, the comparison with Paul's ability to make Felix, his governor and judge, "tremble" matches the divine judgment that Garrison prophesized against his enemies and the earthly justice that he promised to carry out himself. This latter point is especially true in the case of Garrison's May 13, 1830, letter to Judge Nicholas Brice, the chief justice of the Baltimore City Court. Garrison's outrage at his perceived wrongful imprisonment leads him to threaten Judge Brice with a different form of prosecution for silencing advocates for Christ and his ruling principles. He promises to devote his leisure time to reviewing the judge's life and conduct towards others: "even here, barren as is the place," he writes, "I daily discover new beauties springing up in your character, which shall certainly embellish my essays. Nay, I will erect your statue even in your lifetime."[123] And so, when the textbook compares William Garrison to the Apostle Paul, this is a carefully chosen analogy that is the product of a rhetorical tradition that, by 1922, was close to 100 years old. These comparisons are the same ones that Garrison makes between himself and his followers in the pages of *The Liberator* in the 1830s, 40s, 50s, and 60s, and it's the same appeal that is used to emphasize Garrison's righteousness (and, by association, Massachusetts's important role in emancipation) following the war's conclusion and the emergence of a northern culture of commemoration that honored its anti-slavery activism. It is also important to remember that this reference to a story from the book of Acts was preceded by Parker Pillsbury's narrative of Garrison in *Acts of the Antislavery Apostles*, which tells Garrison's story through the narrative structure of and through allusions to the Biblical *Acts of the Apostles*. The fact that a school textbook approved by the Boston Board of Education circulates these claims as part of the city's standardized curriculum suggests that the comparison was taken for granted or at least deemed as common knowledge.

An emphasis on Garrison's suffering and pain also creeps into the book's narrative account of antebellum anti-slavery activism in the region. The threats against Garrison's life from angry southern readers are covered and described in graphic detail. The book points out that one threat against Garrison's life promised that southerner's would "clip their hands in his heart's blood" if the opportunity presented itself.[124] The humanistic rationale behind the anti-slavery impulse is ignored and what remains is an account of abolitionism that is, ironically, devoid of a discussion of slavery. The chapter's title "The Abolitionists" is telling in this regard, since the principle focus is on mythologizing the historical figures of New England abolitionism in a manner that represents them as grander than the cause itself. Quotes attributed to Garrison stress his willingness to die for the cause and do so through a sacred language of Christ's original example. One rousing sentiment attributed to Garrison, in regard to his own determination and that of his followers, proclaims that "We will die in such a cause, only as martyrs to the truth. In this, our blessed Saviour has set the example."[125]

Such is the message of the book—Garrison the apostle and devout evangelist (through the comparisons with Paul) and Garrison the redeemer who spreads an anti-slavery message and whose sacrifice played an active role in guiding regional and national spiritual reconciliation. The latter representation of Garrison appears in otherworldly descriptions of his voice ("it went up in trumpet tones"), his steadfast faith ("the dampness of his cell did not repress the energy of his spirit"), his writing in *The Liberator* ("its pages flashed light and truth far and wide ... darkness and gloom fled before it"), and the lasting effect of his efforts and sacrifice ("the effects of these efforts is seen and felt this moment").[126] Garrison's work appears so encompassing and unmatchable that the only avenue left for "Colored Americans" and for New England citizens of this era is to *remember,* which is a process rooted in forgetting slave pain and avoiding a serious discussion of the region's own complacency in the slave trade.

A history of abolitionism that stresses the work of Garrison and his followers is not necessarily an emancipationist history of the war, especially if the most vivid pain is that of a white reformer. David Blight's argument in *Race and Reunion: The Civil War in American Memory* that an early 20th century focus on shared military experience overshadowed the emancipationist legacy of the Civil War should be equally applied to abolitionist histories produced in early 20th century Massachusetts.[127] Lionizing past white reformer efforts through sacred language, metaphors, and comparisons precludes the possibility of black agency and erases a history of black abolitionist efforts.[128] These popular and institutional Garrisonian narratives also distance histories of abolitionism from the wide breadth of northern responses, both productive and unproductive, to the issue of slavery.

Garrison's pain and sacrifices remain most vivid because by 1922 they had become an essential part of Massachusetts' narrative of the Civil War. A vision of pure sacrifice and redemption, like the Biblical narrative of Christ, offered a less complicated and decidedly more appealing understanding of how to relay the causes and the meaning of a divisive and destructive war to a new generation of Boston children. As southern leaders and states struggled to find an appropriate way to properly historicize their own experience with the war, the narrative that emerged in Massachusetts proved to be culturally and institutionally stable.[129] Of the major curriculum debates that consumed the school board between the late 19th and early 20th century none involved the presentation of the Civil War or the depiction of abolitionist activities in their state. And so, while some religious groups would continue to protest well into the early 20th century their view that the Massachusetts standardized curriculum privileged Unitarian beliefs more than those expressed by other New England churches, there was no dissent concerning the scope or language of their curriculum's narration of the Civil War.[130]

Post-bellum debates surrounding standardized curriculum viewed education as a means to reunite the nation through shared values, stories, and histories. The curriculum taught in Boston public schools during the turn-of-the-century realized this vision on the regional level by instilling within all children, both black and white and wealthy and poor, a sense of pride in the sacrifices of those who came before. Garrison's history became their region's history and the region's lofty past became intrinsically linked to the next generation's best aspirations for the future. An important legacy of the region's past and the Civil War became the willingness of William Lloyd Garrison to lead a region and a nation in standing up to the tyranny of southern practices.

Nevertheless, it is still remarkable to observe the alarming degree of continuity between the language used to describe William Garrison's life in political speeches, commemorations, popular culture, and institutional knowledge. Since 1866, every occasion marking a historical milestone tied to Garrison's life has become an opportunity to remember and reinforce this dominant sentiment. In a December 11, 1905, address to the Boston Suffrage League an AME pastor delivered a rousing sermon celebrating the 100-year anniversary of Garrison's birth.[131] He discussed the "sacred trust" imparted to the current generation and then, invoking a story the congregants would have known well, went on to the remind them of Garrison's legacy:

> His friends and neighbors looked upon him as one who brought a stigma upon the fair name of the city in which he lived. The business interests regarded him as an influence, which disturbed and injured the relations of commerce and of trade; the Church opposed him; the press denounced him; the State regarded him as an enemy of the established order; the North repudiated him; the South burned him in effigy. Yet, *almost singlehanded and alone,* Garrison continued to fight on, declaring that "his reliance for the deliverance of the oppressed universally is upon the nature of man, the inherent wrongfulness of oppression, the power of truth, and the omnipotence of God" ... William Lloyd Garrison has passed from us, but the monumental character of his work and the influence of his life shall never perish. While there are wrongs to be righted, despots to be attacked, oppressors to be overthrown, peace to find and advocate, and freedom a voice, the name of William Lloyd Garrison will live.[132]

The emphasis on Garrison's "single-handed" management of the fight against slavery is a strong characteristic of Massachusetts historical and educational narratives produced between 1867 and 1922. Such sentiments remain firmly entrenched in the region today. The language used at an April 24, 2011, festival that honored Garrison's legacy in Newburyport, Massachusetts demonstrates that this story continues to occupy an important role within the Massachusetts popular imagination and still informs their historical understanding of the Civil War and their narrative of the region's anti-slavery activism. "Freedom Narrative" was the festival's theme and the opening speaker was Frank Garrison, the great-great grandson of William Garrison. Just as Garrison's children fought to protect and promote their father's legacy in the late 19th and early 20th century, Garrison's contemporary descendants continue this tradition. Vicki Hendrickson, one of the event's organizers, spoke to the *Boston Globe* about the necessity of such an event: "I think people need to be reminded that there were some courageous people out there working towards something that was just."[133]

# 4

## Ross Lockridge's *Raintree County*
### American Abolitionism as Epic Origin Narrative

As we saw in the preceding chapters, an explosion in the production of popular and institutional narratives that addressed the historical role of William Garrison and New England abolitionists in the American Civil War's causes and meanings took place between the late 19th and early 20th century in Massachusetts and throughout the nation. By the 20th century, Garrisonian abolitionism increasingly became synonymous with American abolitionism. Memoirs of former Garrisonians, funerary eulogies and odes, biographies, state holidays and festivals, mass produced fictional representations, and Massachusetts school textbooks all played a role the production of a new history which stressed the redemptive nature of abolitionist suffering as the saving grace of the union and of the newly emancipated slaves.

The boundaries that dictated who could rightly be called an abolitionist expanded during the postwar years in proportion to the wider circulation that Garrisonian narratives received until, of course, this historical memory could encompass virtually all efforts to preserve the Union. In other words, this *new* national anti-slavery narrative became the popular history of the war for audiences outside of Massachusetts. Abolitionist history now included Union political figures like Abraham Lincoln and military heroes like Ulysses S. Grant.[1] Northern leaders who published postwar memoirs went to great lengths to stress the connection between their work and anti-slavery reform. For instance, the 1885 publication of Ulysses S. Grant's two-volume collection, *Personal Memoirs of U.S. Grant*, demonstrates the extent to which former Union leaders used abolitionist narratives and history as a means to claim a sacred and morally superior justification for their participation in the Civil War. Grant writes unequivocally: "the cause of the great War of the Rebellion against the United States will have to be attributed to slavery."[2] In his memoirs, Grant portrays himself as an emancipator backed by Union moral fortitude and military might.[3] He concedes that many in the north were not "hostile ... out and out abolitionists," but he specifically stresses that following the Mexican War, "the great majority of people in the North, where slavery did not exist, were strongly opposed to the institution, and looked upon its existence in any part of the country as unfortunate."[4] He compares the practitioners of "Southern religion"—meaning those who viewed slavery as a divinely sanctioned institution—to Mormons in their misguided understanding of Christianity: "for there were people who believed in the 'divinity' of human slavery, as there are now people who believe Mormonism and Polygamy to be ordained by the Most High. We forgive them for entertaining such notions, but forbid their practice."[5] Such rhetoric had the effect of transforming the historical abolitionist into a patriotic symbol of Unionism and a guardian of Christian and American virtues. This language also marks a shift towards a more malleable representation of antislavery activism. "Radical" abolitionists like Garrison defined themselves in clear opposition to the United States government and its Constitution, but this new label allowed instruments of the state to retrospectively claim membership and affiliation with the antislavery movement.

Abolitionist language and history informed the way living Union officials, like Grant, defined themselves and provided others a conduit for remembering and framing the sacrifices of those who lost their lives fighting to protect the union during the Civil War. This is especially true in the case of Abraham Lincoln. Unlike Grant, Abraham Lincoln was unable to pen his memoirs and in the postwar period northern and southern audiences engaged in a highly contested battle over the relationship between his legacy and northern abolitionism. This desire stemmed from the actions of late 19th century southern thinkers and politicians who attempted to firmly situate Lincoln within a tradition of white supremacy. In 1890 Matthew Butler, a U.S. senator from South Carolina, introduced congressional legislation that called for Africans residing in America to be sent back to the regions from which they were taken.[6] Butler hailed his plan as a way to "fix the new negro problem" while also making amends for any past wrongdoing that occurred in the original removal of Africans from their native homelands.[7] Butler repeatedly invoked Lincoln during his legislative presentation and during his subsequent attempts to garner public support and argued that his proposed "humanitarian" law represented the strongest step towards a fuller realization of "Lincoln's solution."[8]

In contrast, northern politicians and works of popular culture placed Lincoln at the center of a progressive American historical evolutionary movement away from the injustices and regressive beliefs of southern culture and values. In this narrative, Lincoln is frequently linked to Garrison and to Massachusetts's culture in order to argue that his life represented a forceful and heroic effort to free slaves from bondage and to more fully incorporate them into American life.[9] Thomas Nast's 1867 print "Emancipation" visually captures this understanding of the war by contrasting the slave's experience under the Confederacy with the new life that national union and freedom promised.[10] "Emancipation" features a large portrait of a Lincoln who is surrounded by a variety of small scenes that depict aspects of post–Civil War African American life. Nast uses Lincoln's image to imagine a society in which former slaves are fully integrated into all aspects of American society: attending public schools and receiving equal wages for labor are two of the outcomes that his drawing depicts.[11]

By the early 20th century African Americans celebrated Lincoln's legacy on Emancipation Day and by doing so they linked the former president's memory with a vision of equality that most fully expressed their own ideals and aspirations.[12] When Emancipation Day later became Negro History Week, Carter Woodson, the celebration's initiator, chose the second week of February in a move that symbolically linked Lincoln with the abolitionist Frederick Douglass.[13] The point is that between the late 19th and early 20th century a variety of political and military figures became increasingly identified with the abolitionist movement and the fight to rid the country of slavery. Both Grant and Lincoln are but two examples of the way that the struggles over the memory of northern abolitionist efforts, visions, and sacrifices expanded into a broader regional conflict between union and confederate sympathizers.

As northern writers and audiences beatified former Union heroes they routinely discussed slavery as a cause of the Civil War and reserved a special place of honor for those who opposed this institution. The widespread contemporary visibility of this understanding of the war is a testament to the power of this type of postwar literature and rhetoric. As recently as January 10, 2011, in an article for *The Washington Post* titled, "Five Myths About Why the South Seceded," James W. Loewen cites the abolitionist narrative of the war as one of the greatest widely-held popular misconceptions: "since the Civil War did end slavery, many Americans still think abolition was the Union's goal. But the North initially went to war to hold the nation together. Abolition came later."[14]

As northern narratives stressed the abolition of slavery as the Union's primary aim a growing body of southern literature attempted downplayed slavery as one of the Civil War's principal causes. An investment in a language of suffering linked both of these otherwise different understandings of the conflict. The northern emphasis on slavery as *the* cause of the war placed the blame for the death and destruction that followed on the plantation culture of the south, which led northern writers to increasingly link valor with the willingness to suffer, and perhaps die, in order to rid the country of this contemptible practice. Southerners, on the other hand, stressed the union's plundering of their land and their individual heroic willingness to die fighting a hostile federal government that refused to honor past obligations.[15]

Postwar abolitionist rhetoric stressed Union valor and relegated the Confederate cause and its leaders into an antagonistic role in the new national Civil War narrative. Writers who objected to the South's villainous characterization in the popular press reacted with fictional and non-fictional histories of the war that nostalgically looked back to the region's chivalric antebellum agrarian culture as an alternative to the dominant New England-focused stories of the war, which privileged abolitionist pain and northern heroism.[16] Collectively, these counter-narratives became known as the "Lost Cause" mythology of the war. Lost Cause narratives argued that slavery was not the cause of the war and that southerners should harbor no shame for their defeat at the hands of northern, industrial-based, military aggression.[17] Between 1900 and 1950 lost cause narratives reached their peak in popularity and became an important way to revise history from a confederate perspective.[18] Southern literature and monuments produced during this era emphasized confederate courage, duty, and honor.[19] New histories like Allen Tate's *Stonewall Jackson: The Good Soldier* (1928), which lionized Jackson's military heroism and leadership, while also stressing his gentle, faith-based humanity, provided southerners sympathetic portraits of figures demonized in the northern press.[20] Other works, like F. Scott Fitzgerald's short stories "The Night at Chancellorville" (1935) and "The End of Hate" (1940), along with Robert Penn Warren's

*John Brown: The Making of a Martyr* (1929) and Margaret Mitchell's *Gone with the Wind* (1936) stood as southern counter-narratives to the dominant abolitionist-centered reunion story.[21] Robert Penn Warren, in particular, expressed outrage at the way in which the northern celebration of abolitionist "fanatics" like John Brown made "the gallows ... glorious like the cross."[22] For Warren, the popular focus on Brown's martyrdom overshadowed the man's mental instability, arrogance, and misguided interpretations of scriptural "higher law."[23] He viewed the suffering-laden narrative tropes used to resuscitate Brown and other abolitionists during this era as part of a disturbing larger and growing trend within the popular culture of uncritically heralding abolitionist pain.

It is within this tumultuous era of contesting visions of the war that Ross Lockridge publishes *Raintree County ... which had no boundaries in time and space, where lurked musical and strange names and mythical and lost peoples, and which was itself only a name musical and strange* (1948), an epic American origin narrative that mythologizes the abolitionist movement by allegorically aligning individual Union sacrifice with the redemption, resurrection, and rebirth of the republic.[24] John Wickliff Shawnessy, Lockridge's protagonist, embodies the northern desire of this era to retrospectively imagine every antebellum profession, from writer to politician to minister to teacher to soldier as part of the historical "unified" northern moral and ethical efforts to stop the spread of slavery. The novel's story spans the entire 19th century, from abolitionist antebellum protest to the postwar Reconstruction, and the nation's entire history and suffering during these years is expressed through abolitionist John Shawnessy's personal triumphs and pain. Lockridge's fragmented prose style, his allegorical use of Biblical creation narratives and metaphors, and his protagonist's self-conscious, Whitman-esque, ruminations on the nature and boundaries of self, consistently invite the reader to see Shawnessy's personal story as their own and his narrative of his hometown of Raintree County as the history of the American republic.

This chapter examines *Raintree County* to show how by 1948 the literary trope of the "suffering abolitionist" had become intertwined with the popular vocabulary used to represent historical abolitionist efforts. Shawnessy's principle means of activism, I argue, is repeatedly understood through highly sexualized scriptural imagery of penetration, wetness, virginity, and subjugation that conflate his desire for victimization with America's best hopes of restoring its covenantal relationship with all its peoples. His physical pain and suffering is both a source of sexual ecstasy and a marker of difference that signifies his selfless patriotic principles. The novel uses Shawnessy's pronounced ability to empathize with slave pain and his strong commitment to abolitionist ideals and republican values as means to transform his promiscuity into innocence, his suffering into penance, and his painful movement into adulthood into the analogous re-birth of the republic. In doing so, the abolitionist is understood in elusive and mysterious messianic terms that position him as the source of national reconciliation and at the center of a new American mythology.

*Raintree County* is self-aware in its exploration of historical memory, with the majority of the action composed of John Shawnessy's reminisces over a 24-hour period on July 4, 1892. Festivities mark this day as the fictional town of Waycross celebrates America's independence and honors local heroes who played a role in the Union's Civil War victory. The town's festival is itself an occasion of commemoration and remembering and this atmosphere leads Shawnessy to recall his adolescence and coming of age, his first love, the tragedy of his first marriage, his years as a teacher and a soldier, and his ill-conceived campaigns for political office. These painful recollections of life, love, and misadventures narrate the entire 19th century through Shawnessy's personal experiences. These memories demonstrate his capacity to empathize with slaves, to love freely, and they highlight his strong sense of social justice and morality. The novel's author, Ross Lockridge, contrasts these virtues with the lives and values of Shawnessy's closest friends, who offer alternatives which he ultimately disavows: Professor Jerusalem Stiles, his former teacher and mentor, whose cynicism, intellectual coldness, and worldly pragmatism stand as a foil to Shawnessy's protected innocence and idealism; Cassius P. Carney, a financier whose sole pursuit is the accumulation of wealth; and Senator Garwood B. Jones, an opportunistic politician who quickly adopts and vociferously mirrors popular public sentiment while simultaneously ingratiating himself to whoever can help him to retain political power.

Lockridge portrays Shawnessy's quest as more "pure" than that of his friends and his painful struggles to define his own life are intermingled with attempts to define the America that emerges from the refining fire of the Civil War. *Raintree County's* premise would have been unthinkable before 1866 but in the post-bellum period Garrison's resuscitation produced a new conception of American abolitionism that understood 19th century antislavery activities as an origin and expression of quintessential American values of selfless sacrifice. As Shawnessy struggles to express himself he repeatedly reverts to nationalistic imagery and rhetoric. His thoughts of self lead him outward to thoughts about national identity. On the occasion of his 50th birthday Shawnessy's character observes that, "America is still waiting to be discovered. America is a perpetual adventure of discovery. I've spent fifty years of life trying to discover America."[25] Jeanette Vanausdall argues that Shawnessy, as a self-sacrificial dreamer, is a uniquely American messianic figure that embodies "something about the American dream" that 19th and 20th century Americans longed for, namely mythic participation in the events taking place around them, driven by the belief that individual experience could become "the collective dream of all mankind."[26] The novel's 1892 setting is also a reminder that the fictional story takes place during an era of U.S. imperialism, which is a cultural period that Amy Kaplan succinctly characterizes as consistently expressing a desire for empire and "an anti-modern desire to retrieve primitive origins."[27] The abolitionist here is at the center of efforts to locate an authentic source of contemporary American life.

Ross Lockridge's 1948 novel appeared roughly 88 years after the Civil War and its interest in American origins is also a product of a post–World War II American culture that celebrated its military superiority, its worldwide moral leadership, and its economic prosperity following the defeat of Nazi Germany and its allies. America's entrance into World War II and its subsequent military victory coincided with a surge in fictional representations of the Civil War that looked back to the 19th century as a way to imagine a long history of heroic and willing American suffering for democratic and egalitarian principles. Clearly the late 19th century abolitionist narrative of the Civil War remained attractive to 1940s audiences and authors searching for a historical genealogy of selfless American sacrifice. Accordingly, many novels during these years focused on the abolitionist as a general patriotic figure who could originate from either the north or the south and who could generally appeal to a variety of Americans.

The "conversion story" is a common convention of abolitionist fiction of this era and encompasses all fictional stories that focus on the unlikely transformation of regular citizens who, despite their upbringing and culture, become crusaders for racial justice. Henrietta Buckmaster's popular novel *Deep River* (1944), for instance, tells the story of a Georgia mountaineer who, despite his southern upbringing and his marriage to a woman who grew up on a plantation, becomes an ardent abolitionist. The novel celebrates the conversion of Buckmater's hero that leads to his heroic willingness to risk his life for the sake of the slave's freedom.[28] The *New York Times* praised the selflessness of Buckmaster's protagonist and called the novel an important work about American history "in which events have moral values."[29] The *Times* reviewer, Orville Prescott, especially approved of the way Buckmaster avoided "crude sensationalism" and instead relies on realistic descriptions of the brutality of slavery that vividly convey "the fear and hope and desperation of the Negroes."[30]

Similarly, Jessamyn West's 1945 novel *The Friendly Persuasion* celebrates a group of Indiana Quakers and their staunch pious and patriotic opposition to the institution of slavery despite great outside pressures.[31] The climax of West's novel occurs when Josh Birdwell, a pacifist, diminutive Quaker, defies his religion's prohibitions against violence in order to fight confederate troops.[32] West imagines abolitionist principles as a higher calling that is part of an innate American conscience that takes precedent over denominational religious traditions. Josh defiantly tells his Quaker parents, who object to his decision to fight, that "any man is my enemy who kills innocent men and makes slaves."[33] During this same period, novels like Stephen Longstreet's obsessively detailed account of the Battle of Gettysburg, *Three Days* (1947), used the Civil War as an opportunity to celebrate and to construct a history of American military power as a tool to promote social equality.[34]

Other 1940s writers, like Muriel Rukeyser, wrote poems that looked back to historical abolitionist sacrifices as a way to encourage Americans to support the war effort and to stand up to Adolf Hitler. Rukeyser's 1940 poem, "The Soul and Body of John Brown," aligns the abolitionist impulse with the American desire for all people to have freedom and argues that the situation facing 1940s Americans parallels the historical Brown's own heavy burden: "The trial of heroes follows their execution./The striding wind of nations with new rain, new lightning,/destroyed in magnificent noon shining down the fiery pines./ Brown wanted freedom./ Could not himself be free until more grace reached a corroded world./ Our guilt his own."[35] The Garrison directive to abolitionists to embrace otherwise avoidable suffering provided a narrative by which artists and commentators could inspire and interpret America's initially reluctant involvement in an overseas war between European nations.

New England occupied a privileged position in 1940s Civil War literature as a region that successfully confronted tyranny and social injustice through its citizen's unrelenting eagerness to sacrifice for equality. Late 19th century novels like *The Gilead Guards* (1891) by Lucy Jameson Scott featured affectionate fictional dramatizations of the sacrifices of New England towns during the Civil War and provided a template for 20th century novelists with conventions that linked everyday abolitionist suffering with the Union victory.[36]

*Raintree County's* author Ross Lockridge spent the 1940s in Boston as an English professor at Simmons College following the completion of his doctorate from Harvard and this time only intensified his interest in the New England origin of an endlessly altruistic and child-like generosity in American identity and character. It was during his stay in Boston that the author developed a fascination with 19th century anti-slavery reform movements.[37] His son Larry Lockridge writes in his Pulitzer Prize winning biography of his father, *Shade of the Raintree,* that his father's fascination with 19th century America developed as he came to see this period as the genesis of the modern American myth of moral forthrightness and willing self-sacrifice.

In Lockridge's imagination, and in the popular parlance of mid–20th century America, the 19th century produced reformers who worked to rectify America's "betraying its early promise" of equality through the continued existence of the institution of slavery.[38] Lockridge's fascination with New England anti-slavery activism led him to view the 19th century as a moment in which America was able to start anew and live up to the legend of its wistful beginnings and ideals.

Audiences and critics alike responded with overwhelming enthusiasm to Lockridge's everyman abolitionist, lyrical prose style, and epic approach to 19th century American history. *Life* magazine, even before the book's official publication date, only encouraged such public clamor by naming *Raintree County* an important work of "prominence and profusion."[39] Following its official publication, the book went on to win the MGM award and in March of 1948 it topped the *New York Times* bestseller list.[40] *The New York Herald Tribune* wrote that the book, "grips the heart and stirs the mind. By any standard it is a novel of rare stature for these days."[41] *The New York Times Book Review* similarly praised the book's epic scope and ambitions as, "an achievement of art and purpose, a cosmically brooding book full of significance and beauty."[42] *The Saturday Review of Literature* went so far as to crown *Raintree County* as a frontrunner in the search for the "great American novel" when it proclaimed that the book's "breath of life sweeps through its voluminous pages; and it may be that *Raintree County* marks the end of a long slump in American fiction."[43] The only remarkable negative press that the book received in 1948 came from those who objected to Lockridge's strong sexual literary allusions. Such critics still, however, found aspects of *Raintree County's* epic literary ambitions admirable, but they dissented with what they perceived to be the book's reliance on Freud's theories. The *Christian Science Monitor's* reaction is representative of the way the book's frank sexuality (or "eroticism" and "obscenity") tempered the enthusiasm of conservative papers: "there is, incidentally, a functional lustiness of action and word in Mr. Lockridge which to some readers might be offensive."[44]

Of most interest to his book, however, is *Raintree County's* understanding of 19th century American history as the pursuit to realize the nation's "early promise" of equality by aligning the regeneration of the nation with abolitionist suffering and sacrifices. The novel characterizes abolitionism in the broadest possible way and by doing so it dissolves boundaries that would more narrowly limit the term to signify a specific group or people. Lockridge is not interested in crafting a story specifically about New England abolitionism, but is instead interested in a more general, self-sacrificial, aspect of American character.

The raintree and the river are the novel's earliest and central metaphors and together they create a narrative framework in which Shawnessy's suffering and traveling antislavery efforts are understood through eroticized Biblical imagery of pain and ecstasy. The raintree and the Shawmucky river are at the geographical center of the town of Waycross and allude back to the Tree of Knowledge and the Garden of Eden as described in the book of Genesis. The tree in both the Biblical story and in Lockridge's narrative signifies life and knowledge. In the Genesis account, Adam and Eve are given eternal life in the Garden of Eden and in return they are required to abstain from the fruit of the Tree of Knowledge. Eventually, Eve's curiosity and both of their lust for knowledge (along with the coaxing of a conspiring serpent) lead them to partake in the forbidden fruit. This disobedient action causes God to banish them from the garden and to also withdraw his gift of immortality. In the protestant Christian tradition the paradoxical legacy of this "fall" is that by disobeying God Adam and Eve necessitate the earthly return of a "suffering servant" or savior as a mean to redeem these and all of mankind's sins. Christ's sacrifice, according to this logic, had the positive effect of allowing man to develop a closer relationship with God. It represents a "fall forward" which means that the pain that resulted from the fall is also inextricably linked to the promise and pleasure of eternal union with God.

The raintree and the river are similarly the site of Shawnessy's ultimate forbidden pleasure, the origin of his suffering, and the catalyst for his redemptive quest. The Shawmucky River in the novel is whimsically described as a source of life and mystery for Shawnessy: "part of the secret was that all things that came from the Shawmucky River were one thing, all were subtle reminders of himself and all were perfect in their way, and all had been forever in the river, and the river was the ancient valley of his being, and everything that came from its waters was intolerably beautiful."[45] The formless, mythic, quality attached to the river is associated with an American ideal of innocence and an uncomplicated source of fundamental ethical principles. Yet the tree and the river it overlooks are also the site where Shawnessy is first awakened to his own sexuality when he accidentally comes upon Nell Gaither, a classmate of his, as she bathes nude in its waters. She is the principle focus of his adolescent love, infatuation, and undirected sexual energies. At that moment, Nell and the river are linked in Shawnessy's mind: "the river was there when the great ice sheet withdrew and left the land virginal, dripping, and devoid of life. The river was there when the first green life surged up from the south. The river was full of shining fleshes when the first man came from wandering into the forest country that was now called Raintree County."[46] In such passages, Lockridge situates Shawnessy through his "pure" love and desires for Nell as the masculine origin of the republic.

The tree and the river are also, however, associated with Susanna Drake, the daughter of a Southern plantation owner, who arrives in Waycross and promptly seduces Shawnessy into a drunken sexual encounter by its banks. During his sexual tryst with Susanna he begins to see the river as "fullbodied."[47] As he succumbs to Susanna's temptation and penetrates into her he awakens parts of himself ("it seemed to him dimly that he had thrust his way to the secret heart of life") but this transgression also ultimately forces him to leave Raintree County on a quest for redemption.[48] Guided by his abolitionist principles this encounter is the catalyst that causes him to abandon all "empty" sexual pleasure in favor of the ecstasy that comes from righteous suffering. In doing so, over the course of his journey, Shawnessy transforms from an Adamic figure into a messianic reformer.

The Edenic imagery associated with the novel's setting looks to the late 19th century utopian characterization of American abolitionism. The second half of the book's lengthy title hints at this elusive quality and *Raintree County's* tenuous spatial and spiritual boundaries: "... which had no boundaries in time and space, where lurked musical and strange names and mythical and lost peoples, and which was itself only a name musical and strange."[49] The spatial aspect of the Civil War (north-south) divided the country into definable regions that were characterized by either their support or opposition to the institution of slavery. The post-bellum commemoration of Garrison complicated such easy geographical distinctions. In the late 1860s, *Harpers' Weekly* and other magazines of this era described abolitionism as being "everywhere."[50] The entire country was retrospectively imagined by such publications as an "antislavery society."[51] Regional divisions collapsed in these discourses as different groups sought to align themselves with the Union's military victory and with the abolitionist's righteous suffering. Lockridge's title, then, is part of a tradition that stresses the mythical "boundary-less" quality of abolitionist reform. The title also mirrors the novel's expansive definition of the American abolitionist by alternately situating anti-slavery advocacy through the jobs and the roles that its protagonist John Shawnessy takes up: as a newspaper reporter, as a teacher, a Union soldier, as a politician, and as a local historian. The history of the 19th century and the history of the Civil War are mediated through Shawnessy who, like the town in which he resides, is a figure without boundaries that is capable of standing in for many types of peoples.

John Shawnessy's mythic aura is enhanced by the novel's frequent doubling of his namesake and personal story with the life of the 14th century Christian reformer and Bible translator John Wycliff and with the legend of Johnny Appleseed. Shawnessy's narration explains early on that Johnny Appleseed supposedly passed through the Raintree County region during one of his westward travels and planted a tree that inspired the region's name. He remarks that "no one ever found the eponymous tree of Rain tree County" while also stressing that he is one of two people who ever showed any interest in locating it.[52] Shawnessy "never doubted the truth of the legend" and "felt sure that a wondrous tree grew in secret somewhere in the county ... by a man whose name was also Johnny."[53] In fact, one of the novel's many storylines involves Shawnessy's obsession with locating this tree, which he believes will reveal a "wondrous secret" that will help him better understand himself.[54] Lockridge uses Raintree County as an allegory for the republic and Shawnessy's search for the fabled origin of the county parallels his search for what is authentically American. He seeks to excavate an America that lives up to the mythical, lofty, ideals of the founders and sees this process as one that necessarily involves purging the institution of slavery.

John Shawnessy's youthful quest to find the "tree" of Raintree County becomes a way to mark him as a reformer and this association is heightened by the name he shares with the first man to translate the Latin Vulgate Bible into English. Shawnessy's recognition of the doubling of his name with that of the 14th century Wickliff stirs in him an awareness of the mediated nature of his identity. His father T.D., the town's Protestant minister, explains to an adolescent Shawnessy the origins of his name through a copy of the family Bible. He recalls feeling at that moment that "his whole life had been woven from the pages of this august book ... his very substance was shaped from its archaic language."[55] At the most basic level, Lockridge's use of the "double" here suggests that Shawnessy's identity is unstable. But the implications of this dynamic are more complex: realizing that the novel's many storylines, images, and thematic structures explicitly reference specific 19th century abolitionist narratives like *Uncle Tom's Cabin,* implicitly cite Garrisonian rhetorical appeals, and draw on the literary trope of the "suffering abolitionist" of the late 19th and 20th century, more richly situates Shawnessy's identity as a series of imitative performances.[56]

Shawnessy's search for self-knowledge is explored through his self-conscious engagement with the way his personal identity is dependent upon other stories and tied to citation and imitation. The young Shawnessy is particularly fascinated with the Biblical story of the Garden of Eden and the tree of forbidden fruit that his mother reads to him nightly. These Biblical allusions anticipate the narrative arc of his "fall" but on a simpler level they also convey the novel's thematic interest in origins. America in this novel is the lost Eden that God has distanced from his grace due to the sin of slavery, which necessitates a sacrifice that is grand enough to atone for the country's many spiritual wrongs. In early chapters the young Shawnessy increasingly confuses the "sins of American history" with the "bloody, exciting and irrational legends of the Bible."[57] As he tells his own story he alternately imagines himself as Adamic and messianic. His understanding of America and the possibility of it becoming "the greatest republic since the beginning of time" is intrinsically tied to his Christian understanding of Christ's sacrifice on the cross and the role of suffering in this political and spiritual drama of salvation.[58] He yearns for "definite answers" about why "God's gentle son ... had been nailed to a cross for being good."[59] He concludes that American union and individual sacrifice are inseparable and his melding of the religious and the secular creates a context in which the abolitionist becomes the conduit for the nation's healing and redemption.

Shawnessy's narration continuously returns to the question of his personal history and his character expresses optimism that an awakening to his own identity has larger implications beyond the boundaries of the self. These ruminations demonstrate a high degree of cultural consciousness, that is to say, the ways in which his name recalls certain cultural archetypes, myths, and legends: "What did it mean? If the sounds and meanings that it once had were traced back far enough, it too perhaps would return into the primitive garden of the race, back to the parent word."[60] Such moments recall a 19th century historical romance literary tradition that used the individual as a vehicle by which to imagine national identity.[61] In "The Presence of the Past in the Heartland: *Raintree County* Revisited," Joel M. Jones points out that "Shawnessy's biography becomes the region's and the nation's ... his is the heart of the heartland," and argues that "Lockridge's most impressive aesthetic achievement is the extensive temporal and structural parallels he establishes between the personal experiences of Shawnessy and public events in the national experience."[62] Shawnessy is described as "life's eternal young American" and the novel repeatedly identifies him as embodying the potential and the collective essence of the republic's origin.[63] Shawnessy's introspective search leads him to see in himself, "a murmurous reminder of the common source and common destiny of man."[64]

The novel's narration reminds of its constructed nature and its debt to other texts and in doing so Lockridge challenges the reader to examine the myths and legends of American history that the novel recirculates. Such tendencies reinforce his protagonist's outspoken "holy faith in the printed word" as a source of inspiration for the production of self-knowledge and mythology.[65] Patricia Ward Julius writes in her essay "The Southern Myth in Ross Lockridge, Jr.' s *Raintree County*" that the novel's reworking of popular texts privileges personal, individual, mythology as the only narrative capable of producing a greater degree of understanding of the republic.[66] Shawnessy even writes a meta-narrative of his life that serves as a parallel commentary to the major events of the novel, which he calls the *Mythic Examiner*. But it is not simply for internal musing that the book self-reflexively engages its writerly quality; it is also a device that examines and reuses the important foundational texts of 19th century abolitionism. For example, *Uncle Tom's Cabin* first appears early in the story, chronologically during the summer of 1852, when Shawnessy's father T.D. brings home a copy of the book and begins using its story in his sermons. Shawnessy remembers the controversy the book caused in his father's church as one of the "great spiritual events of Raintree County."[67] He explains that his father's Uncle Tom-based anti-slavery sermons produced many Christian conversions and new abolitionists, including the young Shawnessy himself, and he offers his "conversion story" in a matter-of-fact and detached third person voice: "after he read *Uncle Tom's Cabin* he was never confused again about the question of slavery. He knew where and what slavery was, he knew that it was bad, he knew also that it would one day be destroyed."[68]

The majority of Shawnessy's memories are mediated by other stories, particularly by 19th century anti-slavery sentimental fiction. After the war Shawnessy names his first daughter Eva, he tells us, after the character from Stowe's story. He explains that he admires Stowe's character Eva because she is, "too simple to be real and thus more true than life."[69] *Raintree County* uses familiar sentimental narratives as yet another layer of expression. The archetypal tropes of these stories become the foundation for Shawnessy's own story and emphasize the role of personal experience, language, and narrative in the production and transmission of national self-definition. From the mythic origins of *Raintree County* to the naming of Shawnessy's daughter Eva, characters and events are shadowed by their fictional traces.[70] In doing so, *Raintree County* becomes a novel that participates in the circulation of 19th century narrative traditions of American abolitionism for 20th century audiences, while also drawing attention to the repetition and the use of narrative itself, highlighting the limits of the contemporary culture's knowledge and understanding.

*Raintree County's* anti-slavery message is expressed through the personal suffering that Shawnessy experiences through his two most significant romantic relationships: with his star-crossed love Nell Gaither and with his first wife, the southern temptress, Susanna Drake. This love triangle draws on genre conventions popularized by other 20th century Civil War novels like *The Soul of Abe Lincoln* (1923), *The Stranger* (1907), and *Kitty Dixon* (1907) that each dramatized the unlikely courtship and romantic pairing of northern anti-slavery men with southern women who sympathized with slavery and the Confederacy. Such stories transformed America's historical drama of sectional dissent into a fictional drama of conciliation and resolved the conflict through the mechanisms of sentimental fiction.[71] Yet, *Raintree County's* two romances deny tidy reunions. Nell Gaither dies without ever marrying or consummating her forlorn relationship with Shawnessy and Susanna Drake's southern sensibilities and dangerous sexual allure nearly destroy Shawnessy both emotionally and spiritually.

The expression of Shawnessy's personal suffering as a form of national sacrifice is heightened through the absence of a satisfying romantic resolution. His personal suffering and his careful exploration of his self becomes a way for him to understand national atrocities and to discover a greater degree of clarity on issues like slavery. "Here where the two roads cross," he gently speaks under his breath in one memorable passage following news of the Kansas-Nebraska Act, "I study and study the riddle of the sphinx, the intersection of my life with the republic."[72] Shawnessy struggles to make sense of the cultural tensions and sectional debates over race happening around him and he concludes that he can best participate by understanding his own life and suffering. The outward events of the world become little more than "fragments of the immense puzzle of myself" and his narration argues that republican wholeness is only possible through his self-knowledge.[73] This understanding of antislavery activism is a product of Garrison's appeals that stressed slave passivity and the redemptive quality of abolitionist pain and its use here demonstrates the extent to which this language had become a part of commonly held heroic Civil War literary conventions. It imagines the suffering abolitionist figure as the foundation for the optimistic expectation of bringing about the birth of a new nation. The anti-slavery struggle becomes a moment for self-reflection, understanding, growth, and exaltation for those who fight the tyranny of southern religious and cultural practices.

Shawnessy's strong abolitionist and democratic ideals are contrasted with those of his first wife Susanna Drake. She is the daughter of an aristocratic Southern family in New Orleans that maintains one of the city's largest plantations. She settles in Raintree County following a prematurely terminated engagement and upon arriving in town she aggressively pursues Shawnessy's attention. Shawnessy is alternately charmed by Susanna's genteel Southern manners and horrified by her outspoken support of slavery. Susanna dominates all of their early conversations, which Shawnessy characterizes as "a whole repertoire of stories intended to show that the Negro was not a human being and that there was no use to talk of emancipating him."[74]

Susanna's brutal and strangely nostalgic southern stories diverge from John Shawnessy's appetite for ideas and thinkers "fresh from New England," which he first encounters and adopts during the early years of his formal schooling under the tutelage of Professor Jerusalem Stiles, who argues that New England culture represents that which is "foremost American."[75] Susanna, in contrast, owns two young slave girls and her interactions with them repeatedly reveal a malicious and masochistic side of her temperament. For instance, she reserves her most violent racial stories and her most severe physical treatment of the girls for moments when Shawnessy is in her presence to witness them. Shawnessy himself realizes that, "the most offensive stories concerning black people were told in the presence of the Negro girl who carried the tea service in and out."[76] Susanna takes particular pleasure in plantation stories of rape and sexual atrocities perpetrated by slave men against women from the "finest families in New Orleans" and recounts in startling detail how they were attacked, had their clothes ripped off, and were forced to submit to their attackers to save their life.[77] Shawnessy repeatedly turns inward as Susanna reaches the climax of her stories and returns to his preoccupation with an internal mythological language of birth, renewal, and republic and imagines his soul and his physical body as inseparable from the abstract idea of the republic. He ponders his physical appearance, for instance, and describes his face as a "palimsest" that is "also a memory of a million other faces."[78] By looking inward Shawnessy simultaneously distances himself from the violence conjured in Susanna's stories and assumes the pain of others and makes it his own. His description of himself as a "palimsest" only reinforces the idea that the pain of others is, in a sense, already his own pain. It need only to be peeled back within in order to reveal and approach it. The novel adopts the Garrisonian model of the abolitionist as the suffering ethical witness and does so to express the central paradox of Shawnessy's ideology: the redemptive work of imagining the tyranny of slavery without really seeing or experiencing it.

Shawnessy's narration presents his personal life with Susanna as a sacrifice for the union cause. Lockridge constructs and enhances Shawnessy's martyr narrative arc through juxtapositions between his protagonist's personal plight and the work of recognizable historical anti-slavery "martyrs," like John Brown, whose narrative appears throughout the story. The first news of John Brown's raid in Harper's Ferry sparks excited conversations at the local post office when Shawnessy anxiously arrives to check his mailbox for a letter from Susanna

Drake. Townspeople stand on all sides of him debating the legality and wisdom of John Brown's revolutionary work and ponder its possible effect on union stability. The letter that Shawnessy anxiously awaits is Susanna's response to his proposal of marriage. Weeks earlier he lost his virginity to her in a drunken moment of passion following his first taste of alcohol. This moment of sexual indulgence, which offers a crude reference to the Adam-Eve temptation story, leads to Susanna's announcement that she is pregnant. The reader later discovers that this feigned pregnancy was, in fact, part of an elaborate string of calculated lies designed to sexually tempt Shawnessy and to then to force him into marriage.

Shawnessy's decision to propose marriage to Susanna is described as a pivotal resolution that comes at a considerable personal cost. He does not love her and barely knows her. Throughout the novel the virginal Nell Gaither remains the object of his love and affection. In contrast, marrying Susanna becomes a familial duty (maintaining his family's honor and standing in the community) that he assumes with the full knowledge that this arrangement is destined to bring him pain and suffering. He ruminates on the very different lives that a union with each woman offers and describes these divergent paths as representing two different "worlds": "one was the guiltless earth of the river of desire, the earth big with seed, the earth of fruit and flower. The other was the world of memory and sadness, guilt and duty, loyalty and ideas."[79] Marrying Susanna also poses a threat to the abolitionist principles by which he lives, since her family is not only ardently proslavery but also maintains the largest plantation in New Orleans. Shawnessy's decision to follow through with these nuptials is not about his heroic decision to accept societal constraints but a celebration of his self-denial.

Shawnessy's pleasurable rendezvous with Susanna becomes an example of his victimization and the catalyst for his antislavery work. As the townspeople eagerly await a newswire with more information about Brown's raid, Shawnessy waits for the news that will similarly change the course of his life. One man standing near Shawnessy enthusiastically praises Brown's efforts and exclaims: "by god, we need more men with gunpowder in their guts."[80] Another seconds this idea by opining that, "in my opinion, John Brown is the Greatest Living American."[81] Shawnessy's thoughts turn inward as the news of Brown's capture pours into the post office and those around him speculate out loud about Brown's fate. "They'll hang him sure as I'm shootin'," is the sentiment of one bystander, which is affirmed by many nods and grunts.[82] As Shawnessy ponders "a wrong grown sacred in the very measure of its age and enormity" it becomes clear that he is not talking about Brown's predicament but his own.[83] The talk of John Brown becomes a "distant tumult" in Shawnessy's mind that is "lost in the headlines of the onward pressing days."[84] His awareness of the news concerning Brown's capture and Brown's wounds and suffering (for a cause that he himself advocates) slowly recedes and is replaced with thoughts of his own potential martyrdom and his own anxiety and suffering that will result from his pending nuptials with Susanna Drake. Shawnessy ponders his spiritual anguish and parallels it with Brown's actual suffering over the course of the hour in narrative time that elapses. He comes to believe that he understands Brown's pain by struggling to make sense of his own bad fortune.

The novel draws an explicit parallel between Shawnessy's pending nuptials and John Brown's encroaching execution by juxtaposing his wedding with the spectacle of Brown's march to gallows and in doing so reminds of Shawnessy's unique internal form of antislavery activism. Shawnessy even begins to confuse the frenzied public discussions of Brown's looming fate by townspeople on Waycross's main street with his own imaginings (and fantasies) in a way that leads him to believe that these people are actually discussing his own destiny and plotting *his* death and demise. After re-reading Susanna's letter he quickly tucks it away in his coat pocket and spends several moments collecting himself before he walks into the outer commotion that abounds on the town's main street. His personal angst in this moment of loneliness is described in Christ-like language: "he didn't want to leave this passageway. Outside there were a thousand eyes. People who had no worries were on the lookout for tender flesh to crucify."[85] Shawnessy remains physically separated from John Brown's revolutionary revolt in Harper's Ferry against the institution of slavery but common pain and anguish links the two men together. Shawnessy the abolitionist is a figure large enough to be a kinsman of all anti-slavery dissent (including Brown's violent actions) but he is also consigned to a different kind revolution that consistently favors internal spiritual struggle and witnessing. The politics of revolution here are grounded in personal domestic crises of subjective and more generalized pain. Personal suffering through self-denial becomes a revolutionary form of protest. Shawnessy is consumed with guilt over his sexual experience with Susanna (afterwards they "put on their clothes and with them shame and a sense of guilt") but it is this encounter that leads him to leave the idyllic Raintree County and by doing so he embarks on a journey of self-discovery that, like the Biblical narrative of Adam and Eve, anticipates the emergence of a redemptive "suffering servant."[86]

The threatening fanaticism of the historical John Brown fades into the background of the narrative among the images of other controversial figures like Nat Turner and the vision of abolitionist protest that remains is that of the domesticated revolutionary and ethical witness. There is a mythic purity associated with Shawnessy's quiet suffering and his eventual exile that aligns and distances himself from John Brown. After returning home from the post office Shawnessy contemplates his situation with Susanna Drake and does so with John Brown's impending execution foremost in his thoughts. As he thinks about his situation and John Brown's fate he sees them as similar but ultimately concludes that his suffering outweighs that of the man who will soon be dead. Consider how these two disparate narrative lives are intermingled, but Shawnessy's personal suffering finally overshadows Brown's "martyrdom":

> Do lovers really possess each other in the night? Do they really become one? Do the bride and groom really marry and belong to each other forever? He was thinking then of John Brown, who had fought for the freedom of a few million nameless black men, shadowy projections of the Southern earth where they toiled. Perhaps it was better to make a few concessions and live a little longer than to be once brave and forever dead. John Brown must die terribly alone as all men must. But John Shawnessy was alive.[87]

Shawnessy's thoughts emphasize his responsibility to "live," to carry out his duty, and to witness as he compares his fate with that of Brown and soberly observes that each man would soon "go to far strange places."[88] He speculates that as Brown is lowered into a "dirty grave" he would be proposing to Susanna Drake.[89] Brown's literal death becomes a vehicle for Shawnessy to imagine his symbolic death.

The novel's insistence that Shawnessy's marriage vows to Susanna Drake are completed at the exact moment of John Brown execution accentuates the transference of suffering from Brown to Shawnessy.[90] Shawnessy adopts Brown's suffering and history as his own. This occurs both inwardly (in Shawnessy's first person narration) and in a brief commentary by the omniscient third person narrator (Ross Lockridge, the novel's author). The third person narration aggressively makes this connection: "so long as John Wickliff Shawnessy could spring up joyous in the springing day, John Brown could never die, and one heroic soul was enough to sustain the whole mass and fabric of the world."[91] Shawnessy's personal suffering, his marriage to Susanna, John Brown's death, and the increasing political reality of national disunion and civil war then collapse into one complex image in Shawnessy's wedding night dream concerning his marriage license:

> The print ran blurred. The parchment [of the marriage license) was a map of Raintree County. A red gash had been torn in it, the wound was bleeding, staining his hands and covering him with shame and a hideous fear from which he kept trying to awaken with small choked cries.[92]

The boundaries between the individual and the state dissolve here. The angst that Shawnessy will experience in his marriage anticipates the secession of southern states and the bloody drama of the Civil War. Raintree County stands in for the nation and there is the suggestion in this image of a lost mythical place of origins. Shawnessy now must leave the home that he is so closely tied with and experience the pain that his abolitionist ideals require him to assume.

Shawnessy's honeymoon with Susanna to New Orleans takes him away from the idyllic town of his youth and allows him to directly witness southern plantation culture for the first time; he repeatedly processes and articulates his observations about these foreign sights through the spectacular and traumatic language of fictional 19th century anti-slavery narratives. For example, as he begins his sojourn through the south he repeatedly references Harriet Beecher Stowe's *Uncle Tom's Cabin* as a way to broadly order his environment and his experiences. As he stands on the railing of the steamboat that is taking him and his new wife to New Orleans he can't help but feel that he is living "scenes of a new *Uncle Tom's Cabin*, starring in the principal role Mr. John Wickliff Shawnessy from *Raintree County*."[93] When he finally arrives in New Orleans he is horrified by the sight of freshly auctioned slaves in chains and continues to revert to *Uncle Tom's Cabin* as a way to process this new information. He equates those he meets with characters from the story and he sees their entire way of life as strange and melodramatic. Plantation owners, labor supervisors, and slaves are described as playing parts in a "barbarous cruel old melodrama, which for some reason or other all the actors and the audience passionately believe in."[94]

Such passages demonstrate the interdependence of Shawnessy's abolitionist beliefs with the narrative tropes of sentimental literary heroes and heroines. This tendency looks back to Garrison's own interest in re-writing and re-printing southern accounts of slave suffering within a new context that was interpreted through an abolitionist presence. In Garrison's religious and political activism the text offered a way to see, change, and re-order the "real" environment. The Christian appeals and the altruistic narratives made popular by Garrison, Stowe, and others are all present in Shawnessy's observations of the nameless slaves he observes: "they were all slaves, human beings whose dark skin made it legal for other men to rule them. They were also all Christians."[95] As Shawnessy's boat descends further down through New Orleans he is tortured by the work songs that the slave's chant. He is only able to hear in the songs the "proof of the darkest of all crimes."[96] Shawnessy's descriptions begin with anecdotes concerning slave suffering and conclude with his strong empathy for their pain and circumstance. He hears in the "syncopated rhythms" of their songs the "sad and inerrable misery of their bondage," which produces inside of him a feeling of "great restlessness."[97]

Shawnessy's reformer identity is defined and signaled through his distinct struggles as a witness to slave pain and southern atrocities. His "protest" throughout the story involves very little outward verbal dissent or subversive works. When he first arrives in New Orleans he remembers that he "trained in disputation at the Pedee Academy" in Raintree County and he imagines that perhaps his oratorical skills might be put to use on behalf of the slave.[98] The novel's narration in this section reveals a disconnect between Shawnessy's outwardly polite tone and the moral outrage of his internal ruminations: "as a staunch advocate of Republican principles in the press and elsewhere, John Shawnessy made a tactful effort to present Northern views during his sojourn in the South."[99] And so when his southern hosts take offense with his anti-slavery views he resolves to stop bringing up the subject in conversation. Witnessing and expressing his internal pain in *The Mythic Examiner* and in his thoughts becomes the principle means by which he protests the institution of slavery and the brutal violence committed against the slaves on the plantation where he resides during his stay.

Shawnessy's first experience as a "witness" to slave injustice occurs when Susanna Drake and her family take him to his first minstrel performance, which provides a setting that explicitly draws attention to his passive spectatorial role. "You'll love it, honey," are the words of assurance that Susanna speaks to him before they depart for an experience that produces reactions of horror and confusion in his mind. The vacillation between celebration and denigration in the minstrel drama is a dynamic that Shawnessy is unable to fully reconcile at the end of the show: "I understood dimly why the songs most beloved by the white culture of the South were all simulated darkie songs. Through them all, a nameless darkie toted a weary load and longed for the old plantation. He was the south's primitive, simple hero, laden with chains."[100] Yet these celebratory songs and the "artistic satisfaction" they produce for the admiring audience contrast sharply in his mind with the reality of "a human being sold downriver into exile and slavery, growing old in a land that was not his own."[101]

The feelings of bewilderment that Shawnessy experiences after his first encounter with the plantation culture of the south in a transmissible, condensed, and overtly performative setting emphasizes his status as a foreign observer. The minstrel show haunts him as a reminder of America's failed democratic principles just as it presents a challenge to his own conception of his abolitionist identity and civic responsibilities towards others. After viewing the show he feels as if he is "plunged in a great dismal swamp of human prejudice and error" and he realizes that his belief in the possibility of progress stands at odds with the reality that his country is bereft of basic humanistic values.[102] With that conclusion, Shawnessy begins a process of increasingly identifying with slave pain. What follows during the rest of his time in the south is a series of events that privilege his language and internal unrest over actual slave pain and his imagined autobiographical narratives of suffering over lived experience.

Written into *Raintree County*'s narrative design are a series of nocturnal excursions in which Shawnessy's southern hosts take him on trips to show him the "real south" and these adventures lead the narrator to view his pain as similar to that of the slave. "Come along, Johnny.... I'll protect you. It's something to see, son. Downright educatin'," says Susanna's cousin Bobby Drake as he pleads with Shawnessy to accompany him and the other men on a tour of New Orleans brothels and ballrooms.[103] As a "no account" yankee the New Orleans men promise Shawnessy that he will change his mind about their way of life once he experiences a "stag dinner"—an event punctuated by a night of drinking at several ballrooms that culminates in a visit to a brothel on one of the so called "nigger nights"—when the patrons are taken care of by a staff of all African slave women.[104]

And indeed, it is something "to see" and Shawnessy does experience a symbolic rebirth during these trips that leads him to link his pain with slave pain and to map his subjective experiential suffering onto those whose exploitation he witnesses until the two are indistinguishable. The ride down into the heart of New Orleans parallels Shawnessy's own spiritual transformation and his temporary descent into "blackness." The cab he travels in quickly navigates the winding streets, taking him into new "terrifying depths."[105] The entire company of men spiral "deeper into the nocturnal muck of New Orleans as if to reach its lowest circle of depravity."[106] His southern hosts guide him through a labyrinth of sin only surpassed in the narrator's eyes by the macabre images in Dante's *Divine Comedy*. This parallel is appropriate because what he discovers in the brothel is a kind of hell. It is, in Shawnessy's own words, a "hell of decayed magnificence," a "detestable flower," that unveils what the mythology of the paternal plantation culture temporarily obscures during the daytime hours.[107] Shawnessy observes plantation masters enter the brothel and is repulsed by the unavoidable realization that the brothel is the literal climax of the symbolic rape that begins on the plantation during the workday. He remains outwardly indifferent and passive, but internally he experiences indescribable pain. The smallest details of the brothel bother him as he is awakened to a new level of sensitivity to black suffering. Even the brothel walls seem to ooze sweat and filth as he "watches."[108]

Witnessing the debacle at the saloon so affects Shawnessy that he imagines the words hurled at the slaves as weapons directed at him. He is horrified by the "vile words" of his hosts and the "epithets delivered with savage zeal."[109] The atmosphere in the brothel turns into a scene of carnivalesque horror as slave masters "clinch their teeth" and "excrete drunken words."[110] These words and this troubling scene torture him but he is even more perturbed to find the slave women giggling and playing along. In this moment, Shawnessy's pain of witnessing the whole event becomes more palpable and real than that of the slaves. He feels the words and actions of the slave masters "like a blow of a whip" that is taken to his own back.[111] His ability to experience this pain informs the way he views the entire drama performed before him. It gives the whole scene an "extra brutality" and he is only able to describe what he witnesses as "a baser indignity than the whip."[112] He is grasping for a language of suffering that places the white witness, the abolitionist, at the center of a national story of slavery's wrongs. This idea is especially present in one of the most significant moments in the novel, which occurs as he leaves the brothel, changed and scarred. His experiences that night, he tells the reader, forced him to acknowledge "his equality with the slave."[113] By "equality" he suggests not only his capacity to suffer alongside the slave, but he is also asserting that the pain of the abolitionist witness who is trapped and unable to act is sometimes greater than actual slave pain. Shawnessy feels a kinship with the slave's predicament from this moment forward and it leads him, both in his conscious thoughts and in his dreams, to blur the boundaries between himself and them.

Shawnessy's troubling relationship with Susanna during their sojourn in the south is organized around their mutual desires to experience slave pain. Early in their stay, for instance, as the couple arrives back at the grounds of the Drake plantation in a buggy, Shawnessy physically intervenes to prevent Bobby Drake (Susanna's cousin and the slave overseer on the family plantation) from Whipping a slave who looked at Susanna too long as she dismounted. The scene haunts Shawnessy the rest of the day, but the spectacle sexually arouses Susanna, who harbors fantasies of abuse and degradation that are awakened at the sight of such pain. That night Susanna crawls up to Shawnessy in their bedroom as they discuss the incident. She gets on her knees and begs him to hit her:

"I deserve it. Go on and hit me *hard*, honey."[114] He refuses but he is deeply disturbed by her beseeching request. Shawnessy's feverish dreams that follow indicate the internal power struggle between him and Susanna over the symbolic vocabulary of slave pain.

Shawnessy loses access to both the strength and the personal peril that are essential to his identity as a witness to slave pain in scenes where Susanna's sexual "role-playing" dictates the terms of the narrative. Susanna's southern infused fantasies of sexual abuse ask him to take a more active part in the drama and to play the role of the aggressor and not the spectator. As he wakes in and out of consciousness that night, Susanna's narrative threatens to overtake his: "he looked at her back in the warm dark-soft olive, with its graceful furrow. Suddenly, he imagined it covered with long, cruel gashes."[115] This role reversal represents the first time that Shawnessy wants to immediately leave the south and cut his honeymoon short.[116] His own sense of identity is uncomfortably displaced at the moment that a counter-narrative recasts him in a role outside of his own romantic designs.

The contrast between Susanna Drake's vision of the south, with its symbolic appropriation of slave suffering through sexual role-playing fantasies, and John Shawnessy's understanding of slave pain as a referent to the ecstasy of redemptive abolitionist suffering and witnessing produces an irreconcilable tension that causes the pair to split. In the period preceding the collapse of their marriage Shawnessy tells Susanna that he can no longer tolerate her Southern culture of slavery and that their differing views are representative of a broader, "contest of ideals."[117] These divergent "ideals," however, are each part of southern and northern narratives of power and authority that are equally invested in recalling, reenacting, and using slave pain to each of their own ends.

Susanna's sexual role-playing awakens an anxiety in Shawnessy over the displacing impact of playing a "character" associated with the rebel south, which calls for him to inflict violence as opposed to his ideal of watching and experiencing pain by proxy. What Susanna confronts Shawnessy with is a distorted version of his own internal musing. Shawnessy views Susanna's strange fantasies as proof that she is mentally unstable and delirious and this belief leads to her physical confinement in her bedroom where she is kept tied to her bed in order to force her to get some rest. When Shawnessy comes up to check on her she is unbound from her bed and, to his horror, she sits beside a leather belt on the floor. The exchange that follows demonstrates the volatile challenge that Susanna poses to Shawnessy's narrative of passive, humanistic, and regenerative abolitionist suffering:

> *Whip* me, honey. I deserve it.
> —Johnny picked up the whip and tossed it into a corner of the room.
> —Get up, you crazy little thing, he said.
> Go on and *lash* me, she said with savage intensity.... I wish you'd beat me good and hard.[118]

Such moments serve as a double to Shawnessy's first introduction to the south through the minstrel performance he attended with the Drake family. In the earlier incident Shawnessy expressed horror at the performance he was forced to endure. Here, Shawnessy is asked to explicitly become part of the performance and to do more than passively exist as a witness. Yet, like the earlier minstrel show, the details of their confrontation here have a non-realistic pantomime quality: as he enters Susanna's room he parts the stuffy drapes surrounding her bed, while the "flickering candlelight made dusky shadows."[119]

What this scene presents is an inverted mirror image of the first literal stage performance and the distorted quality of this repetition calls the integrity of the "self" in the first performance into question. Shawnessy's identity is rooted in his ability to witness slave suffering and to adopt that suffering as his own. Lockridge's novel is structured around a telling of American history in which national identity becomes coherent through the memories, pain, and experiences that take place over Shawnessy's life. The birth of the modem republic is intrinsically tied to the abolitionist narrative.

Shawnessy's marriage to and confrontations with Susanna signify the competing narratives of northern and southern audiences that attempt to claim slave pain as their own. Shawnessy's internal narrative and spiritual musings are positioned as redemptive because they produce empathy and self-awareness on the part of the narrator for the slave (through the spectator) and the union cause, while Susanna's efforts to narrate slave pain are disavowed because they end in a misguided and emotionally distant (and disconnected) self-gratification, and not progress. Both Shawnessy's self-imaginings and Susanna Drake's sexual fantasies accentuate the violent commonality at the heart of both northern and southern mythic fantasies: that nostalgia, spectatorship, and desire are carefully intertwined in national narratives of origin and provide a way to overwrite the ambiguities of history (and historical memory) with stories that provide order and continuity.

Shawnessy's meditations on black suffering and his efforts to blur the boundaries between his pain and slave pain climaxes in the emergence of a figure called "Black Johnny," a black version of the narrator who appears in his dreams following the emotional collapse of his marriage to Susanna Drake. Competing narratives that espoused "different ideals" characterized Shawnessy's marriage to Drake and his freedom from her marks his movement towards more intimately experiencing black pain. Upon returning to Raintree County from New Orleans his remarks are triumphal. He describes his suffering as a stabilizing and mediating agent between the violent and chaotic sectional forces taking place around him:

> Yes, all would be well within him now. It was necessary to find one's courage and conviction and to find one's people at the right time. All would be well, too, with the Republic.... It mattered after all whether one was right or wrong. It mattered about slavery. It mattered about the Union. This was the springtime of a solemn new awakening of conscience.[120]

The new "solemn awakening" that Shawnessy experiences is one that removes any doubts about the moral worthiness of Union cause. He enlists in the army, he writes antislavery articles, and he later runs for elected office. But these events are secondary to the drama occurring within his own imagination and the internal tensions that place his suffering and his predicament at the center of the national conflict of the war. He finds outward metaphors or historical equivalences for his inward condition. The tumultuous sectional upheaval occurring around Shawnessy becomes a way for him to express and to better understand himself. As a new Union soldier at the battle of Gettysburg, for instance, he does not ponder the horror or the carnage of the battlefield, but he does discuss his internal spiritual pain and discomfort. It is this private pain that is foremost in his thoughts following the battle: "he smoked, remembering his own private Battle of Gettysburg, the one that never got into the history books."[121]

"Black Johnny" stands as the novel's most explicit and grotesque equation of abolitionist pain with slave suffering. This character repeatedly appears in Shawnessy's dreams following traumatic personal experiences. In these dreams, the moments in his life in which he witnessed slave pain are re-staged (they are mostly from his time spent in the south), with Shawnessy himself "cast" in the role of the slave. Within this dream space he and the slave are literally joined together into one body. White subjectivity and slave pain become identical and interchangeable. "Black Johnny" forces the reader to consider the political dynamics of duplication since Shawnessy's dreams point to the increasing difficulty of distinguishing between inner and outer conceptions (or representations) of self, between the counterfeit and the real person. These sections are written in the style of a minstrel show playscript with character descriptions, dialogue, and stage directions. The first of these dreams occurs on a train as Shawnessy returns to Raintree County. His marriage to Susanna is lost, his child with her is gone, and his hope of one day having a family no longer seems likely. He struggles to express his pain and finds that he is only capable of doing so through a vocabulary borrowed from tragic racial romances (like *Uncle Tom's Cabin*). This realization leads him to increasingly narrate, embrace, and to understand his life through such forms: "gone were the days when hearts were young and gay, all gone, he knew, all lost on the river of years, a dream recaptured in the greatest of sentimental novels or perhaps in the poem of a lost young bard of Raintree County."[122]

Repetition here is performative and is less about the double ("Black Johnny") than it is concerned with the "doubling" as a process that blurs the boundaries between slave and abolitionist. The appearance of "Black Johnny" allows scenes that Shawnessy witnessed in the past to be replayed, with Shawnessy cast as the object of physical persecution, emotional derision, and psychological torment. This doubling produces in Shawnessy a more immediate empathy for general slave pain through internal re-enactments of situations he directly witnessed and scenes that are a combination of witnessed experiences and excerpts from fictional antislavery melodramas; the two become inseparable.

Black Johnny makes his first appearance in a feverish, minstrel-like dream that draws from religious temptation stories (i.e., the Biblical narrative of Adam and Eve), from Shawnessy's personal history (i.e., watching Cousin Bobby's abuse of slaves on Susanna's New Orleans), and from popular slave escape narratives (like *Uncle Tom's Cabin*). These different stories coalesce into a mosaic that mythologizes Shawnessy's movement into adulthood through slave pain. Both Shawnessy or "Johnny," as he is described in the "play-text" of the dream, and Black Johnny both initially appear on stage together in this drama. They converse with "Woman," an Eve-like character who is compared by Johnny to the mythological "Helen," blurring the boundaries between Christian creation stories and pagan narratives. Black Johnny and Johnny remain separate manifestations of the story's narrator and he maintains the privileged power to occupy both black and white versions of himself. Yet the sameness and the connection between the characters is stressed: "you and I were the same and are always the same, being children of the same dark loins."[123] "Black Johnny" becomes a vehicle for sentiment and a symbol of the abolitionist identification with "authentic" African suffering.[124] The link between Johnny and Black Johnny as a performative marker of abolitionist pain is more emotional and theatrical than logical, but the presence of these two simultaneously distinct and inseparable characters express the complex racial exchange of Garrisonian abolitionism: witnessing and evoking African pain as a means to violently claim the carnage of slavery for Anglo-American readers. These dreams, as Leonard Lutwack writes, are the "substance of Johnny's life."[125] Unlike the dreams of Homer's Odyssesus and other mythological characters who learn from their outward travels, "the knowledge Johnny needs cannot be acquired abroad; rather it is bred within him."[126]

The Christian-pagan discussions between Johnny/Black Johnny and "Woman" demonstrate the novel's emphasis on character doubling, which parallels its omnipresent theme of the duplicity of narrative and language. The language here, with both Biblical and mythological references intertwined, is another form of doubling, wherein all speech carries cryptic meanings. Language here fails to stabilize identities or meaning. The destabilization of Shawnessy's identity in these dreams allows him access to black subjectivity in order to explore aspects of his own personality. After all, even within this dream Shawnessy never "becomes" the slave who he witnessed Cousin Bobby torment, but he does take on black skin (he is, after all, Black "Johnny") and does place himself within the scene. The difference is important and suggests that African suffering is a phenomenon that is filled with rich but imprecise significance for white readers. The desire to save the African slave from further injustice and suffering and a fascination with witnessing and inhabiting their torment produces a palpable tension.

Behind Shawnessy's impassioned desire to view himself as the passive victim of violence, and not the aggressor, is the oscillating relationship between pleasure and pain found in Garrrison's Christian abolitionist narratives. The Garrison revival popularized the impulse to preserve and revere those who welcomed persecution on behalf of the antislavery cause. This system of beliefs idealized pain as a source of pleasure and ecstasy because it brought the sufferer closer to God. Garrison and his followers looked to the death of Jesus as an example of willing and voluntary obedience to God. The work of the abolitionist, therefore, became associated with the re-enactment of Jesus' death by volunteering to experience pain and suffering. By the 20th century the explicit religious justifications (and rationale) for antislavery activism faded from popular accounts of abolitionist work, but the notion of abolitionist pain as an effective form of protest remained intertwined with abolitionist representations.

The personal tragedy and injustice of Shawnessy's own life is accessed and performed through his memories of prior black exploitation and the pain that he witnessed on the Drake family plantation. As Black Johnny he is physically assaulted by Susanna's father Robert Seymour Drake and his men as Cousin Bobby watches. These men "hugged him hard and hurled him down, squeezed the breath out of him with their buttocky bodies, gouged him with pistolbutts, clubs, knifehandles."[127] He struggles and screams for help, but these pleas are met with calm, paternal quips of measured indifference from Cousin Bobby, who speaks the same words to Black Johnny that he originally spoke to Shawnessy and Susanna when they accidentally happened upon him disciplining the slave on the plantation: "hell, boy, you got to learn'em young, as my Old Man always said."[128] The literary impact of this doubling is both forceful and imprecise. The scene elicits pity for the slave and emphasizes the pathological cruelty of the Drake family, but it does so through the body and the consciousness of Shawnessy, who shapes this pity, and invests it with new political and personal meaning.

The earlier pain that Shawnessy witnessed is detached from its original context and what remains is an example of southern cruelty towards anti-slavery activists and their altruistic enterprises. In this dream, violence towards the African body performs the same function that Elaine Scarry ascribes to the injured bodies of war: legitimation. "Though it lacks interior connection to the issues," Scarry writes, "wounding is able to open up a source of reality that can give the issue force and holding power."[129] The novel's representation of the physical punishment inflicted on the slave's body, via Shawnessy, allegorically participates in construction and perpetuation of a cultural narrative of national progress that privileges individual abolitionist sacrifice and valorizes the selfless assumption of slave pain by the white witness.

Saidiya Hartman provides useful a useful framework by which to think about Shawnessy's schizophrenic minstrel dreams and other narratives that use black pain as a vehicle that "provide us with the opportunity for self-reflection."[130] "At issue here," she writes, "is the precariousness of empathy and the uncertain line between witness and spectator."[131] Hartman is referring to the tenuous line between spectator and voyeur and suggests that even representations of slave pain that intend to convey a slave's humanity and represent the injustice of their enslavement can also "tether, bind, and oppress" when this process of empathy becomes simply another form of domination.[132]

For Hartman, the most troubling form of empathy is that which, by its very presentation, implies that black suffering is only legible when presented through a white body. She wonders whether, "the white witness of the spectacle of suffering," can "affirm the materiality of black sentience only by feeling for himself?"[133] Her main point is that another person's pain can only be represented and acknowledged to the extent that it can be imagined and "made one's own," but that this process itself substitutes the original trauma or pain for the witnesses' imagined pain.[134] This whole cycle of identification and empathy first obscures and finally replaces the victim's real pain with the witness's imagined pain. The end result is not a more nuanced understanding or identification with slave pain, but a co-opting of the spectacle of slave pain in order to use suffering as a form of self-identification.

Shawnessy's desire to embody, experience, and define himself through his capacity to understand slave pain is explicitly self-conscious in his dreams that re-enact key dramatic scenes from 19th century sentimental abolitionist literature, like *Uncle Tom's Cabin*. In some of his dreams, Shawnessy is inserted into the role occupied by Eliza in Harriet Beecher Stowe's text. The popularity of Stowe's *Uncle Tom's Cabin* for 19th century audiences and for contemporary readers derives from its powerful use of sentimental structures and archetypal characters through which the author makes political and moral arguments against the institution of slavery. The characters from *Uncle Tom's Cabin* were widely familiar to American audiences by the time Ross Lockridge published *Raintree County* in 1948: Uncle Tom, the faithful Christian martyr; Little Eva, a saintly child whose death becomes the impetus for the conversion of both her father and a non-Christian slave girl; and Simon Legree, the prototype for the vicious and tyrannical plantation slave driver.

As a story and as a symbol, *Uncle Tom's Cabin* is an important cultural artifact in the history of 19th century American abolitionism and its continued widespread popularity in the 20th century helped to shape the popular historical memory of anti-slavery activism. Jane Tompkins argues that the lasting power of *Uncle Tom's Cabin* derives from its "jeremiad" theme, which she defines as a "mode of public exhortation" that joined "social criticism to spiritual renewal, public to private identity, the shifting 'signs of the times' to certain traditional metaphors, themes, and symbols."[135] Tompkins claims that novels like *Uncle Tom's Cabin* proved most effective when the sentimental appeal of the narrative defined reality and became its own record of history by convincing readers of its description of the world. Eric Sundquist similarly argues that the complex way Stowe's novel unites sacred and secular anti-slavery appeals rest at the core of the book's "elevation of domestic Christian virtues associated with women over the failed political secular virtues associated with a patriarchal society."[136] Sundquist describes the "knotted complexity" of the relationships between women, blacks, and the Christian tradition in the book and laments "how inadequately *Uncle Tom's Cabin* has been understood and how central it is, as a literary and political document, to the American experience."[137]

In his dreams, Shawnessy re-enacts a modified version of the ordeal faced by the fictional Eliza, a character who Stowe depicts as a loving, but desperate, mother who flees across an icy river with her newborn child in an effort to avoid their sale on the slave market and the resulting physical separation that would follow. Shawnessy leads the mother with child through the river as they are a mob of men guided by bloodhounds loudly trail them. As the dramatic tension from the chase builds the dream becomes less about the perils of slave flight than the narrator's heroics and his sense of obligation in the wake of great danger:

> Bloodhounds bayed in the distance. Lanterns flared. Shotgun blasts ripped the still leaves. A bloodred moon hung low on the horizon. The heaving muds of the swamp shimmered and stank. He was stumbling through the inky water, trying to find a way to freedom.... He was trying to remember how he had come by this unhappy burden. At any rate, it was a sacred charge, and he must find the underground railway and get her to safety on the north shore.[138]

Images of willing abolitionist suffering obscures slave pain in Garrison's original narratives and in Lockridge's fictional portrayal of abolitionist valor. Here Shawnessy bears the "unhappy burden" of helping this mother to escape, his life is in danger as the mob pursues him with weapons, and the decision to assume this burden carries with it a "sacred charge," which implies a divinely sanctioned aspect to this selfless work. The dream dramatically symbolizes Shawnessy's ascent (along with the literary trope of the suffering abolitionist) to a position of divine guardianship and purpose for the slave and the nation.

Yet Shawnessy's co-opting performance of slave pain here is different from Garrisonian precedents because it is framed non-realistically as a dream. Garrisonian narratives transformed the abolitionist witness into a participant by gradually shifting away from the verbal expressions of the slave's pain to the internal musings of the abolitionist's pain, which made the entire movement from slave pain to abolitionist pain invisible. Garrison reprinted and rewrote vivid and detailed southern accounts of slave executions and lynchings in order to ensure the greatest degree of verisimilitude. In contrast, Lockridge's story emphasizes the artifice of the scenario in presentation and narrative. His text is formatted like a playscript, which points to its overtly constructed qualities and his use of widely familiar sentimental stories stresses his novel's performative dimension. The narrative is also very self-conscious about its desire to highlight the structures of sentimental literature. The *Uncle Tom's Cabin* dream, for instance, is punctuated by an appearance by the book's author Harriet Beecher Stowe as a character. In a self-reflexive moment Shawnessy even calls out to Harriet Beecher Stowe for help as he flees his mob of pursuers: "Mrs. Stowe, for God's sake, hurry up and get us out of here! We're drowning Mrs. Stowe!"[139] In such instances the question of authorship is itself called into question by Lockridge:

there is the Lockridge novel that structures this dream like a play to underscore its nonrealistic quality; Shawnessy's narration in which his internal monologues celebrate his own heroism and his attempts to self-mythologize and to create an exemplary moral narrative out of his life and his fantasies of physical sacrifice; and Stowe's presence in this dream serves as a reminder that the moment itself is a re-staging of an earlier story. It is tempting to read these dream sequences as an effort to distance abolitionist activism from the kind of national mythologizing that locates their sacrifice as the birth of the modem, reunited, republic. The multiple layers of authorship, after all, each point to the dream's constructed nature and could be read as an attempt to make visible the tropes, techniques, and structures that advanced and perpetuated stories that exalted abolitionist pain by substituting it for slave pain.

The dream sequences do draw attention to their constructed and performative nature, but these non-realistic moments nevertheless serve as a means for Shawnessy to understand his waking life. For all its thematic and voluminous grandeur, *Raintree County* remains an intensely "small" novel about one man's interiority, which is mapped onto a nation in order to use his personal experiences as a way to narrate and viscerally connect American audiences with the nation's history. Shawnessy describes himself as "life's American" and he compares his personal history of growth and heroism with the abstract idea of the republic itself ("he and the republic reborn together").[140] His self-conscious understanding of himself as a microcosm of the nation leads him to frame himself in messianic language as a savior whose life is offered as a sacrifice and whose eyewitness testimony frames the history of 19th century reform. The tensions, schisms, and the ultimate reunion of Civil War-era America only become understandable through the narrator's life and sacrifice. In a passage that is worth quoting at length, Lockridge, as narrator, describes Shawnessy's role in the production, meaning, and perpetuation of 19th century narrative of national sacrifice and redemption:

> Despite his lonely life during this time, John Shawnessy had come to complete faith in himself, and there welled up in him stronger than ever the assurance that he was the bearer of a sacred fire. He had been meant from the beginning by a messianic birth to be the Hero of the County. Only he could fulfill prophecy and lead his generation to a nobler way of life, a loftier religion than they had known before.
>
> He had always meant to do this great thing while he was young. Keats was dead. At thirty-three, Jesus was crucified. The time had come for John Shawnessy to make a godlike exertion, to produce a masterwork, a book that would usher in the Golden Age of the American Republic.[141]

My point is that even though Lockridge organizes Shawnessy's violent fantasies around a desire to experience slave pain and sometimes, as in the case of the novel's dream sequences, writes in such a reflexive way as to preclude the charge of simplistic voyeurism, the novel itself is heavily invested in mythologizing abolitionist sacrifice, empathy, heroism. Here he is explicitly framed as a messianic figure, comparable to Jesus, and his own life of suffering and toil becomes the only canvas great enough to "usher in the Golden Age of the American Republic."[142]

John Shawnessy's capacity for slave empathy stands in stark contrast to the anxieties about race, racial purity, and racial roles that frame every other major character's dramatic conflict. We are told, for instance, that Susanna Drake, the novel's southern temptress and Shawnessy's first wife, ultimately goes mad because she believes local stories of her father's infidelity with a slave woman and she fears that she is possibly a "negress."[143] Shawnessy's friend Senator Garwood Jones speaks loftily about racial equality after the war, but the novel frames him as an insincere opportunist whose efforts are politically motivated and unstable. John Brown, Harriet Beecher Stowe, and even Abraham Lincoln make appearances throughout different parts of the novel as symbols of a general historical abolitionist tradition but they remain aloof and distant figures.

*Raintree County* draws on sensual religious language and metaphors of humankind's fall and Christ's redemption in order to situate Shawnessy as a messianic figure whose personal sacrifice regenerates the nation. The abolitionist is at the center of humankind's fall and redemption. According to Larry Lockridge, this mythic relationship begins with the faithful temptation and consummation of Shawnessy's relationship with Susanna: "in making love to Susanna under the raintree and paying for it mightily, he [Shawnessy] lives out the Genesis myth."[144] Shawnessy's redemption, then, is related to his selfless desire to witness and assume the pain and the experiences of those he encounters. His marriage to Susanna Drake brought him to the plantation culture of the south and gave rise to the "Black Johnny' character, an African slave version of the hero that could subconsciously re-create and experience black pain. His wounds on the battlefield at Gettysburg as a Union soldier provided him the experience of a more literal physical pain. But just as the novel is interested in doubling and blurring boundaries it is the line between the imagined and the real that remains tenuous. Black pain and white pain are not differentiated but they are instead presented as one in the same. Shawnessy points to the intense connection between his pain and slave pain at the end of the novel when he recalls his life and wonders aloud to himself: "did you think: that a single black man could feel the lash and you not bear the scar?"[145]

Shawnessy's suffering consistently obscures and substitutes for the pain of other groups and in doing so the history of the American experience with slavery and its eradication is experienced, embodied, and told through the history of abolitionist subjectivity. Near the end of the story Shawnessy makes a revealing observation in a passage that typifies the novel's understanding of the connection between the outward events he witnesses and his own experiences and identity: "To look outward at the farthest star is to look inward into oneself. We are merely exploring our immense cupboard."[146] The perils of Shawnessy's expansive abolitionist visions are inherited from the narratives of Garrisonian abolitionists. Slave suffering remains opaque until it is brought into focus through abolitionist embodiment in an act of substitution that displaces more than it clarifies. The last image of the book, of Shawnessy visiting his own tombstone, a marker prematurely installed by friends and family who erroneously believed that he was killed in battle, only reinforces this sense of redemptive suffering. Standing at his own grave he expresses what this novel is ultimately about: personal rebirth and national regeneration. Shawnessy's sacrifice, this image implies, is metaphorically associated with his physical death (or act of martyrdom) and by giving up his innocence and desires he atones for America's past sins and becomes a symbol of the new post-bellum nation. The story of the death of the nation (i.e., sectional schism) is tied to his own personal story of sacrifice, death, and salvation (or national reunion). The "old" America is laid to rest and the abolitionist's heroic personal narrative becomes the epic origin of a new and more egalitarian modem American republic.

# Epilogue: William Lloyd Garrison in the Mid–20th Century and Beyond

This book ends with the 1948 publication of Ross Lockridge's *Raintree County*, but public commemorations of William Lloyd Garrison and stories of abolitionist suffering continued to be retold for new audiences throughout the latter half of the 20th century. The period of time from 1950–1980, in particular, remains one of the most understudied eras of Civil War memory. David W. Blight's recent *American Oracle: The Civil War in the Civil Rights Era* (2011) is the first serious effort to begin to address this pronounced deficiency.[1] Blight points out that this scholarly omission is particularly ironic given that "the Civil War and civil rights have been forever intertwined in American history and mythology."[2] William Lloyd Garrison remained a vital part of Massachusetts's regional narrative and America's national narrative of the Civil War and during these years contemporary politicians and activists alike looked to him as a symbol of uncompromising sacrifices for moral justice.

President John F. Kennedy, a Massachusetts native, prominently invoked Garrison on several occasions throughout 1961 during the first year of his presidency as a way to convey America's staunch resolve in the wake of Soviet military challenges. For instance, on June 5, 1961, the *New York Times* wrote that Kennedy stopped at the William Lloyd Garrison statue that sits on Boston's Commonwealth Avenue to briefly collect his thoughts while in route to give a speech about how America would confront new Soviet challenges in Germany.[3] Kennedy was reportedly moved by Garrison's words (which are engraved on the monument) and in the speech he delivered that night he spoke of Garrison's sacrifices and suffering in the wake of great opposition as a model for all Americans. He compared the contemporary plight of America to the moral dilemma faced by 19th century Massachusetts abolitionists and concluded his speech by reciting the words that Garrison penned over 100 years before: "I will not retreat."[4] As Kennedy's innovation suggests, William Lloyd Garrison continued to appear in civil rights-era and Cold War discourses and such instances deserve the attention of Civil War memory scholars. Less clear, but of equal interest, is how Garrison will be remembered during the current Civil War Sesquicentennial.

Throughout the time I researched and wrote this book American state commissions began early preparations for commemorating the 150th anniversary of the Civil War. In fact, Virginia, North Carolina, and South Carolina appointed state-funded commissions and began planning for a wide variety of sesquicentennial festivities close to 7 years ago.[5] Barack Obama's 2008 election only reinforced the historical importance of the current sesquicentennial celebration. For the first time, an African American president would be in charge of overseeing, participating in, and guiding how the country should remember and think about the war and its lasting legacies. If Obama's April 12, 2011, "Presidential Proclamation of the Civil War Sesquicentennial" is any indication of what is to follow over the next four years then it suggests that this celebration, more than any other in history, will focus, not on soldiers, but on the valor of abolitionists. Obama's first Civil War speech heralded the sacrifices of white and black abolitionists who worked to "extend equal rights to all our citizens and carry out the letter of the law after the war."[6] Unlike past presidential addresses on the Civil War, Obama's speech placed a singular emphasis on celebrating those who worked to abolish slavery and he argued that their sacrifices resulted in the passage of the 13th, 14th, and 15th amendments.[7] Clearly the abolitionist-centered emancipationist narrative of the war was primed to take center-stage.

Massachusetts, however, like many of its bordering northern neighbors, began planning comparatively "late" in the process. No extensive state commissions were organized and only now-roughly one year into the national sesquicentennial celebration-is the state working to quickly schedule events that will take place throughout 2012. I am curious to see how Massachusetts as a whole, and Boston in particular, will narrate its Civil War history in relation to past state celebrations that privileged Garrison as the embodiment of the region's antislavery activism and history. I am also interested in the extent to which William

Lloyd Garrison and the trope of the "suffering abolitionist" will be invoked as a key part of this regional story.

Massachusetts is reportedly organizing a dramatic re-enactment of Garrison's burning of the United States Constitution that will take place later this year, but at this point it remains unclear how Garrison will be read within our current "post-civil rights era."[8] Regardless, William Lloyd Garrison as a historical figure, symbolic model, and synonym for American abolitionism has played and will continue to play a singularly important role in encouraging Americans to honor white abolitionist activism and to herald their witnessing and suffering with the moral and political renewal of America. Massachusetts's failure to engage in the same degree of commemorative pageantry as its southern neighbors only further reinforces the state's comfort with this narrative of its history. The region's historical emphasis on Garrisonian abolitionism as a way to express its participation-explicitly and implicitly— in the tumultuous 19th century has been told and re-told in traditional biographies, fictional representations, and educational textbooks to such an extent that today it remains largely invisible and unquestioned by audiences and scholars alike. Past generations of white and black civil rights activists used Garrison as a way to stress emancipation as the central struggle and legacy of the Civil War. In the late 19th and early 20th century, invoking Garrison's emotionally powerful narrative and fiery rhetoric offered an avenue to combat other popular stories in both the north and the south that erased slavery and emancipation from the nation's history by stressing common Union-Confederate military valor.

Today, as we begin the process of once again remembering the Civil War I want to suggest that we move beyond past abolitionist-centered emancipation narratives. We should, instead, strive to approach traditional abolitionist histories with a greater degree of critical attentiveness to their long history in American culture and to acknowledge their limitations and tendency to reinforce, rather than challenge, past racial prejudice. For most scholars and popular audiences, Garrison is the beginning of American abolitionist efforts and it is my belief that his continued visibility in Civil War narratives deserves the same degree of scrutiny that scholars apply to the other stories that we continuously tell and re-tell as a way to remember and commemorate our nation's participation in this conflict.

# Chapter Notes

## Introduction

1. William Lloyd Garrison, "A Letter to Joseph T. Buckingham," *Courier*, 24 May 1830, Boston, Massachusetts.
2. William Lloyd Garrison, "A Letter to Harriet Farnham Horton," 13 May 1830, William Garrison Papers, Anti-Slavery Manuscript Collection, Boston Public Library, Boston, Massachusetts.
3. William Lloyd Garrison, "To the Public," *Genius of Universal Emancipation*, 29 November 1829. Garrison published other critiques of Todd that same month. See *Genius of Universal Emancipation*, 13 November 1829, edition.
4. William Lloyd Garrison, *A Brief Sketch of the Trial of William Lloyd Garrison, for an Alleged Libel of Francis Todd of Massachusetts* (Boston: Garrison and Knapp, 1834), The Library of Congress, Washington, D.C. This number only accounts for those currently collected in available archives. Several of Garrison's letters make reference to other stories that he sent to various papers, but those have been lost to history. Suffice to say that his time in jail marked a time of enormous productivity and public attention.
5. *Ibid*. "To the Victim of Tyranny": Pris'ner! Within these narrow walls close pent, —/ Guiltless of horrid crime or trivial wrong, —/Bear nobly up against thy punishment,/ And in thy innocence be tall and strong!/ Perchance thy fault was love to all mankind;/ Thou did'st oppose some vile, oppressive law;/ Or strive all human fetters to unbind;/ Or would'st not bear the implements of war:—/ What then? Dost thou so soon repent the deed?/ A martyr's crown is richer than a king's!/ Think it and honor with thy Lord to bleed, And glory midst th' intensest sufferings!/ Though beat—imprisoned—put to open shame—/ Time shall embalm and magnify thy name.
6. Indeed, Garrison's jail sentence partly resulted from his inability to pay the $100 fine that Judge Brice levied at the conclusion of his trial. When faced with the option of paying a fine or serving a prison sentence, he was left with no real options.
7. Garrison wrote his "Brief Sketch" while in prison and papers printed portions of it, but the final book edition was not widely disseminated until 1834.
8. By "culture," I am referring to Raymond Williams' conception of culture as a way to mark and understand the intellectual, spiritual, and aesthetic development of ideas within a specific historical moment. See, Raymond Williams, *Keywords: A Vocabulary of Culture and Society* (London: Fontana Press, 1983).
9. United States Postmaster General Amos Kendall famously viewed Garrison as such a threat to public order that he allowed copies of *The Liberator* to be pulled form official Postal Service mailbags and destroyed. Kendall rationalized his support for this undeniably illegal provision by expressing his overwhelming concern for public welfare: "We Owe an Obligation to the Laws, but a Higher One to the Communities in Which We Live." Quoted from: Clement Eaton, *Freedom of Thought in the Old South* (Durham: Duke University Press, 1940), 126–129. Garrison's paper also briefly wrote about this incident in the August 15, 1835 edition of *The Liberator*.
10. The comparison with Joseph Smith is made in an 1850 article published in the *Democratic Review*. See "The Conspiracy of Fanaticism," *Democratic Review*, May 1850 edition, 391. Channing described Garrison and his supporters as "Pious Fools with Violent Impulses." See Jack Mendehson, *Channing: The Reluctant Radical* (Westport: Greenwood Press, 1971).
11. This label was very much a part of the vernacular shorthand of the 1830s New England anti-slavery debates. Reverend James

T. Woodbury's critique of the false doctrines of Garrison's "Church" is but one of many examples of this trend. See, Rev. James T. Woodbury, "A Clerical Appeal," *New England Spectator*, 17 August 1837, Newspaper and Periodical Division, Library of Congress, Washington, D.C.

12. See, William Lloyd Garrison, "A Letter to Harriott Plummer," 4 March 1833, William Garrison Papers, Anti-slavery Manuscript Collection, Boston Public Library, Boston, Massachusetts. In this letter Garrison made just such a threat, which is a common trait of his appeals in the 1830s. In March of 1833 a Massachusetts law forbidding interracial marriage drew Garrison's ire. He wrote about this in a private correspondence during this year and publicly addressed it in the March 16, 1833 edition of *The Liberator*.

13. Benjamin Lundy's March 30, 1833 letter to Elizabeth M. Chandler is quoted from a reprint in: Merton L. Dillon, *Benjamin Lundy and the Struggle for Negro Freedom* (Urbana: University of Illinois Press, 1966), 189.

14. See *Harper's* 31 (1865), 265–266; *Harper's* 35 (1867), 256–257. From Eugene Exman, *The House of Harper: One Hundred and Fifty Years of Publishing* (New York: Harper and Row, 1967).

15. Ibid. *Harper's* 35 (1867), 256–257. From Eugene Exman, *The House of Harper:One Hundred and Fifty Years of Publishing* (New York: Harper and Row, 1967).

16. See Samuel May, *Some Recollections of Our Antislavery Conflict* (New York: Arno Press and the New York Times, 1968); Parker Pillsbury, *Acts of the Anti-Slavery Apostles* (Concord: Clague, Wegman, Schlicht & Co, 1883).

17. See Joseph Seaman Cotter, Sr., "William Lloyd Garrison" (1895), *The Vintage Book of African American Poetry: 200 Years of Vision, Struggle, Power, Beauty, and Triumph from 50 Outstanding Poets*, Michael S. Harper and Anthony Walton, eds. (New York: Vintage, 2000), 61–62.

18. Garrison's sons Frank and Wendell served as advisors on the design of Olin L. Warner's 1886 statue, which was installed on Boston's Commonwealth Avenue.

19. The Reverend William H. Yeocum wrote a stirring speech that he delivered as part of the annual festivities commemorating the second anniversary of Garrison's death. Reprinted in: Reverend William H. Yeocum, "The Mind That Was in Christ," *Christian Recorder*, 20 October 1881, p.1, Philadelphia, PA, Newspapers and Periodicals Division, The Library of Congress, Washington, D.C. By 1905 African American groups are also regularly celebrating Garrison's birth. See, "William Lloyd Garrison," *Afro-American*, 9 December 1905, p.4, Newspapers and Periodicals Division, The Library of Congress, Washington, D.C.

20. See Katherine Holland Brown, *The Father* (New York: Day, 1928).

21. See Emma Miller Bolenius, ed. *The Boys and Girls Fifth History Reader* (Boston: Houghton Mifflin, 1922), Monroe C. Gutman Library, Historical Textbooks Collection, Harvard University, Cambridge, MA.

22. There is a large body of scholarship that focuses on Civil War memory. Some seminal works include: David W. Blight, *Race and Reunion: The Civil War in American Memory* (Cambridge: Harvard University Press, 2001); W. Fitzhugh Brundage, *Where These Memories Grow: History, Memory and Southern Identity* (Chapel Hill: University of North Carolina Press, 2000); Nina Silber, *The Romance of Reunion: Northerners and the South, 1865–1900* (Chapel Hill: University of North Carolina Press, 1993). See also, Kirk Savage, *Standing Soldiers, Kneeling Slaves: Race, War, and Monument in Nineteenth Century America* (Princeton: Princeton University Press, 1997), and Paul A. Shackel, *Memory in Black and White: Race Commemoration and the Post-Bellum Landscape* (Walnut Creek, CA: AltaMira Press, 2003).

23. Ibid., 24.

24. W. Fitzhugh Brundage, *Where These Memories Grow: History, Memory and Southern Identity* (Chapel Hill: University of North Carolina Press, 2000).

25. Elizbeth B. Clark, "The Sacred Rights of the Weak: Pain, Sympathy, and the Culture of Individual Rights in Antebellum America," *The Journal of American History*, Vol. 2, No. 2 (Sept. 1995), 463–493.

26. Ibid., 470. She writes: "By the Start of the Civil War, Then the Account of Slave Suffering Designed to Evoke a Sympathetic Response Had Established Itself as an Important Social and Cultural Trope in the North."

27. Ibid., 474–476.

28. Karen Sanchez-Eppler, *Touching Liberty: Abolition, Feminism, and the Politics of the Body* (Berkeley: University of California Press, 1993).

29. Ibid., 13.

30. Elizabeth Barnes, *States of Sympathy: Seduction and Democracy in the American Novel* (New York: Columbia Press, 1997).

31. Ibid., 5.

32. Julia A. Stern, *The Plight of Feeling: Sympathy and Dissent in the Early American Novel* (Chicago: University of Chicago Press, 1997).

33. *Ibid.*, 26.

34. John Stauffer, *The Black Hearts of Men: Radical Abolitionists and the Transformation of Race* (Cambridge: Harvard University Press, 2002), 1.

35. This is particularly true of the "Lost Cause" narrative of the war that emerges in the post-bellum era, which stressed northern aggression, southern sacrifice, the south's heroic defense of founding constitutional principles, its idyllic antebellum plantation life, and its adherence to a stringent chivalrous moral code. In contrast, Frederick Douglass, in speeches like "Oration at the Dedication of the Freedmen's Monument to Abraham Lincoln," discussed Lincoln's "martyrdom" as a symbol of a new American "rebirth." In both scenarios, suffering frames why the war was fought, who fought it and who and what sacrifices should be remembered and honored. See, Jefferson Davis, *Rise and Fall of Confederate Government* (New York: D. Appleton and Company, 1881), and Jubal A. Early, *Narrative of the War Between the States* (New York: Da Capo, 1991). See also, Frederick Douglass, "Oration at the Dedication to the Freedmen's Monument to Abraham Lincoln," *Frederick Douglass: Selected Speeches and Writings*, Stephen S. Foner, ed. (New York: Lawrence Hill Books, 2000), 615–625.

36. Drew Gilpin Faust, *This Republic of Suffering: Death and the American Civil War* (New York: Vintage, 2008).

37. *Ibid.*, 16–18.

38. In the fall of 1818 Garrison worked as an apprentice to the editor of the Newburyport Herald. The personal letters and public writings from this year are amongst the earliest of his surviving documents. By 1822 he began to weigh in on the slavery issue, but does so by mimicking the legal arguments of British abolitionists. He scarcely mentions any of the theological justifications that so typify his appeals from 1830 to the end of his life. See William Lloyd Garrison, "Letter to the Editor of the Newburyport Herald," *Newburyport Herald*, 21 May 1822, 43. A reproduction of this letter is part of the Garrison papers at the Boston Public Library.

39. Reprinted as William Lloyd Garrison, "A Letter to Garrison's Free Color Supporters in Boston," 27 August 1831, *The Liberator*, Boston, Massachusetts.

40. For one of many examples, see his letter to Rev. George Shepard of Harford, Connecticut on September 13, 1831. William Lloyd Garrison, "A Letter to Rev George Shepard," 13 September 1831, William Lloyd Garrison Papers, Boston Public Library, Boston, Massachusetts.

41. William Lloyd Garrison, "A Letter to George Benson," 29 August 1832, William Lloyd Garrison Papers, Anti-Slavery Manuscript Collection, Boston Public Library, Boston, Massachusetts.

42. William Lloyd Garrison, "A Letter to George Benson," 12 September 1835, William Lloyd Garrison Papers, Anti-Slavery Manuscript Collection, Boston Public Library, Boston, Massachusetts.

43. William Lloyd Garrison, "A Letter to Amos Phelps," 11 October 1834, William Lloyd Garrison Papers, Anti-Slavery Manuscript Collection, Boston Public Library, Boston, Massachusetts.

44. *Ibid.*

45. *Ibid.*

46. David W. Blight, "If You Don't Tell It Like It Was, It Can Never Be as It Ought to Be," *Slavery and Public History: The Tough Stuff of American Memory*, James Oliver Horton and Lois E. Horton, eds. (New York: New Press, 2006), 22.

47. In March 5, 1832 letter to Sarah Douglass, who was a prominent Black Quaker, Garrison remarks that the rewards for faithfulness are not always "Manifested in Our Physical Welfare." But, courageously maintaining faith offers eternal spiritual defenses that are greater than the any person's "Hand of Violence." William Lloyd Garrison, "A Letter to Sarah Douglass," 5 March 1832, William Lloyd Garrison Papers, Anti-Slavery Manuscript Collection, Boston Public Library, Boston, Massachusetts.

48. Bart D. Ehrman, *God's Problem: How the Bible Fails to Answer Our Most Important Questions—Why We Suffer* (New York: Harper One, 2008), 130–131. He goes on to cite the story of Joseph in Genesis and the story of Lazarus in John as two parables that exemplify this approach to understanding the presence of a Biblical tradition that views suffering as having redemptive qualities.

49. *Ibid.*, 138–139 See also, Romans 3:24–25: "Being justified freely by His grace through the redemption that is Christ Jesus; whom God hath set forth to be a propitiation through faith in His blood, to declare His righteousness for the remission of sins that are past, through the forbearance of God" (King James Version). Here and elsewhere I reference the original King James version of the Bible, which is the only translation that William Lloyd Garrison had access to during his lifetime.

50. *Ibid.*

51. It's important to point out that the term martyr comes form the Greek word, "martus," meaning "to witness." The term is

frequently used in the New Testament and sometimes it is used to describe Christ himself. However as G.W. Bowersock points out, before the age of persecution "No where can it be shown to be used in any sense other than witness." See G.W. Bowersock, *Martyrdom and Rome* (Cambridge: Cambridge University Press, 1995), 14.

52. Quoted from W.H.C. Frend, *Martyrdom and Persecution in the Early Church: A Study of Conflict from the Maccabees to Donatus* (Oxford: Basil Blackwell, 1965), 14–15.

53. "The Refuge of Oppression" is a regular column that appears in *The Liberator* beginning in September 1834, These columns consistently revel in the hostile attitudes that Garrisonian abolitionist encountered from both northern and southern audiences during this period.

54. Several Early American historians discuss the wide prominence of Foxe's *Book of Martyrs* in early American culture. See, Ernest Lee Tuveson, *Redeemer Nation* (Chicago: University of Chicago Press, 1968); Sacvan Bercovitch, *the Puritan Origins of the American Self* (New Haven; Yale University, 1975), 136–163.

55. William Lloyd Garrison, "A Letter to Helen Benson," 5 April 1834, Garrison-Benson letters, William Lloyd Garrison Papers, Anti-Slavery Manuscript Collection, Boston Public Library, Boston, Massachusetts.

56. John Foxe, Foxe's *Book of Martyrs* (Grand Rapids: Zondervan, 1929), 1–3.

57. William Lloyd Garrison, "A Letter to Henry Benson," 15 September 1834, Garrison-Benson letters, William Lloyd Garrison Papers, Anti-Slavery Manuscript Collection, Boston Public Library, Boston, Massachusetts.

58. William Lloyd Garrison, "A Letter to Helen Benson," 5 April 1834, Garrison-Benson letters, William Lloyd Garrison Papers, Anti-Slavery Manuscript Collection, Boston Public Library, Boston, Massachusetts.

59. William Lloyd Garrison, "A Letter to George Benson," 31 May 1834, William Garrison Papers, Anti-Slavery Manuscript Collection, Boston Public Library, Boston, Massachusetts.

60. Oliver Johnson, *William Lloyd Garrison and His Times* (Boston: B. B. Russell & Company, 1879).

61. *Ibid.* pp.

62. *Ibid.*

63. Godwin Smith, *The Moral Crusader: William Lloyd Garrison* (New York: Funk & Wagnalls, 1892).

64. *Ibid.* pp.

65. John Jay Chapman, *William Lloyd Garrison* (New York: Moffat, Yard, 1913).

66. *Ibid.*, 2.

67. *Ibid.*, 7.

68. Henrietta Cordelia Ray, "William Lloyd Garrison," *Poems* (New York: Grafton Press, 1910), 69.

69. "Book Review," *Atlantic Monthly*, January 1886, 57: 121, 121.

70. Gilbert Barnes, *The Anti-Slavery Impulse: 1830–1844* (Goucester: Peter Smith, American Historical Association, 1933).

71. *Ibid.*, 88–89.

72. *Ibid.*, 90.

73. Dwight L. Dumond, *Antislavery: The Crusade for Freedom in America* (Ann Arbor: University of Michigan Press, 1961).

74. *Ibid.*, 170.

75. *Ibid.*, 174.

76. *Ibid.*

77. This is also observable in the surge of post-WWII invocations and representations of Abraham Lincoln as both an emancipator and as a catalyst for an American "Rebirth." As America assumed a postwar position as a global power, Lincoln offered a model for responsible stewardship and duty. See Barry Schwartz, *Abraham Lincoln and the Forge of National Identity* (Chicago: University of Chicago Press, 2000).

78. *The Glenn Beck Show*, CNN, New York, 3 November 2006.

79. *Ibid.*

80. Robert Bellah, "Civil Religion in America, "the *Robert Bellah Reader*, Robert N. Bellah and Steven M. Tipton, Eds. (Durham: Duke University Press, 2006), 235.

81. Russel B. Nye, *William Lloyd Garrison and the Humanitarian Reformers* (Boston: Little, Brown and Company, 1955).

82. *Ibid.* See "Preface," 3–5.

83. *Ibid.*, 199–200.

84. C. Vann Woodward, "The Antislavery Myth," *The American Scholar (*Spring 1962), 31: 320.

85. Walter M. Merrill, *Against Tide and Wind: A Biography of William Lloyd Garrison* (Cambridge: Harvard University Press, 1963).

86. John L. Thomas, *The Liberator: William Lloyd Garrison: A Biography* (Boston: Little, Brown), 1963).

87. George M. Frederickson, *William Lloyd Garrison* (Englewood Cliffs, NJ: Prentice-Hall, 1968).

88. Lawrence J. Friedman, *Gregarious Saints: Self and Community in American Abolitionism, 1830–1870* (New York: Cambridge University Press, 1982).

89. James Brewster Stewart, *William Lloyd Garrison and the Challenge of Emancipation* (Arlington Heights: Ill: Harlan Davidson, 1992).

90. Henry Mayer, *All on Fire: William Lloyd Garrison and the Abolition of Slavery* (New York: St. Marten's Press, 1998).
91. *Ibid.* p. xiii.
92. Louis Filler, *The Crusade Against Slavery, 1830–1860* (New York: Harper and Row, 1960), and Aileen S. Kraditor, *Means and Ends in American Abolitionism: Garrison and His Critics on Strategy and Tactics* (New York: Random House, 1967).
93. Richard S. Newman, *The Transformation of American Abolitionism: Fighting Slavery in the Early Republic* (Chapel Hill: University of North Carolina at Chapel Hill, 2002).
94. *Ibid.*, 1.
95. I see W.E.B. DuBois' *Black Reconstruction in America* (1935), as the beginning of this counter-narrative. DuBois uses this book as a space to address the "moral problem of abolition" and to offer a corrective to histories that are "silent so far as the negro is concerned." See, W.E.B. DuBois, *Black Reconstruction in America* (New York: Russell, 1935), 13–21, 713–719; John Hope Franklin's book *The Emancipation Proclamation* similarly focuses on the work of black abolitionist like Frederick Douglass and relegates Garrison to a smaller role in grander national drama of the abolition of slavery. See John Hope Franklin, *the Emancipation Proclamation* (New York: Double Day, 1963); Paul Goodman's *Of One Blood: Abolitionism and the Origins of Racial Equality* stresses black agency by linking immediate abolition movements with the eradication of slavery and argues that black abolitionists influenced Garrison's own transformation from supporting colonization to immediate abolition. Garrison remains a prominent part of Goodman's story, but Goodman carefully uses Garrison as an expression of black abolitionist ideas. See Paul Goodman, *Of One Blood: Abolitionism and the Origins of Racial Equality* (Berkeley: University of California Press, 1998); Recent works by David Brion Davis and John Stauffer also excavate the influences of black abolitionist on the perceived "leaders" of American abolitionism. See David Brion Davis, *Challenging the Boundaries of Slavery* (Cambridge: Harvard University Press, 2003), and Timothy Patrick McCarthy and John Stauffer, eds, *Prophets of Protest: Reconsidering the History of American Abolitionism* (New York: New Press, 2006).
96. Benjamin Quarles, *Black Abolitionists* (New York: Oxford University Press, 1969), vii.
97. *Ibid.* p. viii.
98. *Ibid.*
99. *Ibid.*, 42.
100. Stephen Greenblatt, "The Circulation of Social Energy," *Shakespearean Negotiations: The Circulation of Social Energy in Renaissance England* (Berkeley: University of California Press, 1988), 1–21.
101. *Ibid.*, 6–8.
102. See Robert Azbug, *Cosmos Crumbling: American Reform and the Religious Imagination* (New York: Oxford University Press, 1994), 129–162; see also Wendell Phillips Garrison and Francis Jackson Garrison, *William Lloyd Garrison, 1805–1879: The Story of His Life Told by His Children* (New York: The Century Company, 1885).
103. *Ibid.* Azbug cites this text over 35 times in one short chapter.
104. William Lloyd Garrison, "A Letter to Harriet Farnham Horton," 12 May 1830, William Lloyd Garrison Papers, Boston Public Library, Boston, Massachusetts.
105. W.E.B DuBois, "Opinion," *Crisis*, August 1922, Vol. XXIV, No. 4, 151–155.
106. W.E.B. DuBois, "Triumph," *Crisis*, September 1911, Vol. II, No. 5, 195–197 (for the problems with black voting); "As the Crow Flies," *Crisis*, June 1927, Vol. XXXIV, No. 4 (for a discussion of Sacco and Vanzetti); and "The Winds of Time," *Chicago Defender*, 27 January 1945 (for a discussion of the Boston school system).
107. W.E.B DuBois, "Opinion," *Crisis*, August 1922, Vol. XXIV, No. 4, 151–155.
108. David Blight extensively discusses the way narratives of the Civil War the focused on the shared Union and Confederate military valor overshadowed the emancipationist history and legacy of the conflict. See David W. Blight, *Race and Reunion: The Civil War in American Memory* (Cambridge: Harvard University Press, 2001).
109. Walter Johnson, *Soul by Soul: Life Inside the Antebellum Slave Market* (Cambridge: Harvard University Press, 1999), 217.
110. Sadiya Hartman, *Scenes of Subjection: Terror and Self Making in Nineteenth Century America* (New York: Oxford University Press, 1999), 19.
111. *Ibid.*
112. In fact, Garrison's personal life is altogether ignored in Russel B. Nye's *William Lloyd Garrison and the Humanitarian Reformers* (Boston: Little, Brown, and Company, 1955), and in George M. Frederickson's *William Lloyd Garrison* (Englewood Cliffs, NJ: Prentice-Hall, 1968). The work of Walter M. Merril made important strides towards understanding Garrison's complex relationship to his homelife but his book does so through a Freudian framework that is so pronounced that it overly relies on heavy-handed

psychoanalytic images of the "controlling mother" and the "rebellious son." See Walter M. Merril, *Against Tide and Wind: A Biography of William Lloyd Garrison* (Cambridge: Harvard University Press, 1963).

113. See Allen Tate, *Stonewall Jackson: The Good Soldier* (New York: Minton, Blach, and Co., 1928), F. Scott Fitzgerald, *The Complete Stories of F. Scott Fitzgerald* (New York: Scribner, 1989); Robert Penn Warren, *John Brown: The Making of a Martyr* (New York: Payson and Clark, 1929); and Margaret Mitchell, *Gone with the Wind* (New York: Warner Books, 1999).

## Chapter 1

1. As a result, the most influential and effective British abolitionists were politicians, lawyers, and legislators. Wilberforce and Clarkson both served in Parliament; Zachary Macaulay was a well-respected scholar and historian; Thomas Buxton ushered Wilberforce's emancipation bill through Parliament; Stephen Lushington was a distinguished judge and lawyer; as were George Stephen and Daniel O'Connell.

2. This sentiment is most forcefully expressed in his letters to his financier Arthur Tappan during his 1833 trip to England. See, William Garrison, "Correspondence to Arthur Tappan and the Association of Gentlemen," July 28, 1833, Garrison Family Papers, Sophia Smith Collection, Smith College, Northampton, Mass.

3. The New England Anti-Slavery Society sent Garrison to England with a directive to solicit organizational advice and financial support for their American work. The exact details of how Garrison accomplished this feat are not known, but minutes and notes from the New England Anti-Slavery Society's 1832 quarterly meeting in Boston provide some clue. At this meeting he argued that the national attention that *The Liberator* brought to the anti-slavery cause made him an ideal, but also reluctant, spokesman and leader for abolition the cause. He asked to go to England, despite the fact that, "my friends are full of apprehension and disquietude ... [but] I tremble at nothing but my own delinquencies, as one who is bound to be perfect, even as my heavenly father is perfect." See "New England Anti-Slavery Society Fall Quarterly Meeting Notes," Boston 1832, New England Anti-Slavery Society Manuscripts, Anti-Slavery Manuscripts Collection, Boston Public Library, Boston, Mass. It is an interesting coincidence that Wilberforce died during Garrison's four-week stay. He actually met Wilberforce at his home two to three days before the elder statesman's death. Garrison attended Wilberforce's funeral as the guest of George Thompson. His letters to Arthur Tappan provide the only account of experiences at Wilberforce's funeral. See, William Garrison, "Correspondence to Arthur Tappan and the Association of Gentlemen," July 28, 1833, Garrison Family Papers, Sophia Smith Collection, Smith College, Northampton, Mass.

4. In a letter to Harriot Plummer dated November 4, 1833 Garrison describes how his trip to England impressed upon him the reality of the horrors of the slave trade, leading him to describe the United States as "an African Golgotha." Garrison pleads with Plummer to do what she can in her own community to "excite the interest and curiosity" of those around her to work for the" deliverance of those in bonds." In a similar letter written to John B. Vashon on November 1, 1833 Garrison discusses the importance of religious language and moral influence in the anti-slavery movement, telling Vashon that "it is true that some of us will lose our lives; but it is also true that the martyr's blood's the seed of freedom's tree." See William Garrison, "A Letter to Harriot Plummer," 4 November 1833, Ms. Folder 8: "Mission to England," Anti-Slavery Manuscript Collection, Rare Books Division and Special Collections, Boston Public Library, Boston, Massachusetts. See also William Garrison, "A Letter to John Vashon," 1 November 1833, Ms. Folder 8: "Mission to England," Anti-Slavery Manuscript Collection, Rare Books Division and Special Collections, Boston Public Library, Boston, Massachusetts.

5. See John R. McKivigan and Stanly Harrold, *Anti-Slavery Violence: Sectional, Racial, and Cultural Conflict in Antebellum America* (Knoxville: University of Tennessee Press, 1999), 15.

6. *Ibid.*

7. *Ibid.* Lawrence Friedman's *Gregarious Saints* argues that Garrison's unbending pacifism is related to his desire to protect the womanhood of the female members of his circle, who fully participated in his anti-slavery activities. See Lawrence Friedman, *Gregarious Saints: Self and Community in American Abolitionism*, 1830–1860 (New York: Cambridge, 1982), 158, 201, 220–22 More recent scholarship argues that Garrison's immediatist positions, though they invoked violence and controversy in the 1830s, were adopted out of a desire to prevent a large scale race war in the south. See Robert Abzug, "Garrisonian Abolitionists' Fears,"

*Cosmos Crumbling: American Reform and the Religious Imagination* (New York: Oxford University Press, 1994), 15–28.

8. See James Brewster Stewart, *William Lloyd Garrison and the Challenge of Emancipation* (Arlington Heights, Ill: Harlan Davidson, 1992); Russel B. Nye, *William Lloyd Garrison and the Humanitarian Reformers* (Boston: Little, Brown, and Company, 1955); and Walter M. Merrill, *Against the Tide and Wind: A Biography of William Lloyd Garrison* (Cambridge: Harvard University Press, 1963).

9. See, for instance, William Garrison's October 19, 1831 letter to Henry Benson in which he laments the ineffectiveness of "anonymous letters and petitions" as a way to forcefully and fully address the "abominable and bloody sentiments" of slavery. He instead advocates a more direct route that bypasses congress and seeks to win over the hearts of the American people. At this particular moment he maintains an optimistic assessment of *The Liberator's* progress: "The disturbances at the South still continue. *The Liberator* is causing the most extraordinary movements in the slave States among the whites, as you are doubtless aware." William Garrison, "A Letter to Henry Benson," 19 October 1831, ms. A. 9.1 v. 5, 12, Anti-Slavery Manuscript Collection, Rare Books Division and Special Collections, Boston Public Library, Boston, Massachusetts.

10. The writings of 18th century Pennsylvania Friends often cite Quaker founder George Fox's 1676 ethical complaint against the practice of slavery: "Do not slight... Ethyopains, the Blacks now, neither any man or woman upon the face of the Earth in that Christ dyed for all." Quoted from Gary Kornblith, *Slavery and Sectional Strife in the Early Republic, 1776–1821* (New York: Rowan and Littlefield, 2010), 9; For a full account of the tensions and theological debates between 18th century American Quakers on the issue of slavery see, Jean R. Soderlund, *Quakers and Slavery: A Divided Spirit* (Princeton: Princeton University Press, 1985).

11. In *Race and Revolution*, Gary Nash points out that such measures failed despite some prominent support from figures like Benjamin Franklin. In 1790 when Quakers petitioned Congress to abandon the practice of slavery Franklin, who would die less than a year later, presented it and voiced his support. See Gary Nash, *Race and Revolution* (Madison: Madison Horse, 1990), 144–145.

12. Don Fehrenbecher, *The Slaveholding Republic: An Account of the United States Government's Relations to Slavery* (Oxford: Oxford University Press, 2001), 76–77; Fehrenbecher writes that the flow of petitions dramatically increased every year during the 1830s, climaxing around the 1836 debates over the annexation of Texas.

13. Despite persistent criticism, Pickney's "gag rule" was passed by congress at the annual beginning of every session until 1845. Richard Newman in *The Transformation of American Abolitionism: Fighting Slavery in the Early Republic* points out that Pickney's "gag rule" was not without precedent. In 1791 Congress rejected a Quaker petition that called for the abolition of slavery as "out of place" and "improper." Similarly, Newman sees the 1797 congressional decision to cancel plans for the first black memorial as part of a larger government desire to avoid taking part in anti-slavery discourses. See Richard Newman, *The Transformation of American Abolitionism: Fighting Slavery in the Early Republic* (Chapel Hill: University of North Carolina Press, 2002), 57.

14. See *The Emancipator* 16 December 1834 edition, Newspapers and Periodicals Division, The Library of Congress, Washington, D.C.

15. In a September 12, 1835 letter written to George Benson, Garrison expresses his alarm at the visible trend of violence directed towards abolitionists in northern states. Between September 12 and September 17th Garrison writes three letters to George and Henry Benson, lamenting and anxiously following news of their precarious situation. Working in Providence, Rhode Island both men were locked in the local jail to ensure their protection from hostile mobs that threatened their lives. Garrison encourages them to follow the advice of their friends and loved ones and to remain in the jail, "for safe keeping from your enemies." Garrison also relays his efforts to maintain a "lofty spirit," and despite the "tediousness and monotony" of such precautionary measures he concedes that he "dare not to go back to Boston." See William Garrison, "A Letter to George Benson," 12 September 1835, Anti-Slavery Manuscript Collection, Rare Books Division and Special Collections, Boston Public Library, Boston, Massachusetts.

16. Frederick J. Blue, *No Taint of Compromise: Crusaders in Anti-Slavery Politics* (Baton Rogue: Louisiana State University Press, 2005), 18–22; Blue points out that such demonstrations actually proved to be counterproductive and the number of abolitionist organizations continued to grow exponentially throughout the 1830s.

17. Ibid.

18. Ibid.

19. Quoted from Leonard Richards, "*Gentlemen of Property and Standing*": *Anti-Abolition Mobs In Jacksonian America* (New York: Oxford University Press, 1970), 82.

20. Stanley Harrold argues that the northern violence of the mid 1830s demonstrates that abolitionism should be studied and understood by its northern origins rather than by its southern protests. That underscoring the violence of the 1830s is a desire on the part of New England and New York based abolitionists to "renew" or change themselves and the culture immediately around them. See Stanley Harrold, *The Abolitionists and the South, 1831–1865* (Lexington: University of Kentucky Press, 1995), 85.

21. Lydia Marie Child, "A Letter to William Lloyd Garrison," 15 May 1835, ms. A. 9.2, 42, Lydia Marie Child Correspondence, ID: 3298818, Anti-Slavery Manuscript Collection, Rare Books Division and Special Collections, Boston Public Library, Boston, Massachusetts.

22. See *The Liberator* 8 November 1834 edition, Periodicals and Newspaper Division, The Library of Congress, Washington, D.C.

23. Ibid.

24. Ibid.

25. "The Refuge of Oppression" is a regular column that appears in *The Liberator* beginning in September 1834. These columns consistently revel in the hostile attitudes that Garrisonian abolitionist encountered from both northern and southern audiences during this period.

26. John N. King, *Foxe's Book of Martyrs and Early Modern Print Culture* (Cambridge: Cambridge University Press, 2006), 1–5.

27. Ibid.

28. Ibid. p.1.

29. Several Early American historians discuss the wide prominence of Foxe's *Book of Martyrs* in early American culture. See, Ernest Lee Tuveson, *Redeemer Nation* (Chicago: University of Chicago Press, 1968); Sacvan Bercovitch, *The Puritan Origins of the American Self* (New Haven: Yale University, 1975) 136–163.

30. William Warren Sweet, *The Methodist Episcopal Church and the Civil War* (Cincinnati: Methodist Book Concern Press, 1912), 19–21.

31. Ibid.

32. Ibid.

33. Ibid.

34. Jan Willem Van Henten and Friedrich Avemarie, *Martyrdom and Noble Death: Selected Texts from Greco-Roman, Jewish, and Christian Antiquity* (London: Routledge, 2002), 100–101. See also: Ariel Glucklich, *Sacred Pain: Hurting the Body for the Sake of the Soul* (Oxford: Oxford University Press, 2001); W.H.C. Trend, *Martyrdom and Persecution in the Early Church* (Oxford: Blackwell, 1965).

35. James Tabor, *A Noble Death: Suicide and Martyrdom Among Christians and Jews in Antiquity* (San Francisco: Harper Collins, 1992), 115.

36. See W.R. Schodel, *Igantius of Antioch: A Commentary on the Letters of Ignatius of Antioch* (Philadelphia: Fortress Press, 1985), 85.

37. James Tabor, *A Noble Death: Suicide and Martyrdom Among Christians and Jews in Antiquity* (San Francisco: Harper Collins, 1992), 119.

38. J. Perkins, *The Suffering Self: Pain and Narrative Representation in the Early Christian Era* (London: Routledge, 1995), 53.

39. Maurice Halbwachs, *The Social Frameworks of Memory*, trans. Francis J. Ditter and Vida Yazdi Ditter (New York: Harper and Row, 1980).

40. In an August 14, 1838letter to Oliver Johnson he points out that the trouble with convention New England congregation is that they comfortably denounce slavery but attack those who are called to deal with the issue directly as having "riotous spirit." Garrison goes on to express his belief that their diluted theology has downplayed their "fear of God" and their ability to evince "real sympathy for the cause of bleeding humanity." See William Lloyd Garrison, "A Letter to Oliver Johnson," 14 August 1838, William Garrison Papers, Anti-Slavery Manuscript Collection, Rare Books Division and Special Collections, Boston Public Library, Boston, Massachusetts.

41. Quoted from William Garrison, "The Guilt of New England," from *William Lloyd Garrison and the Fight Against Slavery*, ed. Charles Christensen (New York: St. Martin's Press, 1995), 84.

42. William Garrison, "Declaration of the National Anti-Slavery Convention," *The Liberator 14* December 1833, Periodicals Collection, Library of Congress, Washington, D.C.

43. Ibid.

44. See *The Liberator* 8 November 1834 edition, Periodicals and Newspaper Division, The Library of Congress, Washington, D.C.

45. Richard Greaves, "Bunyan and the Ethic of Suffering," *John Bunyan and His England, 1628–88*, ed. Lawrence, Owens, and Sim (London: Hambledon Press, 1990), 63, 70–76.

46. Ibid.

47. Louis Filler, *The Crusade Against Slavery, 1830–1860* (New York: Harper, 1963), 58, 76.

48. William Garrison, "A Letter to George Benson," 12 January 1835, ms. A. 9.2 v. 8, 4–5, William Garrison Papers, Anti-Slavery Manuscript Collection, Rare Books Division and Special Collections, Boston Public Library, Boston, Massachusetts.
49. Ibid.
50. Ibid.
51. Ibid.
52. Ibid.
53. William Garrison, "A Letter to Samuel J. May," 17 January 1837, ms. A. 9.2, 6 William Garrison Papers, ID: 3409354, Anti-Slavery Manuscript Collection, Rare Books Division and Special Collections, Boston Public Library, Boston, Massachusetts.
54. Ibid.
55. Ibid.
56. By 1844 Garrison would not express the same degree of kinship with Birney, but as late as 1838 Birney is still writing letters of staunch support for Garrison's appeals to his supporters asking them not to acknowledge allegiance to any human government.
57. William Garrison, "A Letter to Samuel J. May," 17 January 1837, ms. A. 9. 2, 6 William Garrison Papers, ill: 3409354, Anti-Slavery Manuscript Collection, Rare Books Division and Special Collections, Boston Public Library, Boston, Massachusetts.
58. In the Bible the term "apostle" refers to those individuals chosen by Jesus Christ to travel and minister with him during his 3.5 years of earthly service, between the time of his baptism and his final ascension. There are twelve apostles in the Bible and, unlike disciples, they maintain special powers (i.e., to cast out demons) and special authority (i.e., to teach and baptize). Garrison's frequent use and claim of the term "apostle" for himself and his closest followers is an important invocation of his (and their) unique authority to proclaim the gospel. Apostolic lineage-that is, special knowledge of the Apostle's teachings and seeing oneself in their tradition-rhetorically confers Jesus' authority upon Garrison, most notably the "gift" of teaching and prophetic utterance.
59. William Garrison, "A Letter to Lewis Tappan," 18 February 1836, ms. A.9.2. v. 25, 60B, William Garrison Papers, ID: 3333775, Anti-Slavery Manuscript Collection, Rare Books Division and Special Collections, Boston Public Library, Boston, Massachusetts.
60. Paul values death and suffering as a process of sanctification. 2 Corinthians (1.8–11) is particularly invested in the place of suffering and death in the process of salvation. For Paul, suffering is a necessary form of preparation for future glory (4.17–18). Since Christ's death and resurrection dissolve the bonds between humankind and physical death, suffering and physical death should be embraced and eagerly awaited. For the believer, Christ's earthly work and divine promise for all people is not fulfilled until physical death. Therefore, one should "rejoice in suffering." See, Romans 5.3; 2 Corinthians 1.5–7; 4.17–18.
61. The embrace of suffering as a pathway to a greater intimacy with Christ is at the core of the Christian church's teachings, with origins in Paul's epistles. In letters to Christian communities in Ephesus and Corinth Paul rallies Christians to "rejoice" in their pain. As the church continued to grow, followers began to venerate those who followed Paul's admonishment as either saints or martyrs. St. Catherine of Siena (1347–1380) is an exemplary version of this theology and her narrative is an important reminder of the continuity that narratives of suffering have played throughout church history. Catherine is most famous for her work with the poor (she is the patron saint of doctors), particularly those with leprosy and various forms of skin cancers. During her ministry to the sick, Catherine would beat herself with whips and other devices, endure unnecessary and extraordinarily long fasts, and even drink the infected discharge from the patients in her care. Like the Garrisonian relationship to the slave, Catherine's pain equaled and surpassed that of her patients. All of these acts are tied to the belief that human suffering is the bridge between Christians on earth and Christ is heaven. See Paul Burns, *Lives of the Saints* (Collegville: Liturgical Press, 2003); *The Letters of Catherine of Siena,* Tr. Suzanne O.P. Noffke (Ithaca: Cornell University Press, 2001).
62. William Garrison, "A Letter to James Birney" 6 April 1836, ms. A. 9.2 v. 11, William Garrison Papers, ill: 3285273, Anti-Slavery Manuscript Collection, Rare Books Division and Special Collections, Boston Public Library, Boston, Massachusetts.
63. Ibid.
64. Ibid.
65. Ibid.
66. William Garrison, "A Letter to Oliver Johnson" 18 December 1835, ms. A. 9.2. v.11, 74, William Garrison Papers, 1D: 3415182, Anti-Slavery Manuscript Collection, Rare Books Division and Special Collections, Boston Public Library, Boston, Massachusetts.
67. C. Peter Ripley, ed., *The Black Abolitionist Papers: Volume 1, 1830–1865* (Chapel

Hill: University of North Carolina Press, 1985), 95.
68. *Ibid.*, 92–93.
69. *Ibid.*, 114.
70. William Lloyd Garrison, "A Letter to Sarah Douglass," 5 March 1832, William Garrison Papers, Anti-Slavery Manuscript Collection, Rare Books Division and Special Collections, Boston Public Library, Boston, Massachusetts.
71. *Ibid.*
72. Francis Ellen Watkins Harper, *Poems on Miscellaneous Subjects* (Philadelphia: Merrihew & Thompson, 1857), Microfiche, Gelman Library, The George Washington University, Washington, D.C.
73. Shirley J. Yee, *Black Women Abolitionists: A Study in Activism, 1828–1860* (Knoxville: University of Tennessee Press, 1992), 101–105.
74. *Ibid.*
75. *Ibid.*
76. "To William Garrison," *The Liberator* 16 January 1836, Newspaper and Periodicals Collection, Library of Congress, Washington, D.C.
77. Wendell Phillips, *Remarks of Wendell Phillips at the Funeral of William Lloyd Garrison* (Boston: Lee and Shepard Publishers, 1884), The Library of Congress Rare Books Division, Washington, D.C.; Lucretia H. Newman, "William Lloyd Garrrison," *The Christian Recorder 27* March 1884, Newspapers and Periodicals Division, The Library of Congress, Washington, D.C.; Reverend William H. Yeocum, "The Mind that Was in Christ," *Christian Recorder* 20 October 1881, Newspapers and Periodicals Division, The Library of Congress, Washington, D.C.; Joseph Seaman Cotter, Sr., "William Lloyd Garrison," *The Vintage Book of African American Poetry: 200 Years of Vision, Struggle, Power, Beauty, and Triumph from 50 Outstanding Poets,* Michael S. Harper and Anthony Walton, eds. (New York: Vintage Books, 2000), 61–62.
78. William Garrison, "A Letter to Henry Benson," 26 January 1836, ms. A. 9.2 v. 9, 17, William Garrison Papers, ID: 3279804, Anti-Slavery Manuscript Collection, Rare Books Division and Special Collections, Boston Public Library, Boston, Massachusetts.
79. Note here on Garrison's relationship to the founders or directors of the Emancipator and the Spectator. Also stress that Garrison is traveling during this period giving lectures and organizing anti-slavery groups. As a result, the day-to-day editorial role during this period is mostly carried out by Isaac Knapp, a close friend and longtime ally. However, Knapp and Garrison constantly write to each other. Garrison sends articles to Knapp for publication and is sent every issue of *The Liberator* after its publication and supplies Knapp with feedback and the overall vision of the paper and its rhetorical strategies against slavery.
80. The term "Garrison Man" and the more gender neutral "Garrisonian" and "Garrisonite" are very much a part of the popular parlance of 1830s New England culture. James Woodbury's August 1, 1837 letter to Garrison describes and critiques this cultural phenomenon in great deal. See Rev. James T. Woodbury, "A Clerical Appeal," *New England Spectator,* 17 August 1837, Newspaper and Periodicals Division, Library of Congress, Washington, D.C.
81. Mary Benson, "A Letter to William Garrison," 14 January 1837, ms. A.9.2 v.25, p.6, Garrison Family Letters, ID: 3418635, Anti-Slavery Manuscript Collection, Rare Books Division and Special Collections, Boston Public Library, Boston, Massachusetts.
82. Garrison's theology is paradoxically experiential and fundamentally textual. His own attempts to define his theological beliefs in public confrontations positions his movement as restorationist-the desire to "restore" the "authentic" early church as opposed to the heretical and corrupted contemporary beliefs and practices. His main beliefs (on slavery and other issues) emerge from "correct" biblical readings. Yet, these readings lead Garrison to take an immediatist stand on the question of slavery that separates him from many of his anti-slavery peers, most notably the Society of Friends. His "intemperate" beliefs results in persecution from both northern and southern audiences and churches, which informs the way he sees himself (as an exemplary sufferer in the tradition of early Christians) and the work of his followers (to redeem the world and the slave through personal sacrifice and suffering).
83. William Garrison, "A Letter to Anne Benson," 4 February 1837, ms. 9.2.v.8, 21, William Garrison Papers, ID: 3669345, Anti-Slavery Manuscript Collection, Rare Books Division and Special Collections, Boston Public Library, Boston, Massachusetts.
84. *Ibid.*
85. Douglass Strong, *Perfectionist Politics: Abolitionism and the Religious Tensions of American Democracy* (Syracuse: Syracuse University Press, 1999), 36–38.
86. *Ibid.*
87. During the latter months of 1837 James Woodbury and William Garrison exchanged at least 8 letters. This correspondence began

in private but quickly became a public debate with Woodbury published extracts of one of Garrison's letters, along with his reply to it, in the August 17, 1837 edition of the *New England Spectator*. From that point on the debate was made public, with Garrison printing his responses in *The Liberator*. Woodbury's central complaints against Garrison were (1) his lack of training in Biblical interpretation and his lack of authority to preach as a representative of Christ; (2) that his "peculiar theology," to borrow Woodbury's phrase encouraged such an outpouring of devotion from his followers that his own suffering usurped Christ's role as the principal agent in the drama of salvation.

88. Reverend James T. Woodbury, "A Clerical Appeal," *New England Spectator*, 17 August 1837, Periodicals Collection, Library of Congress, Washington, D.C.

89. *Ibid.*
90. *Ibid.*

91. William Garrison, "A Letter to James T. Woodbury," *The Liberator*, 1 September 1837, Periodicals Collection, Library of Congress, Washington, D.C.

92. *Ibid.*
93. *Ibid.*
94. *Ibid.*
95. *Ibid.*
96. *Ibid.*

97. " The Conspiracy of Fanaticism," *Democratic Review* 1850 May p.391.

98. *Ibid.*
99. *Ibid.*

100. Smith published his new "translation" of the King James New Testament through his own church printing press in Ohio in 1830. However, once news of his text became widely known in 1833 he was forced to secretly transfer the copies to Jackson, Missouri and to label the boxes they were transferred with the simple label "Bible" in order to avoid the crowds who sought to find his translation and destroy it. For the full text of Smith's New Testament and for the story of its conception, publication, and reception, see Thomas A. Wayment, ed., *The Complete Joseph Smith Translation of the New Testament* (Salt Lake City: Deseret Books, 2005).

101. Smith's own feelings on anti-slavery beliefs are tempered in the pages of the Nauvoo Expositor. His followers were already the subject of a great deal of persecution and violence. Engaging in strong anti-slavery rhetoric, he feared, would only lead to more violence. As a result, Smith allowed articles into the paper that sympathized with the pro-slavery position, though the paper largely remained detached from the heated rhetoric that filled the pages of pro and anti slavery periodicals. For a full discussion of the complexities of the Mormon relationship to abolitionism in the 1830s, see Newell G. Bringhurst, *Saints, Slaves, and Blacks: The Changing Place of Black People Within Mormonism* (Westport: Greenwood Press, 1981).

102. Richard Lyman Bushman, *Joseph Smith: Rough Stone Rolling, a Cultural Biography of Mormonism's Founder* (New York: Vintage, 2005), 178–180.

103. *Ibid.*, 167.

104. The masthead of the February 1, 1863 edition of *The Liberator* proclaimed the Constitution "A Covenant with Death, and An Agreement with Hell."

105. Smith ability to even consider such an ambitious plan, according to Robert V. Remini, is a testament to the significant number of converts and follower that he gained, not only in America but also in Europe, by the early 1840s. See, Robert V. Remini, *Joseph Smith* (New York: Penguin, 2002), 162–163.

106. Joseph Smith, *Doctrine and Covenants*, 87: 1,3.

107. "Abolitionism vs. Christianity and the Union," *Democratic Review* 1850 July 4.

108. Sarah Barringer Gordon, "Blasphemy and the Law of Religious Liberty in Nineteenth Century America," *American Quarterly* (December 2000), 685.

109. *Ibid.*

110. This attitude towards violence remained consistent throughout Garrison's public life. Garrison's ultimate disavow of John Brown's October 1859 raid on Harper's Ferry is one representative example of the limits of his support for certain forms of violent anti-slavery resistance. In his published response to the incident in The Liberator he sympathetically acknowledges the slave's desire for freedom at any cost: "no one who glories in the revolutionary struggle of 1776" could "deny the right of the slaves to imitate the example of our fathers." Yet he concludes that "even in the best of causes" violent slave resistance is inappropriate. Garrison reserves his harshest words for John Brown, the leader of the insurrection, calling him "misguided, wild, and apparently insane." See *The Liberator 21* October 1859, Newspaper and Periodicals Division, The Library of Congress, Washington, D.C.

111. William Garrison, "To The Editor of the Boston Courier," *The Liberator*, 18 March 1837, Newspaper and Periodicals Collection, Library of Congress, Washington, D.C.

112. *Ibid.*
113. *Ibid.*

114. See David Robinson, "The Legacy of

Channing: Culture is a Religious Category in New England Thought," *Harvard Theological Review* 74 (1981), 230, 235–239. See also Jack Mendehson, *Channing: The Reluctant Radical* (Wesport: Greenwood Press, 1971).

115. *Ibid.*

116. *Ibid.*

117. William Garrison, "A Letter to George Benson," 5 September 1835, ms. A.9.2 v.6, 66, William Garrison Papers, Anti-Slavery Manuscript Collection, Rare Books Division and Special Collections, Boston Public Library, Boston, Massachusetts.

118. *Ibid.*

119. For a full discussion of this phenomenon, see William E. Huntzicker, *The Popular Press, 1833–1865* (Westport: Greenwood, 1999); and especially Meredith L. McGill, *American Literature and the Culture of Reprinting, 1834–1853* (Philadelphia: University of Pennsylvania Press, 2003). McGill rightly and exhaustively argues that cultural perceptions of reprinting and a widely held aversion to copyright and intellectual property laws produced a distinct American literary form.

120. *Ibid.*

121. William Garrison, "A Letter to George Benson," 11 January 1836, ms. A. 9.2 v. 8 6, William Garrison Papers, Anti-Slavery Manuscript Collection, Rare Books Division and Special Collections, Boston Public Library, Boston, Massachusetts.

122. *Ibid.*

123. *Ibid.*

124. William Garrison, "A Letter to Isaac Knapp," 28 February 1836, ms. A.7.3, 124, William Garrison Papers, ID: 3343879, Anti-Slavery Manuscript Collection, Rare Books Division and Special Collections, Boston Public Library, Boston, Massachusetts.

125. *Ibid.*

126. Here I am thinking specifically about the contentious relationship between William Lloyd Garrison, the founder of *The Liberator*, and Frederick Douglass. In his Introduction to *My Bondage and My Freedom*, John David Smith writes that, "Douglass proved to be so individualistic and such a keen critic of American institutions that even William Lloyd Garrison, the dean of American abolitionists, could not control him." See John David Smith, introduction, *My Bondage and My Freedom* by Frederick Douglass (New York: Penguin, 1993), xxiv.

127. Kenneth Greenberg, "Name, Face, Body," *Nat Turner: A Slave Rebellion in History and Memory*, Kenneth Greenberg, ed. (New York: Oxford University Press, 2003), 9.

128. See Ira Berlin, *Many Thousands Gone: The First Two Centuries of Slavery in North America* (Cambridge: Harvard University Press, 1998). Berlin points out that slaves in South Carolina, for instance, comprised over 80 of the state's total population.

129. Herbert Aptheker, "The Event," *Nat Turner: A Slave Rebellion in History and Memory*, Kenneth Greenberg, ed. (New York: Oxford University Press, 2003), 49–50. Apetheker quotes a Southern writer's observation that "Garrison always disclaimed any intent of inciting slave insurrection," he also described the Turner revolt "in so truculent a manner as fairly to justify the Southern suspicions of his motives."

130. Drew Faust rightly points out that anti-slavery violence was viewed as a challenge to the South's "philosophical, moral, and social" perspective of that nation as a whole. Drew Gilpin Faust, *The Ideology of Slavery: Proslavery Thought in the Antebellum South, 1830–1860* (Baton Rogue: Louisiana State University Press, 1981), 2.

131. "The Burning of William: Slave Execution by Fire," *Daily South Carolinian* 24 October 1856, Issue 22, Col. B.

132. *Ibid.* The paper reports that a town dance and other local festivities followed the execution.

133. *Ibid.*

134. John Kingsley, "A Slave Whipped and Burned to Death," *The Liberator* 23 Jan. 1857, Issue 4, Col. D.

135. *Ibid.*

136. David Potter, "Martyrdom as Spectacle, *Theater and Society in the Classical World*, ed. R. Scudel (Ann Arbor: University of Michigan Press, 1993), 53–88.

137. Saidiya Hartman, *Scenes of Subjection: Terror, Slavery, and Self-Making in Nineteenth Century America* (New York: Oxford University Press, 1997), 17–18.

138. Augustine, *Confessions*, R. Pine-Coffin, trans. (London: Penguin, 1961), 6.7–8.

139. *Ibid.*

140. John Kingsley, "A Slave Whipped and Burned to Death," *The Liberator* 23 Jan. 1857, Issue 4, Col. D.

141. *Ibid.*

142. John Kingsley, "A Slave Whipped and Burned to Death," *The Liberator* 23 Jan. 1857, Issue 4, Col. D.

143. "The Execution of Washington Goode," *The Liberator* 1 June 1849, 89, Issue 2, Col. C.

144. *Ibid.*

145. *Ibid.*

146. *Ibid.*

147. *Ibid.*

148. *Ibid.*

149. "The Execution of Washington Goode," *The Liberator* 1 June 1849, 89, Issue 2, Col. C.

150. James T. Mcintosh, ed., *The Papers of Jefferson Davis, Vol. 3: 1846–1848* (Baton Rogue: LSU Press, 1981), 358.

151. *Ibid.*

152. William Garrison, "A Letter to Nathan R. Johnson," 15 October 1860, ms. A.9.2 v.13, 12, William Garrison Papers, ill: 3416893, Anti-Slavery Manuscript Collection, Rare Books Division and Special Collections, Boston Public Library, Boston, Massachusetts. Johnson wrote to Garrison in the hopes of securing him as the keynote speaker for the 4th Annual Vermont Anti-Slavery Convention that took place in Bradford, Vermont the last week of October. For unknown reasons Garrison chose not to attend at the last moment, but he did support the convention's efforts and republished its roll call and extracts for the speeches that were delivered in the November 2, 1860 edition of *The Liberator*.

153. *Ibid.*

154. See Michel Foucault, *Discipline and Punishment*, trans. Alan Sheridan (New York: 1979), 29.

155. While conceding that victims of persecution are shaped by their experiences (the book of 1 Peter describes Christian faith as one "refined like gold in the fire" ), I nevertheless question the extreme of Foucault's position which locates meaning solely in the exercise of power. Christian martyrs are acting, after all, *Out* of a faith grounded in what he or she believes to be a superior power and reality.

156. See Elaine Scarry, *The Body in Pain: The Making and UnMaking of the World* (Oxford: Oxford University Press, 1985). Here I am referring to one of Scarry's central points: that pain should be understood as a marker of absolute difference between people, what she describes as an "ontological division." In this particular case, Garrisonian abolitionists rely on the visible pain in someone else (whether a Christian martyr image, or even Jesus Christ's narrative) to make their own personal experience with pain understandable, and they then ascribe these feelings and understandings of pain to someone else (i.e., the slave), producing a remarkable degree of sameness, legibility, and understanding.

## Chapter 2

1. *The Rachel Maddow Show*, "A Conversation with Rand Paul," MSNBC, Original Air date: 19 May 2010.

2. In a May 22,2010 Op-Ed for the *New York Times*, titled, "The 'Randslide' and Its Discontents," Frank Rich expresses bewilderment at the public's shock concerning Paul's racial views. He compares Paul's views of the Civil Rights Act of 1965 with those of, his "hero," Barry Goldwater finding both a troubling parallel to the rise of Barack Obama. He also points out that Paul's controversial views on race date back to interviews given in 2002. See Frank Rich, "The 'Randslide' and Its Discontents," *New York Times*, OP-ED, 22 May 2010. Similarly, Republican National Committee Chairman Michael Steele characterized Paul's comments as "misplaced" and attacking Paul's liberatarian views as a philosophy that "got in the way of reality." See James Gordon Meek, "Rand Paul's civil rights remarks are 'misplaced' says RNC Chairman Michael Steele, *New York Daily News*, Washington Bureau Column, 23 May 2010.

3. *The Rachel Maddow Show*, "A Conversation with Rand Paul," MSNBC, original air date: 19 May 2010.

4. *Ibid.*

5. *Ibid.*

6. Timothy Patrick McCarthy and John Stauffer, eds., *Prophets of Protest: Reconsidering the History of American Abolitionism* (New York: New Press, 2006), xvii.

7. *Ibid.*

8. Bruce Laurie, *Beyond Garrison: Antislavery and Social Reform* (Cambridge: Cambridge University Press, 2005), 1.

9. *Ibid.*, 2–5. For Laurie, whose work analyzes the intersections between abolitionism and 19th century labor reform movements, the dominant focus on Garrisonian abolitionism, "with its endless pursuit of self-purification... of moral cleansing of individual souls," is a near impenetrable American myth.

10. Timothy Dwight, 'Greenfield Hill: A Poem in Seven Parts," (New York: Childs and Swaine, 1794). Microfiche. Library of American Civilization, Gelman Library, The George Washington University, Washington, D.C.

11. *Ibid.*

12. Robert G. Deamer, *The Importance of Place in the American Literature of Hawthorne, Thoreau, Crane, Adams, and Faulkner* (Lewistown, NY: E. Mellen Press, 1990), 45.

13. William Garrison, "The Death of Slavery," *The Liberator* 10 February 1865.

14. *Ibid.*

15. *Ibid.*

16. *Ibid.*

17. *Ibid.*

18. *Ibid.*

19. *Ibid.*

20. He began telling this story on the eve of the Civil War when he speculated about what kind of future the war might bring: "oh, how it delights my heart that the worst thing we propose to do for the South is the very best thing that God or man can do! Yes, we will make it possible for them to be a happy and prosperous people, as they never have been, and never can be, with slavery. We will make it possible for them to have free schools, free presses, and free institutions. ".

21. *Ibid.*

22. Phillips and Garrison remained close friends despite clashing personally and publically throughout 1866 and 1867 over the discontinuation of the Massachusetts Anti-Slavery Society, the American Anti-Slavery Society, and *The Liberator*. In the February 3, 1866 edition of the *Independent* Garrison wrote a scathing letter that condemned Phillips' position and in a February 11, 1866 private letter to James Miller McKim, Garrison describes the toll of these disagreements on their longstanding friendship: "the breach is now, doubtless ... past healing." See William Garrison, "A Letter to James Miller McKim," 3 February 1866, William Garrison Papers, Anti-Slavery Manuscript Collection, Rare Books Division and Special Collections, Boston Public Library, Boston, Massachusetts. Garrison's concerns about an unfixable division with Phillips proved to be unfounded. The two would reconcile during Garrison's last years, a process that culminated with Phillips' touching and eloquent funeral eulogy to his friend in 1879.

23. William Lloyd Garrison, "Editorial," "Valedictory: The Last Number of *The Liberator*," *The Liberator* 29 December 1865, Newspapers and Periodicals Division, The Library of Congress, Washington, D.C.

24. *Ibid.*
25. *Ibid.*
26. *Ibid.*
27. *Ibid.*
28. *Ibid.*
29. *Ibid.*
30. *Ibid.*

31. William Garrison, "Letter to Oliver Johnson," 23 December 1865, William Garrison Papers, Anti-Slavery Manuscript Collection, Rare Books Division and Special Collections, Boston Public Library, Boston, Massachusetts.

32. *Ibid.*

33. Oliver Johnson, "Valedictory: The Last Number of *The Liberator*," *The Liberator* 29 December 1865, Newspapers and Periodicals Division, The Library of Congress, Washington, D.C.

34. William Garrison, "Letter to Theodore Tilton," 14 December 1865, William Garrison Papers, Anti-Slavery Manuscript Collection, Rare Books Division and Special Collections, Boston Public Library, Boston, Massachusetts.

35. *Ibid.*

36. Theodore Tilton, "Valedictory: The Last Number of *The Liberator*," *The Liberator* 29 December 1865, Newspapers and Periodicals Division, The Library of Congress, Washington, D.C.

37. And some did both. Lydia Maria Child's essay, "Through the Red Sea into The Wilderness" nostalgically recites and celebrates the history of *The Liberator* and Garrison's movement ("it seems but yesterday that the South called Massachusetts to account for allowing the publication of a newspaper that expressed sympathy of the slave...") and cautiously hopes that this sacrifice is not squandered by the nation's political leaders ("may heaven preserve them from the old chronic disease of Congress—weakness of the spine!). See Lydia Maria Child, "Through the Red Sea into The Wilderness," Valedictory: The Last Number of *The Liberator*, 29 December 1865, Newspapers and Periodicals Division, The Library of Congress, Washington, D.C.

38. Cited from Ernest K. McKay, *The Civil War and New York City* (Syracuse: Syracuse University Press, 1990), 295.

39. *Ibid.*

40. James D. Tabor and Arthur Droge, *A Noble Death: Suicide and Martyrdom Among Christians and Jews in Antiquity* (San Francisco: Harper Collins, 1992), 132–135.

41. See William Lloyd Garrison, "Editorial," *The Liberator* 10 February 1865.

42. See *Harper's Weekly* 18 February 1865 edition.

43. All of these references are cited from *Harper's Weekly* issues reprinted in Eugene Exman, *The House of Harper: One Hundred and Fifty Years of Publishing* (New York: Harper and Row, 1967). For particular issues referenced here, see *Harper's* 31 (1865), 265–266; *Harper's* 35 (1867) 256–257,665–666; *Harper's* 36 (1868) 813.

44. *Ibid.*
45. *Ibid.*
46. *Ibid.*

47. *Ibid. Harper's* 35 (1867), 256–257, 665–666.

48. See *New York Times* 28 January 1868, Newspapers and Periodicals Division, The Library of Congress, Washington, D.C.

49. Alice Fahs, *The Memory of the Civil War in American Culture* (Chapel Hill: University of North Carolina Press, 2004), 2.

50. Drew Gilpin Faust argues that the unprecedented death, suffering, and bloodshed that American's witnessed, read about, and experienced firsthand transformed and informed virtually all cultural productions and powerfully shaped the new modem union. She writes, "but for those Americans who lived in and through the Civil War, the texture of the experience, its warp and woof, was the presence of death. At the war's end this shared suffering would override persisting differences about the meanings of race, citizenship, and nationhood to establish sacrifice as its memorialization as the ground on which North and South would ultimately reunite" (xii). See Drew Gilpin Faust, *This Republic of Suffering: Death and the American Civil War* (New York: Vintage, 20008).

51. *Brooklyn Eagle* 28 January 1870, Newspapers and Periodicals Division, The Library of Congress, Washington, D.C.

52. *Ibid.*

53. Benjamin E. Mays, *The Negro's God as Reflection in His Literature* (New York: Atheneum, 1975), 49.

54. *Harper's Weekly* 15 April 1870; Cited from Eugene Exman, *The House of Harper: One Hundred and Fifty Years of Publishing* (New York: Harper and Row, 1967).

55. See John Greenleaf Whittier's "To William Garrison," *The Complete Poetical Works of John Greenleaf Whittier* (New York: Cornell University Press, 2010), 262.

56. Henry Stanton's *Random Recollections* is one of the most public attacks against Garrison by a former member of his circle. Pillsbury mentions Stanton directly in his memoirs and based on his prior public denunciations of him it's safe to assume that this book was at least part of the impetus for his decision to tell his own story. Stanton's memoir downplays the success of Garrisonian focuses on "moral suasion" and instead offers a counter-narrative that emphasizes the role of political figures in the eradication of slavery.

57. Parker Pillsbury, *Acts of the Anti-Slavery Apostles* (Concord: Clague, Wegman, Schlight, & Co., 1883), iii–v; also 41, 47.

58. *Ibid.*, 379–380.

59. Henry Mayer argues that Garrison failed to produce a memoir because he ultimately found such works to be too egotistical. See Henry Mayer's *All on Fire: William Lloyd Garrison and the Abolition of Slavery* (New York: Norton, 2008), 634. I find this position difficult to reconcile with the care that Garrison devoted to crafting and to celebrating his own work and sacrifices at *The Liberator*. It is true that as the paper progressed he became weary about writing articles under his own name that explicitly celebrated his work, but he certainly encouraged others to do so throughout the history of the paper.

60. Quoted from Jean H. Baker and Michael F. Holt, *The Civil War and Reconstruction* (New York: Norton Press, 2001), 617–621.

61. Samuel May, *Some Recollections of Our Antislavery Conflict* (New York: Arno Press and the New York Times, 1968), 16.

62. *Ibid.*, 18.

63. *Ibid.*

64. *Ibid.*, 19.

65. *Ibid.*

66. *Ibid.*, 20.

67. *Ibid.*, 30. The excerpt that May quotes is from Pope's *Essay on Man* (ep. IV, I., 264). See also Alexander Pope, *Essay on Man and Other Poems* (New York: Dover, 1994).

68. *Ibid.*

69. *Ibid.*, 34.

70. *Ibid.*

71. Augusta Rohrbach, *Truth Stranger than Fiction: Race, Realism, and the U.S. Literary Marketplace* (New York: Palgrave Press, 2000), 55.

72. Lydia Maria Child, "Book Review," *National Antislavery Standard* 25 December 1869.

73. *New York Times* 8 September 1869.

74. For a brief description of the events of this festival, see Ira V. Brown, *Mary Grew: Abolitionist and Feminist, 1813–1896* (Selinsgrove: Susquehana University Press, 1991), 119–120.

75. Parker Pillsbury, *Acts of the Anti-Slavery Apostles* (Concord: Clague, Wegman, Schlicht, & Co, 1883), iii.

76. A version of this debate takes place within the academia during the 1950s when scholars attack the Barnes-Dumond thesis that similarly takes exception with the central role of William Garrison in antislavery histories.

77. Gilbert H. Barnes, *The Antislavery Impulse, 1830–1844* (Goucester: Peter Smith, American Historical Association, 1933).

78. *Ibid.* p. iv.

79. *Ibid.* p. iii.

80. *Ibid.* pgs. iii, Pillsbury's memoir is filled with references to the Biblical book of *Acts*. The frontispiece of his original 1883 manuscript even references the book directly with a quotation from the eighth chapter: "and they went everywhere, preaching the word."

81. In *Acts*, St. Stephen becomes the first martyr of the newly formed church. His story is recounted and mentioned by both Paul and Peter, who describe his stoning and his refusal to renounce his devotion to Christ.

82. Parker Pillsbury, *Acts of the Anti-Slavery Apostles* (Concord: Clague, Wegman, Schlicht, & Co, 1883), iii.
83. *Ibid.* pgs iii, v.
84. *Ibid.*
85. *The Liberator* here and elsewhere in Pillsbury's memoir is used as a historical reference point to date different aspects of the abolitionist struggle.
86. Samuel May's memoir offers a similar timeline and organization. Though more chronologically organized than Pillsbury's memoir, which is more thematic, May also begins his memoir with a chapter on Garrison, titled "The Rise of Abolitionism."
87. Parker Pillsbury, *Acts of the Anti-Slavery Apostles* (Concord: Clague, Wegman, Schlicht, & Co, 1883), 10–27.
88. *Ibid.*
89. *Ibid.*,12.
90. *Ibid.*
91. *Ibid.*
92. *Ibid.*, 18.
93. lbid., 20–21. Pillsbury explains that Garrison's theological beliefs are fairly orthodox and are consistent with those "professed by the whole Evangelical Church" (20). He believes, for instance, in the "inspiration and the authority of the Bible, the Trinity and the Atonement, and the teachings and precepts of Jesus Christ" (20). He then goes on to demonstrate Garrison's love for the Bible by presenting, in full, his poem, "Sonnet to the Bible": "O book of books! Though skepticism flout! They sacred origin, thy worthy decry;/ Though transcendental folly give the lie/To what though teachest: though the critic doubt! This fact; that miracle and raise a shout/Of triumph o'er each incongruity/He in thy pages may perchance espy:/ As in his strength, the effulgent sun shines out,/ Hiding innumerous stars, so dost thou shine/ With heavenly light all human works excelling'/Thy oracles are holy and divine,/Of free salvation through a Savior telling.! All truth, all excellence dost enshrine;/ The mists of sin and ignorance expelling."
94. See Mark 8: 34–35 (Kjv).
95. Robin Lane Fox, *Pagans and Christians* (New York: Alfred A. Knopf, 1987), 435.
96. *Ibid.*
97. Pillsbury's 1883 letter to Frederick Douglass is quoted from Stacy M. Robertson, *Parker Pillsbury: Radical Abolitionist, Radical Feminist* (Ithaca: Cornell University Press, 2000), 180.
98. *Ibid.*
99. The first of these pamphlets was written by Parker Pillsbury himself, the second, *Brotherhood of Thieves, Or, a True Picture of the American Church and Clergy* was written by Stephen Foster, and the *American Churches: The Bulwarks of American Slavery* was written by James Birney. All provided scathing critiques of the practices of northern churches and, in the late 19tb century, served to undercut contemporary claims by northern clergy that stressed Christianity as a force largely responsible for the eradication of slavery.
100. Parker Pillsbury, *Acts of the Anti-Slavery Apostles* (Concord: Clague, Wegman, Schlicht, & Co, 1883).
101. *Ibid.*
102. *Ibid.*
103. *Ibid.*
104. Scott E. Casper, *Constructing American Lives: Biography and Culture in Nineteenth Century America* (Chapel Hill: University of North Carolina Press, 1999), 1–19. Casper offers a compelling cultural history of the 19th century "biographical mania" and the many overlapping conventions, goals, and markets for these books. See also Richard Brodhead's *Cultures of Letters: Scenes of Reading and Writing in Nineteenth Century America* (Chicago: University of Chicago Press, 1993); William J. Gilmore, *Reading Becomes a Necessity of Life: Material and Cultural Life in Rural New England, 1778–1835* (Knoxville: University of Tennessee Press, 1989).
105. In an August 16, 1880 letter to William Garrison, Jr., Phillips apologizes for the attention that this eulogy received and informs Garrison That he plans to donate the "surplus numbers" of his eulogy and other related papers to the Boston Public Library and the Library of Congress. See Wendell Phillips, "A Letter to William Garrison, Jr.," 16 April 1880, William Garrison Papers, Anti-Slavery Manuscript Collection, Rare Books Division and Special Collections, Boston Public Library, Boston, Massachusetts.
106. Wendell Phillips, *Remarks of Wendell Phillips at the Funeral of William Lloyd Garrison* (Boston: Lee and Shepard Publishers, 1884), 3–4. the Library of Congress Rare Books Division, Washington, D.C.
107. *Ibid.* P. 4.
108. *Ibid.* P. 6. Phillips also argues that Garrison's converts held up the movement and carried it on in a more sustained and unified way, leading him to conclude that Garrison's work "is without parallel in history since Luther." (6).
109. *Ibid.*
110. *Ibid.*
111. *Ibid.* P 7–8.
112. *Ibid.* P. 8.
113. *Ibid.* P. 10.

114. "Theological and Literary Intelligence," the *Unitarian Review and Religious Magazine* Feb 1886; 25, 2; P. 173.
115. *Ibid.* Samuel May, himself a Unitarian minister, strongly criticized the general lack of enthusiasm and the slow pace that Unitarians' exhibited when it came to joining the anti-slavery movement. The Unitarian's lack of a rigid hierarchical structure, may reasoned, should have expedited their foray into anti-slavery politics, rather than hinder it.
116. *Ibid.*
117. *Ibid.*
118. Of course, the relationship between Douglass and Garrison was far from consistently supportive and at times their demeanor towards one another became hostile. By May 1851 Douglass pulled away from Garrison and publicly rejected his claim that the U.S. constitution was a "covenant with death" that supported slavery. this debate caused a significant division with the black anti-slavery movement. those who supported Garrison, like Robert Purvis and William C. Nell, accused Douglass of ignoring the immorality of the legal system (particularly in the wake of the passage of the fugitive slave law). Douglass responded by calling Purvis "a contemptible tool of William Lloyd Garrison." The feud continued throughout 1851 and William Powell (a Garrison sympathizer) and others used their positions with newspapers like the *North Star* and the *Liberty Party Paper to* attack Douglass' critique of Garrison. See Robert Purvis, "A Letter to William Lloyd Garrison," 12 September 1853, William Garrison Paper, Anti-Slavery Manuscript Collection, Boston Public Library, Boston Massachusetts. See Also, the August 15, 1851, edition of the *North Star.*
119. " Great Men: James Forten," the *North Star* 10 March 1848, Rochester, NY, 2, Newspapers and Periodicals Division, the Library of Congress, Washington, D.C.
120. *Ibid.*
121. *Ibid.*
122. James Brewer Stewart, *Garrison at Two Hundred* (New Haven: Yale University Press, 2008).
123. Frederick Douglass, "Speech on the Death of William Lloyd Garrison," at Garrison Memorial Meeting, 15th Street Presbyterian Church, 2 June 1879, Frederick Douglass Reel 15, Library of Congress, Washington, D.C.
124. *Ibid.*
125. *Ibid.*
126. "William Lloyd Garrison," *Farmer's Cabinet* 3 June 1879, vol. 77, issue 48, p.2, Newspaper and Periodicals Division, The Library of Congress, Washington, D.C.
127. *Ibid.*
128. Reverend William H. Yeocum, "The Mind That Was in Christ," *Christian Recorder* 20 October 1881 Philadelphia, PA 1, Newspapers and Periodicals Division, The Library of Congress, Washington, D.C.
129. *Ibid.*
130. *Ibid.*
131. "From a child thou hast known the Holy Scriptures, stir up the gift that is in thee, do the work of an evangelist, make full proof of thy ministry, endure hardness as a good soldier, fight the good fight of faith, lay hold on eternal life."
132. See Phil. ii, v.5.
133. Reverend William H. Yeocum, "The Mind that Was In Christ," *Christian Recorder* 20 October 1881 Philadelphia, PA 1, Newspapers and Periodicals Division, The Library of Congress, Washington, D.C.
134. *Ibid.*
135. "A Colossal Statue of Bronze, Nine Feet High, Will Be Erect," *The Christian Recorder* 29 March 1883. The article goes on to compare the magnificence of the statue with the other major artistic monuments in Boston designed by St. Gaudens.
136. *Ibid.*
137. Lucretia H. Newman, "William Lloyd Garrison," *The Christian Recorder* 27 March 1884 2, Newspapers and Periodicals Division, The Library of Congress, Washington, D.C.
138. *Ibid.*
139. *Ibid.*
140. "William Lloyd Garrison," *Afro-American* 9 December 1905 4, Newspapers and Periodicals Division, The Library of Congress, Washington, D.C.
141. *Ibid.*
142. *Ibid.*
143. *Ibid.*
144. Joseph Seaman Cotter, Sr., "William Lloyd Garrison," *The Vintage Book 0/ African American Poetry: 200 Years of Vision, Struggle, Power, Beauty, and Triumph from 50 Outstanding Poets*, Michael S. Harper and Anthony Walton, eds. (New York: Vintage Books, 2000), 61–62. This poem is reprinted in the Vintage collection from *A Rhyming,* Cotter's first published collection of poetry in 1895. Cotter was born in Bardstown, Kentucky in 1861, began his formal schooling in 1883, and spent much of his life as a writer, teacher, and activist. He is most notably remembered for his work as an outspoken teacher and advocate of African American education in the Louisville, Kentucky public school system. He did in 1949. (57).
145. *Ibid.,* 61.
146. *Ibid.,* 61–62.
147. See R.W.B. Lewis, *The American*

*Adam: Innocence, Tragedy, and Tradition in the Nineteenth Century* (Chicago: University of Chicago Press, 1955). Lewis describes the Adamic American as "a figure of heroic innocence and vast potentialities, poised at the start of a new history."

148. *Ibid.*, 62.

149. Henrietta Cordelia Ray, "William Lloyd Garrison," *Poems* (New York: The Grafton Press, 1910), 69, The Civil War Fiction Collection, The University of North Carolina at Chapel Hill, Chapel Hill, North Carolina.

150. *Ibid.*

151. *Ibid.*

152. *Ibid.*

153. William E. Barton, *Pine Knot* (New York: Appleton, 1900). Wilmer Collection of Civil War Fiction, Rare Books Department, University of North Carolina at Chapel Hill, Chapel Hill, North Carolina.

154. See Ann Douglas, *The Feminization of American Culture* (New York: Knopf, 1977), 92, 255; Jane Tompkins, *Sensational Designs: The Cultural Work of American Fiction, 1790–1860* (New York: Oxford University Press, 1985), pp. xi, 130. The crux of the Douglas/Tompkins debate is as follows: Douglas views the rise in sentimental literature within a cultural context of a movement away from intellectual sophistication, as embodied in Calvinist sermons and preaching. For Douglas, sentimental fiction is all about the "commercialization of inner life." Tompkins, on the other hand, analyzes sentimental novels as a legitimate form of intellectual discourse in which women were empowered to be a part of and to "change the world." Other notable works on sentimental fiction include: Nina Baym, *Woman's Fiction: A Guide to Novels by and About Women in America, 1820–1870* (Urbana: Cornell University Press, 1993). Other scholarship that challenges Douglas's thesis that sentimental fiction lacked intellectual depth: Andrew Burstein, *Sentimental Democracy: The Evolution of America's Romantic Self-Image* (New York: Hill and Wang, 1999).

155. William E. Barton, *Pine Knot* (New York: Appleton, 1900), 20–22; 58. Wilmer Collection of Civil War Fiction, Rare Books Department, University of North Carolina at Chapel Hill, Chapel Hill, North Carolina.

156. *Ibid.*

157. Elizabeth Avery Meriwether, *The Sowing of the Swords* (New York: Neale, 1910). Wilmer Collection of Civil War Fiction, Rare Books Department, University of North Carolina at Chapel Hill, Chapel Hill, North Carolina.

158. *Ibid.*, 83–87.

159. *Ibid.*, 15–16.

160. Elizabeth Avery Meriwether wrote a number of novels from her Tennessee home that lamented the collapse of the Old South, and which featured a nostalgic plantation setting. *Master of the Red Leaf* (1872), *Black and White* (1883), and *The Ku Klux Klan, or the Carpetbagger in New Orleans* (1877) are all representative examples of her fiction. Copies of these novels, as well as her non-fiction essays on the Civil War are housed at the Wilmer Collection at The University of North Carolina, Chapel Hill, North Carolina and the Civil War Fiction Collection and Louisiana State University, Baton Rouge, Louisiana.

161. Katherine Holland Brown, *The Father* (New York: Day, 1928), Wilmer Collection of Civil War Fiction, Rare Books Department, University of North Carolina at Chapel Hill, Chapel Hill, North Carolina.

162. He is, for instance, thrown from a train in one instance of mob violence. This story, incidentally, was used by Garrison in his own self-narration and referenced by Rand Paul during his now infamous *Rachel Maddow Show* interview.

163. Katherine Holland Brown, *The Father* (New York: Day, 1928), 8. Wilmer Collection of Civil War Fiction, Rare Books Department, University of North Carolina at Chapel Hill, Chapel Hill, North Carolina.

164. *Ibid.*

165. For a comprehensive examination of the postwar construction of the paternal Lincoln image and the ways that black and white audiences utilized this image to different ends, see Merrill D. Peterson, *Lincoln in American Memory* (New York: Oxford University Press, 1994); the epilogue of Allen C. Guelzo's *Abraham Lincoln: Redeemer President* similarly explores the emergence of this language, pointing out that the familial imagery permeated public reactions to Lincoln's assassination, with many people and newspaper mourning the murder of America's "father." See Allen C. Guelzo's *Abraham Lincoln: Redeemer President* (Grand Rapids: William B. Eerdmans Publishing, 2003): 439–465; Scott A. Sandage's article "A Marble House Divided: The Lincoln Memorial, the Civil Rights Movement, and the Politics of Memory, 1939–1963," analyzes the complex relationship between African Americans and the immortal paternal monuments to Lincoln during the modern Civil Rights movement. Sandage describes Civil Rights' leaders attempts to produce a usable public memory of Lincoln in order to contextualize and strengthen their cause. See Scott A. Sandage, "A Marble House Divided: The Lincoln Me-

morial, the Civil Rights Movement, and the Politics of Memory, 1939–1963," *Time Longer than Rope: A Century of African American Activism, 1850–1950*, eds. Charles M. Payne and Adam Green (New York: New York University Press, 2003), 492–536.

166. James McPherson, *The Abolitionist Legacy: From Reconstruction to the NAACP* (Princeton: Princeton University Press, 1995), 3; This question is also addressed by McPherson's earlier work. See James McPherson, *The Struggle for Equality: Abolitionists and the Negro in the Civil War and Reconstruction* (Princeton: Princeton University Press, 1964).

## Chapter 3

1. Wendell Phillips Garrison and Francis Jackson Garrison, *William Lloyd Garrison, 1805–1879: The Story of His Life Told by His Children* (New York: The Century Company, 1885).

2. Wendell Phillips Garrison, *Letters and Memorials of Wendell Phillips Garrison: Literary Editor of the Nation, 1865–1906* (Cambridge: Riverside Press, 1908), 7.

3. At issue here was the dismissal of Secretary of State Edwin M. Stanton and the appointment of his successor without consulting Congress. Garrison viewed such action as "tyrannical" and as a blatant disregard for American law. See, William Lloyd Garrison, "A Letter to Wendell Phillips Garrison," 23 March 1868, Garrison Papers, Anti-Slavery Manuscripts Collection, Boston Public Library, Boston, Massachusetts.

4. Wendell Phillips Garrison, "A Letter to William Lloyd Garrison," 4 April 1868, Garrison Family Papers, Anti-Slavery Manuscripts Collection, Boston Public Library, Boston, Massachusetts.

5. This conversation can be constructed by examining Garrison's long and careful reply to Nell in his April 23, 1867 letter, which makes reference to the former's invitation. See William Lloyd Garrison, "A Letter to William C. Nell," 23 April 1867, Anti-Slavery Collection, Garrison Papers, Boston Public Library, Boston, Massachusetts.

6. *Ibid.*

7. *Ibid.* Nell was particularly grateful and cites his friendship as a reason why he was able to become the first black postmaster of Boston earlier that year.

8. William Lloyd Garrison, "A Letter to Wendell Phillips Garrison," 18 December 1867, Anti-Slavery Collection, Garrison Papers, Boston Public Library, Boston, Massachusetts.

9. William Lloyd Garrison, "Editorial," *The Independent*, 21 July 1875, Boston, Massachusetts. Portfolio #8, Boston Public Library Newspaper Collection, Boston, Massachusetts.

10. *Ibid.*
11. *Ibid.*
12. *Ibid.*

13. Wendell Phillips Garrison, "A Letter to William Lloyd Garrison," 7 February 1875, Garrison Papers, Anti-Slavery Manuscripts Collection, Boston Public Library, Boston, Massachusetts.

14. *Ibid.*

15. Wendell Phillips Garrison, "A Letter to William Lloyd Garrison," 2 April 1878, Garrison Papers, Anti-Slavery Manuscripts Collection, Boston Public Library, Boston, Massachusetts.

16. *Ibid.*

17. Henry Mayer's *All on Fire: William Lloyd Garrison and the Abolition of Slavery* attributes Garrison's failure to write his memoir with a deep abiding fear that such a work by appear egotistical. This explanation does not sufficiently account for Garrison's expressed desire to sign a contract and publish his account, nor does it reconcile with the extreme care that Garrison devoted to crafting and to celebrating his own work and sacrifices as the Civil War drew to a conclusion. See Henry Mayer, *All on Fire: William Lloyd Garrison and the Abolition of Slavery* (New York: Norton, 2008), 634.

18. As opposed to the commemorative works published in the popular press and the major literary works undertaken by Garrison's friends Samuel May (in 1866) and Parker Pillsbury (in 1883). See Samuel May, *Some Recollections of the Anti-Slavery Conflict* (New York: Arno Press, 1968) and Parker Pillsbury, *Acts of the Anti-Slavery Apostles* (Concord: Clague, Wegman, Schlicht, & Company, 1883).

19. Wendell Phillips Garrison and Francis Jackson Garrison, *William Lloyd Garrison. 1805–1879: The Story of His Life Told by His Children* (New York: The Century Company, 1885).

20. *Ibid.* p. ix.
21. *Ibid.* p. xi.
22. *Ibid.* p. xiii.
23. *Ibid.*

24. James Marten, *Children for the Union: The War Spirit and the Northern Home Front* (Chicago: Ivan Dee, 2004), 41–43.

25. *Ibid.* Marten also tackles the impact of the war on northern children who grew up during the conflict in his book, *The Children's Civil War* (Chapel Hill: University of North Carolina Press, 1998). In this book, as in his

others, Marten is principally concerned with understanding the way children were taught to express patriotic sentiments that were framed by the wider culture as an essential part of the broader 'war effort" from the home front.

26. *Ibid.* p. xii. It is amazing to see the degree to which Wendell and Frank's voluminous work alternates between such grand claims and more intimate personal sentiments regarding their father. After lamenting here their father's "invisibility" in "manuals of American history," they go on to explain that most of their own book concerns the "profoundly religious nature" of their father (xiii). This speaks to the degree to which their father's personal life and public activism were difficult to separate. Even discussions of seemingly trivial family events that William Garrison participated in, within this context, become not only a part of his personal history, but also a part of the anti-slavery movement.

27. *Ibid.* p. xii. From a literary, writing, perspective they also claim that they "aimed at nothing more than clearness, sequence, and proportion."

28. This appointment is discussed in Wendell Phillips Garrison's letter to Frank on February 2, 1886. See Wendell Phillips Garrison, "A Letter to Francis Garrison," 2 February 1886, Ms. 123.49, folder 94, Garrison Family Papers, Anti-Slavery Manuscript Collection, Boston Public Library, Boston, Massachusetts.

29. *Ibid.* And also discussed in letters sent from Wendell to Frank dated February 19, March 10, and April 3rd, Garrison Family Papers, Anti-Slavery Manuscript Collection, Boston Public Library, Boston, Massachusetts.

30. *Ibid.*

31. Wendell Phillips Garrison, "A Letter to Francis Garrison," 3 April 1886, Garrison Family Papers, Anti-Slavery Manuscript Collection, Boston Public Library, Boston, Massachusetts.

32. *Ibid.*

33. *Ibid.* In these same letters he also suggests to Frank that they advertise in Boston newspapers and periodicals asking for people to come forward with stories and/or letters about their father since they were in the process of researching and writing the final two volumes of their biography.

34. Wendell Phillips Garrison, *Bedside Poetry: A Parent's Assistant in Moral Discipline* (Boston: D. Lothrop, 1887).

35. *Ibid.*

36. Wendell Phillips Garrison, *Letters and Memorials of Wendell Phillips Garrison: Literary Editor of the Nation, 1865–1906* (Cambridge: Riverside Press, 1908), 77.

37. *Ibid.*

38. Despite his busy schedule, he managed to produce a significant number of children's books, poetry, and other non-fiction memoirs related to his family. Other titles include: *A Parent's Assistant in Moral Discipline; the Mother's Register* (1887); *Sonnets and Lyrics of the Ever-Womanly; Parables for Home and School* (1897); *The New Gulliver* (1898); and he helped to edit, *The Memoirs of Henry Villard (1904).*

39. Wendell Phillips Garrison, *Parables for Home and School* (New York: Longman's, Green, and Company, 1897).

40. *Ibid.* p. vii.

41. *Ibid.* p. viii.

42. *Ibid.*

43. *Ibid.*

44. *Ibid.*

45. Charles W. Eliot, *Journal of the Proceedings and Addresses of the National Education Association, Session of the Year* 1892, 617–625, Monroe C. Gutman Library, Historical Textbooks Collection, Harvard University, Cambridge, M.A.

46. *Ibid.* Discourses that stressed importance of textbooks occurred within a period of dramatic increases in the volume and circulation of magazines and newspapers. In the 1870s, for instance, the number of American newspapers doubled and by 1892 there were seven newspapers with a circulation greater than 150,000 readers. Magazines like *Ladies Home Journal* boasted of staggering readership numbers that exceeded 700,000. The printed word and the print culture, in other words, played a significant role in the construction and maintenance of ideas related to regional and national identity. As Richard Brodhead points out, the 19th century rise in literacy rates and the development of new printing techniques and transportation technologies placed the printed word in a prime position to shape the "cultural identity" of its readers. See, Frank Luther Mott, *A History of Magazines Volume 3: 1864–1880* (New York: D. Appleton and Company, 1930), 13–35, 56. See also Richard H. Brodhead, *Cultures of Letters: Scenes of Reading And Writing in Nineteenth-Century America* (Chicago: University of Chicago Press, 1993), 6.

47. Caroline F. Lavender, *Cradle of Liberty: Race, the Child, and National Belonging from Thomas Jefferson to W.E.B. Du Bois* (Durham: Duke University Press, 2006), pp.10–11 Lavender argues, for instance, that pro-Union discourses during the Civil War that the figure of the child allowed the United States to advance an ideology of white supremacy "without undermining the nation's racial principles."

48. *Book of Fables for the Amusement and Instruction of Children* (Hartford: Oliver D. Cooke, 1820).

49. William Samuel Cardell, *Charles Ashton, the Boy That Would Be a Soldier* (Boston: N.S. and J. Simkins, 1823).

50. For a discussion of the types of moral appeals used in children's fiction of this era, see Anne Scott MacLeod, *A Moral Tale: Children's Fiction and American Culture, 1820–1860* (Hamden: Archon Press, 1975). For a more specific discussion of how moral lessons linked patriotic ideals to American gender conceptions, see Lorinda B. Cohoon, *Serialized Citizenship: Periodicals, Books, and American Boys, 1840–1911* (Oxford: Scarecrow Press, 2006).

51. This politics of this process are thoroughly discussed in Carl F. Castle's *Pillars of the Republic: Common Schools and American Society* (New York: Hill and Wang, 1983).

52. *Ibid.*

53. For a history of the creation of the public school system in the United States, see Lawrence A. Cremin, *American Education: The National Experience, 1783–1876* (New York: Harper and Row, 1980); and Robert L. Church and Michael Sedlack, *Education in The United States: An Interpretive History* (New York: Free Press, 1976).

54. Benedict Anderson, *Imagined Communities: Reflections on the Origin and Spread of Nationalism* (London: Verso, 1991).

55. David Tyack, *The One Best System* (Cambridge: Harvard University Press, 1974), 74–90.

56. *Ibid.*

57. Michael B. Katz, *The Irony of Early School Reform: Educational Innovation in Mid-Nineteenth Century Massachusetts* (Cambridge: Harvard University Press, 2001), 120.

58. Lawrence A. Cremin, *American Education: The National Experience, 1783–1876* (New York: Harper and Row, 1980), 103–147.

59. For a full discussion of the debates between Catholic leaders in New York educational reforms during the mid-19th century see, Diane Ravitch, *The Great School Wars: New York City, 1805–1973* (New York: Basic Books, 1974), 20–76; and for an exemplary example of these conflicts in Chicago see, James W. Sanders, *The Education of an Urban Minority: Catholics in Chicago, 1833–1965* (New York: Oxford University Press, 1977).

60. Quoted in David Brion Davis, ed., *Antebellum American Culture: An Interpretive Anthology* (Lexington: D.C. Heath, 1979), 36.

61. Ruth Miller Elson, *Guardians of Tradition: American Schoolbooks of the Nineteenth Century* (Lincoln: University of Nebraska Press, 1964), 203.

62. Michael B. Katz, *The Irony of Early School Reform: Educational Innovation in Mid-Nineteenth Century Massachusetts* (New York: Columbia University Press, 2001), 41–43.

63. William Sydney Mount's 1835 painting *The Truant Gambler* offers a decidedly unoptimistic assessment of the effectiveness of educational reforms. In his painting, a group of boys skip school in order to remain outside, gamble, and play games. Their happiness is not tied to the rigidity of the classroom atmosphere. In contrast, Charles Frederick Bosworth's *The New England School* imagines a classroom that is comfortable and an ideal place to grow intellectually and socially. Students casually walk around the classroom talking with one another, a variety of ages are intermingled, and a teacher gives her undivided attention to tutoring a single student. For Bosworth, intellectual growth is not necessarily tied to the wider culture's preoccupation with efficiency, standards, and regulations.

64. Winslow Homer, *Country School*, 1873, Addison Gallery of American Art, Phillip Academy, Andover, Massachusetts.

65. Horace Mann, *The Life and Works of Horace Mann*, Volume IV (Boston: Walker, Fuller, and Company, 1867), 259.

66. Quoted from Nicolai Cikovsky, "Winslow Homer's School Time: 'A Picture Thoroughly National,'" *Essays in Honor of Paul Mellon*, ed. John Wilmerding (Washington, D.C.: National Gallery of Art, 1986), 65.

67. *Ibid.*

68. Drew Gilpin Faust, *The Creation of Confederate Nationalism: Ideology and Identity in The Civil War South* (Baton Rouge: Louisiana State University Press, 1989). Faust's book examines the way Confederate periodicals and a variety of other texts "explored parallels between the Confederacy and other fledgling nations or independence movements," in order to "disassociate the South from genuinely radical movements" (13). As means of examining how the south viewed (or wanted to view) itself the author examines the Confederate national seal, their earliest postage stamps, the aesthetics of Jefferson Davis' inauguration, and other expressive documents that gave the Confederate states a unique identity and history apart from the United States of America (14–15).

69. Of course, everyone did not embrace the image of the schoolhouse and classroom as a model of American values. Mark Twain's *The Adventures of Tom Sawyer* and *Adven-*

*tures of Huckleberry Finn* are two of the most prominent examples of counter-narratives that celebrated wild, free, and unmanageable children who consistently rebel against their teachers and frustrate the efforts of adults in positions of authority. In *Adventures of Huckleberry Finn*, the relationship between Huck and the escaped slave Jim reminds of the book's thematic interest in ideas of slavery and freedom. Huck's distaste for school and other forms of oversight leads him to fake his own death and, along with Jim, to pursue the freedom of living outside of the confines of traditional "civil" life. Similarly, in *The Adventures of Tom Sawyer*, Mr. Walters, Tom Sawyer's stringent superintendent and Sunday school teacher, embodies many of Twain's concerns about the effectiveness of a classroom-centered learning atmosphere. Mr. Walters instructs children to "sit up just as straight and pretty as you can." His pupils are expected to behave by giving him their undivided attention, which means training them to curtail their natural inclination to play outside. And so when one young girl finds herself gazing out a classroom window she is promptly chastised and her attention refocused on the teacher: "I see one little girl who is looking out of the window—I am afraid she thinks I am out there somewhere—perhaps up in one of the trees making a speech to the little birds." There is a narcissistic quality to Mr. Walters's instruction that the book's narrator ascribes to a general tendency of male teachers to "show off," with "all sorts of official bustlings and activities, giving orders, delivering judgments, discharging directions here, there, everywhere that he could find a target." *Tom Sawyer* lampooned and questioned the widely propagated notion that structure, standardized curriculum, and individual growth could exist in a harmonious relationship. In each novel Twain correlates, both explicitly and implicitly, the image of the child in the classroom with slavery and oppression and life outside of school as freeing and adventurous. See, Mark Twain, *The Adventures of Tom Sawyer* (New York: Broadview, 2006); see also, Mark Twain, *The Adventures of Huckleberry Finn* (New York: Norton, 1998).

70. See Will Carleton, *Young Folks Centennial Rhymes* (New York: Harper and Brothers, 1876), Children's Books from 1876 Collection, The Philadelphia Public Library, Philadelphia, PA; Will Carleton, *The Centennial Frog and Other Stories* (Philadelphia: Claxton, Remsen, & Haffelfinger, 1876), Children's Books from 1876 Collection, The Philadelphia Public Library, Philadelphia, PA.

71. During the Civil War years Southerners came to resent the presence and widespread dominance of northern narratives of the war. By the end of the war the south had fewer journalist and papers than the north and many of those papers were put out of business by Union military victories. By September of 1864 it is common for Southern newspapers to decry their lack of visibility. For an example, see the Editorial pages of the *Charleston Daily Courier*, October 25, 1864 edition or the *Daily Richmond Enquirer*, September 27, 1864. In both instances these editorials optimistically hope that the end of the war will restore the quality of southern journalism.

72. " Review Clipping," *New York Tribune*, 9 February 1889.

73. "Book Notes," *The Philadelphia Ledger*, 11 February 1889.

74. "Books and Authors," *Boston Daily Examiner*, 10 December 1889, 6.

75. Wendell Phillips Garrison and Francis Jackson Garrison, *William Lloyd Garrison, 1805–1879: The Story of His Life Told by His Children* (New York: Houghton, Mifflin, and Company, 1894). These copies still exist at the Boston Public Library and the Library of Congress.

76. *Ibid.*, "Preface," pp. ix–xiv.

77. *Ibid.*

78. Melvin Hix, *The Approved Selections for Supplementary Reading and Memorizing* (Boston: Noble and Eldredge: 1905), 82, Monroe C. Gutman Library, Historical Textbooks Collection, Harvard University, Cambridge, M.A.

79. *Ibid.*, 83.

80. John Greenleaf Whittier, "Oh None in All the World Before," *Poems in Wartime from Volume III: The Works of Whittier: Anti-Slavery Poems and Songs of Labor and Reform* (New York: Houghton and Mifflin, 1892), 139.

81. Melvin Hix, *The Approved Selections for Supplementary Reading and Memorizing* (Boston: Noble and Eldredge: 1905), 83, Monroe C. Gutman Library, Historical Textbooks Collection, Harvard University, Cambridge, M.A.

82. *Ibid.*, 82.

83. *Ibid.*

84. William Lloyd Garrison, *The Words of Garrison: A Centenary Selection, 1805–1905* (Boston: Houghton, Mifflin, 1905), The Library of Congress, Washington, D.C.

85. *Ibid.*, 10.

86. In 1896 Marry Terrell founded the National Association of Colored Women. On the first day of the Garrison Centenary she is listed as one of the first speakers. "Garrison Centenary Program," box 15, file 404, William

Garrison Collection, Boston Public Library, Boston, Massachusetts.

87. *Ibid.*

88. David Blight, "The Dead and the Living," *Race and Reunion: The Civil War in American Memory* (Cambridge: Harvard University Press, 2001), 6–30. In this chapter Blight astutely analyzes the Blue Gray Reunion that took place on July 1–4 on the fiftieth anniversary of the Battle of the Gettysburg. Blight reads in Wilson's suggestion that the meeting should "celebrate the end of all feeling as well as the end of all strife between sections" the movement towards a white supremacist vision of the war that erases the specter of slavery, skirts the possibility of racial reconciliation, and brings the union together by stressing a innocuous and vague form of white heroism that is broad enough to encompass and celebrate both confederate and union soldiers.

89. James M. McPherson, *The Abolitionist Legacy: From Reconstruction to the NAACP* (Princeton: Princeton University Press, 1975), 389–390.

90. Parker Pillsbury, *Acts of the Anti-Slavery Apostles* (Concord: Clague, Wegman, Schlicht, & Company, 1883).

91. *Ibid.* McPherson argues that the children of abolitionists lent the organization's new push for rights a continuity with and connection to past reform efforts. He quotes one speech made at the Wendell Phillips Centenary that makes this connection explicitly: "[we] have reason to believe that the master spirits of the earlier crusade are with us now ... In every charge we make against the forces of oppression we have a right to feel that Garrison and Phillips ... are riding at our side" (390).

92. *Ibid.*, 392. He also cites other important work that Garrisonian abolitionists accomplished concerning the election of 1872, the Civil Rights Act of 1875, and Hayes Southern policy in 1877. These issues took place during a period of time when the elder William Garrison was gravely ill and largely inactive. The continued work of his children and the children of other Garrisonians after their founders death in 1879 provided a surprising degree of perceived continuity, or what McPherson describes as a "cyclical pattern in the history of race reform."

93. See Harriet Hyman Alonso, *Growing Up Abolitionist: The Story of the Garrison Children* (Boston: University of Massachusetts Press, 2002), 306–307. Alonso explains that Helen was particularly angry with her father's provision that she would only receive $25,000 and that this amount would be slowly distributed to her in the form of a monthly allowance. The author explains that Helen's letters to friends expressed her rage at her father's actions, viewing them as manipulative and unfair.

94. Henry Villard, *Memoirs of Henry Villard: Journalist and Financier, 1835–1900*, Helen Garrison-Villard, ed. (New York: Da Capo Press, 1969).

95. " The Villard Will Fight," *New York Sun,* 4 December 1903, 1.

96. *Ibid.* See "Preface," vi.

97. See Harriet Hyman Alonso, *Growing Up Abolitionist: The Story of the Garrison Children* (Boston: University of Massachusetts Press, 2002), 314. Alonso points out that the relationship between Fanny and government officials was complicated. Just as Fanny used her name to advance progressive social causes, the state also called on her to speak or testify in order to use her family name to gamer support or credibility for legislation. The author writes: "whenever leaders found an opportunity they asked her to say a few words, to sit on a platform, to walk at the head of a demonstration, to be part of a delegation to a government leader."

98. *Ibid.,* 315.

99. " The New York Diet Kitchen Association," *Social Service,* November 1903 ed., 85–89, m1321, folder 896, Garrison-Villard Papers, William Lloyd Garrison Collection, Boston Public Library, Boston, Massachusetts.

100. Fanny Garrison Villard, *William Lloyd Garrison on Non-Resistance Together with a Personal Sketch by His Daughter Fanny Garrison Villard* (New York: Nation Press Printing, 1924).

101. W.E.B. Du Bois, "National Negro Conference," *Horizon,* (November 1909), Vol. 5, No. 1, 1–2, 8–9.

102. For a few representative examples, see W.E.B. Du Bois, "National Negro Conference," *Horizon,* November 1909, Vol. 5, No.1, 1–2,8–9; *Crisis,* November 1910, Vol. 1, No.1; *Crisis,* April 1912, Vol. 3, No.6; *Crisis,* July 1912, Vol. 4, No.3; *Crisis,* August 1922, Vol. XXIV, No.4 in "Opinion"; *Crisis,* June 1928, Vol. XXXV, No.6, 202; Du Bois offers a special retrospective of *The Liberator* on the centenary of its first publication in *Crisis,* February 1934, Vol. XXXVIII, No.2, 65–66.

103. W.E. B. Du Bois, "Men of the Month," *Crisis,* July 1912, Vol. IV, No.3, pp.129–132.

104. Garrison's relationship to Douglass became strained in 1847 when he moved to New York and began to publish the *North Star.* When his paper merged with the *Liberty Party Paper* the tensions between the two

men grew. Douglass sought more intellectual autonomy, while Garrison preferred to present a unified challenge to the institution of slavery. Garrison also perceived Douglass' move to be a personal challenge and an act of disrespect. These feelings were only amplified by Douglass' 1851 reading of the U.S. Constitution, which he interpreted as an antislavery document-a belief that stood in stark contrast to Garrison's charge that this document represented a "covenant with death." Garrison's paper *The Liberator* and other publications subject to Garrisonian influence (like the *Pennsylvania Freeman*) wrote scathing attacks on Douglass. Douglass, in turn, responded with denunciations of Garrison's despotic tendencies: "If a black man dares to show manliness enough to think for himself, as to his field and mode of labor, he must be denounced." The two men's relationship never fully recovered and Garrisonian's never fully embraced Douglass again. See William Garrison, *The Liberator,* 4 July 1851; *Frederick Douglass Paper* 24 July 1851; *Pennsylvania Freeman,* 25 June 1851; see also Benjamin Quarles, *Frederick Douglass* (New York: Da Capo Press, 1997), 70–79.

105. W. E. B. Du Bois, "Opinion," *Crisis,* August 1922, Vol. *XXN,* No.4, 151–155. Du Bois does concede in this article that New England is far from realizing educational equality and laments the rise of racism in institutions of higher education. Nevertheless, even this understanding does not prevent him from looking to the past as a way to fondly and optimistically think about the rich progressive history of the region, especially to 19th century New England abolitionists.

106. Emma Miller Bolenius, ed., *The Boys and Girls Fifth History Reader* (Boston: Houghton Mifflin, 1922), Monroe C. Gutman Library, Historical Textbooks Collection, Harvard University, Cambridge, M.A.

107. *Ibid.,* 90.

108. *Ibid.,* 142.

109. *Ibid.,* 120.

110. *Ibid.,* 129.

111. See Brian Santana, "Chapter 3: Commemorating Garrison: Origins of the Garrison Revival in Post-Bellum American Memory, 1867–1910," *Sacred Sacrifice: William Garrison and American Abolitionism in Memory and Literature.*

112. *Ibid.*

113. See Brian Santana, "Chapter 4: Ross Lockridge's Raintree County: American Abolitionism as Epic Origin Narratives," *Sacred Sacrifice: William Garrison and American Abolitionism in Memory and Literature.*

114. This narrative became increasingly more important in the early 20th century during the Great Depression, when literary and film representations linked Lincoln's simple decency to his Midwest roots. Carl Sandburg's *Abraham Lincoln: The Prairie Years* (1926) and Robert E. Sherwood's Pulitzer Prize winning play, *Abe Lincoln in Illinois* (1938) are two prominent literary examples. John Ford's *Young Mr. Lincoln (1939)* accomplished similar work by showing how his roots instilled in him a compassionate, yet stoic leadership resolve. See Carl Sandburg, Abraham Lincoln: The Prairie Years (New York: Harcourt, 1926); Robert E. Sherwood, *Abe Lincoln in Illinois* (New York: Dramatist Play Service, 1938); John Ford (dir.), *Young Mr. Lincoln,* Twentieth-Century Fox, 1939.

115. *Ibid.,* 128.

116. *Ibid.,* 120.

117. *Ibid.,* 121 The italics here are used within the actual text and indicate a passage in which Garrison's words from the first issue are used in tandem with the text's language.

118. *Ibid.*

119. *Ibid.,* 122.

120. "The Book of Acts," *The King James Version of the Holy Bible* (Nashville: Gideons International, 1971), 996.

121. William Lloyd Garrison, "To the Public," *Genius of Universal Emancipation,* 29 November 1829. Garrison published other critiques of Todd that same month. See *Genius of Universal Emancipation,* 13 November 1829, edition.

122. William Lloyd Garrison, "A Letter to Henry Thompson," 30 May 1830. William Garrison Papers, Boston Public Library, Boston, Massachusetts. There is a written copy of this letter in the Garrison Papers at the Boston Public Library. Benjamin Lundy also publicly reprinted a copy of this letter in the July 1830 edition of *The Genius of Universal Emancipation.*

123. William Lloyd Garrison, "A Letter to Nicholas Brice," 13 May 1830, William Garrison Papers, Boston Public Library, Boston, Massachusetts. Like the Thompson letter, there is a written copy of this letter in the Garrison Papers at the Boston Public Library. Benjamin Lundy also publicly reprinted a copy of this letter in the July 1830 edition of *The Genius of Universal Emancipation.* Collectively, the paper published three letters written to people associated with the trial in this issue, and each of which contained some veiled and some explicit threats of reprisal from Garrison.

124. Emma Miller Bolenius, ed., *The Boys and Girls Fifth History Reader* (Boston: Houghton Mifflin, 1922), 124 Monroe C.

Gutman Library, Historical Textbooks Collection, Harvard University, Cambridge, MA.

125. *Ibid.*, 125.

126. *Ibid.*, 125–127.

127. David W. Blight, *Race and Reunion: The Civil War in American Memory.* (Cambridge: Harvard University Press, 2001). Blight writes about this phenomenon in a memorable description of the semi-centennial: "The veterans, as well as the gazing crowds, had come to commemorate a glorious fight; and in the end, everyone was right, no one was wrong, and something so transforming as The Civil War had been rendered a mutual victory of the Blue and Gray by what Virginia governor Mann called the 'splendid movement of reconciliation.' Behind the podiums and bunting, out beyond the throngs of beautiful, if old and frail, men, beyond, the spectacle of the tent city and smells of campfires, was a society riven with racial strife ... Any discussion of the war's extended meanings in America's omniscient "race problem" was simply out of place.... At this remarkable moment when Americans looked backward with deepening nostalgia and ahead with modem excitement and fear, Jim Crow, only half-hidden, stalked the dirt paths of the veterans' tent city at Gettysburg.... The Civil War had become the nation's inheritance of glory, Reconstruction the legacy of folly, and the race problem a matter of efficient schemes of segregation" (385–387).

128. By the mid-20th century a number of African American scholars produced works that challenged conventional histories of the anti-slavery struggle by producing histories of black abolitionist work. A classic example is Benjamin Quarles, *Black Abolitionists* (New York: Oxford University Press, 1969).

129. Eugene Genovese's *A Consuming Fire: The Fall of the Confederacy in the Mind of The White Christian South* makes a compelling argument that southern Christians believed that God gave the institution of slavery as "the best hope for the vital work of preparation for the kingdom" (xiv). They believed that God entrusted them with the great responsibility of maintaining a racialized social order. However, Genovese points out that many Christian ministers did not believe that slave owners treated their slaves in a manner consistent with Christ's directives. As a result, some members of the Confederacy came to view the outcome of the Civil War as God's punishment for not giving their responsibilities as slaveowners proper contemplation. This created a schism in southern consciousness in the postwar period. They still viewed slavery as a divinely instituted social hierarchy, but they were also forced to reconcile their belief that God aided the union army to punish them for forsaking his commands. See Eugene Genovese, *A Consuming Fire: The Fall of the Confederacy in the Mind of the White Christian South* (London: University of Georgia Press, 1998). Contemporary manifestations of the south's trouble creating a coherent historical narrative include the debates concerning the meaning of confederate flag and whether it is appropriate for a southern government building to fly it. South Carolina and Alabama first began flying the confederate flag in the 1960s and protest greeted it then, culminating with a legal showdown in the 1990s. In 2000 the NAACP circulated "A Resolution on the Confederate Battle Flag and the Confederate Battle Emblem" that called for the removal of the flag from all public sites and buildings in South Carolina. This resolution, an affirmation of an earlier 1991 resolution on the same matter, incited a debate within the south over the meaning of the flag, with some southern newspapers attempting to distance the flag and the confederacy from race. Charley Reese's 1997 article "Purge the South of Its Symbols? You're Barking up Wrong Flagpole" for the *Orlando Sentinel* captures this perspective, with the author dismissing the attempt to link the confederacy with racism as "nonsense" and making an affirmative appeal for presenting southern history without shame. He writes, "Well, we southerners have always been willing to be reconciled, but we won't be reconstructed. We are not going to allow people to obliterate our history and its symbols. We strongly advise our fellow Americans in other parts of the republic to defend their history and symbols." See Charley Reese, "Purge the South of Its Symbols? You're Barking up Wrong Flagpole," *Orlando Sentinel*, 20 February 1997 edition.

130. For a detailed discussion, see Carl F. Kaestle and Maris A. Vinovskis, *Education and Social Change in Nineteenth-Century Massachusetts* (Cambridge: Cambridge University Press, 1980), pp.230–232.

131. Rev. Ransom, "An Oration on William Garrison," 11 December 1905, Garrison Centennial Celebrations, William Garrison Papers, Boston Public Library, Boston, Massachusetts.

132. *Ibid.*

133. Joel Brown, "An Abolitionist Recalled: William Lloyd Garrison to Be Honored at Literary Festival in Newburyport," "Local News," *The Boston Globe*, April 24, 2011 edition.

## Chapter 4

1. See Alice Fahs and Joan Waugh, eds., *The Memory of the Civil War in American Culture* (Chapel Hill: University of North Carolina Press, 2004). Fahs and Waugh pay particular attention to the way that Civil War memory is constructed and contested within fictional and non-fictional representations of the war. In the introduction, the authors write that: "Finally, books have been both physical and symbolic spaces mapping out the contested historical and emotional terrain of the Civil War. Ulysses S. Grant's famous memoirs, late-nineteenth-century southern textbooks, and children's Civil War fiction can all be see as contributing to an ongoing argument over the war's meaning within American culture" (2).

2. Ulysses S. Grant, *Personal Memoirs of U.S. Grant Vol. 2* (New York: C.L. Webster, 1886), 773.

3. *Ibid.*

4. Ulysses S. Grant, *Personal Memoirs of U.S. Grant Vol. 1* (New York: C.L. Webster, 1886), 213–214.

5. *Ibid.*, 217–218.

6. See A. Newby, *Jim Craw's Defense: Anti-Negro Thought in America, 1900–1930* (Baton Rogue: LSU Press, 1965), 74–74; See also Edgar Eggleston, *The Ultimate Solution Of the American Negro Problem* (New York: AMS Press, 1913), and also the writings of Thomas Dixon, which offer similar versions of this interpretation of Lincoln's history.

7. *Ibid.*

8. *Ibid.*

9. For a more in depth discussion, chapter 3 discusses Lincoln's appearance and use in relation to Garrison in early 20th century school textbooks.

10. Thomas Nast, "Emancipation," Philadelphia, 1867. Rare Prints and Photographs Division, The Library of Congress, Washington, D.C. LC-USZ62-2573.

11. Thomas Nast, 'Emancipation" (1867): The south is characterized through a language of unspeakable pain and suffering. In the lower left comer a slave woman is flogged, while a young man is branded. Above this image a man is sold on the auction block and separated from his family. The northern vision-Lincoln's vision-is characterized by a strong egalitarian imagery associated with the restoration of the family (in the center) and paid labor.

12. William H. Wiggins, *O Freedom! Afro American Emancipation Celebrations* (Knoxville: University of Tennessee Press, 1987), 127–28.

13. *Ibid.*

14. James W. Loewen, "Five Myths About Why the South Seceded," *The Washington Post*, January 9,2011, see 1.

15. See Alfred W. Blumrosen and Ruth G. Blumrosen, *Slave Nation: How Slavery United The Colonies and Sparked the American Revolution* (Naperville, Ill.: Sourcebooks, Inc., 2005). The Blumrosens show how in the wake of 1772 British Parliament decision surrounding the "Somerset case" southern colonies feared that British law would turn their attention to the prevalence of slavery in the southern colonies. The authors show that the perpetuation of slavery within the new "independent" United was a central assurance that southern colonies demanded from northern colonies (who were mostly concerned with British taxation issues) before they agreed to join together in revolution. Accordingly, the new American republic was born through a concession to the southern desire to protect slavery.

16. The Lost Cause has been well documented in contemporary scholarship. Cultural expressions of the lost cause mythology are not limited to written texts, but also appear in writings, performances, photographs, and other cultural artifacts. For a more in depth discussion of the various ways that "lost cause" mythology continued to develop and evolve in 20th century American popular fiction, non-fiction, and music, see Jim Cullen, *The Civil War in Popular Culture: A Reusable Past* (Washington: Smithsonian Institute Press, 1995), particularly Chapter 3, "Screening the Boo: The Civil War of Margret Mitchell's Gone with the Wind" and Chapter 4 "Reconstructing Dixie: Confederate Mythology in Rock 'n' Roll" ; Tony Horwitz's *Confederates in the Attic: Dispatches from the Unfinished Civil War* offers a compelling and quirky case history of the culture of Civil War re-enactors and the role that embodied performance continues to inform and perpetuate this narrative within modem southern culture. See Tony Horwitz, *Confederates in the Attic: Dispatches from the Unfinished Civil War* (New York: Vintage, 1998).

17. Cynthia Mills and Pamela Simpson argue that this narrative also impacted the physical landscape of the New South, with its many monuments and sculptures that were commissioned and installed throughout the 20th century. The authors view these memorials and monuments as an instrumental part of the resuscitation of "Confederate history as told from a southern white perspective" (xvii). See Cynthia Mills and Pamela Simpson, eds., *Monuments to the Lost Cause:*

# Notes—Chapter 4

*Women, Art, and the Landscapes of Southern Memory* (Knoxville: University of Tennessee Press, 2003).

18. *Ibid.*

19. Examples of these themes in 20th century confederate monuments include: the Robert E. Lee Monument by Marius-Jean Antonin Mercie in Richmond, Virginia; The Monument to Confederate Women in Baltimore Maryland (1918); and George Julian Zolnay's Davis Family Circle at the Hollywood Cemetery in Richmond, Virginia in 1911.

20. Allen Tate, *Stonewall Jackson: The Good Soldier* (New York: Minton, Balch, and Co., 1928).

21. See F. Scott Fitzgerald, *The Complete Short Stories of F. Scott Fitzgerald* (New York: Scribner, 1989); Robert Penn Warren, *John Brown: The Making of a Martyr* (New York: Payson and Clark, 1929); and Margaret Mitchell, *Gone with the Wind* (New York: Warner Books, 1999). Robert Penn Warren's narrative history of John Brown is characteristic of southern revisionist histories that rhetorically discredit or disparage northern "martyrs" and, in so doing, hope to call into question the veracity of the legendary foundations for the union's mythic providential claims. Concerning John Brown, Penn challenges the prevailing representation of him as a divinely anointed prophet who suffered for the sake of the slave. Warren writes that "John Brown and the instincts of the patriarchal despot.... Even Sunday meant no escape for the workmen.... John Brown once recorded that in his own youth he had been somewhat addicted to lying" (23–24). In these and other passages Warren portrays Brown as a tyrant wholly obsessed with "worldly concerns."

22. Robert Penn Warren, *John Brown: The Making of a Martyr* (New York: Payson and Clark, 1929), 391.

23. *Ibid.*

24. Ross Lockridge, Jr., *Raintree County* (Boston: Houghton Mifflin Company, 1948).

25. *Ibid.*, 294–295.

26. Jeanette Vanausdall, *Pride and Protest: The Novel in Indiana* (Indianapolis: Indiana Historical Society, 1999), 108–109.

27. Amy Kaplan, *The Anarchy of Empire in the Making of U.S. Culture* (Cambridge: Harvard University Press, 2002), 97–99.

28. Henrietta Buckmaster, *Deep River* (New York: Harcourt, 1944). Wilmer Collection of Civil War Fiction, Rare Books Department, University of North Carolina at Chapel Hill, Chapel Hill, North Carolina.

29. Orville Prescott, "Books of the Times," *New York Times*, 10 October 1944, 21.

30. *Ibid.*

31. Jessamyn West, *The Friendly Persuasion* (New York: Harcourt, 1945). Wilmer Collection of Civil War Fiction, Rare Books Department, University of North Carolina at Chapel Hill, Chapel Hill, North Carolina.

32. *Ibid.* The specific story I am referring to here is "The Battle of Finney's Ford."

33. *Ibid.*, 64.

34. Stephen Longstreet, *Three Days* (New York: Messner, 1947), Wilmer Collection of Civil War Fiction, Rare Books Department, University of North Carolina at Chapel Hill, Chapel Hill, North Carolina.

35. Muriel Rukeyser, "The Soul and Body of John Brown," *The Collected Poems of Muriel Rukeyser* (New York: McGraw-Hill, 1978), 243–244.

36. Lucy Jameson Scott, *The Gilead Guards* (New York: Hunt & Eaton, 1891). Wilmer Collection of Civil War Fiction, Rare Books Department, University of North Carolina at Chapel Hill, Chapel Hill, North Carolina. Scott's sentimental fiction is particularly adept at showing the threat the war posed to the traditional nuclear family structure. Mother's lose children to the war and children sacrifice their childhood in order to protect the union.

37. Larry Lockridge, *Shade of the Raintree* (New York: Viking Press, 1994), 276.

38. *Ibid.*

39. *Life* 8 September 1947. In this issue, Life even reprinted excerpts of the chapters that feature the footrace that John Shawnessy participates in.

40. This is significant because part of the prize for winning this award (aside from gaining publication and status) was a check for $150,000, a formidable sum of money.

41. James Hilton, "Review of *Raintree County*," *New York Herald and Tribune Book Review*, 4 January 1948, 1.

42. Charles Lee, "Review of *Raintree County*," *New York Times Book Review*, 4 January 1948, 5.

43. Howard Mumford Jones, "Review of *Raintree County*," *Saturday Review of Literature*, 3 January 1948, 9.

44. H.M.R, "Review of *Raintree County*," *Christian Science Monitor*, 5 January 1948, 4.

45. Ross Lockridge, Jr., *Raintree County* (Boston: Houghton Mifflin Company, 1948), 107.

46. *Ibid.*, 95.

47. *Ibid.*, 266.

48. *Ibid.*

49. This is the full title of the novel, but for the sake of brevity, here and elsewhere I simply refer to the novel as *Raintree County*.

Ross Lockridge, Jr., *Raintree County* (Boston: Houghton Mifflin Company, 1948).

50. All of these references are cited from *Harper's Weekly* issues reprinted in Eugene Exman, *The House of Harper: One Hundred and Fifty Years of Publishing* (New York: Harper and Row, 1967). For particular issues referenced here, see *Harper's* 31 (1865), 265–266; *Harper's* 35 (1867), 256–257, 665–666; *Harper's* 36 (1868), 813.

51. *Ibid.*
52. *Ibid.*, 44–45.
53. *Ibid.*
54. *Ibid.*
55. *Ibid.*, 54–55.

56. The notion of the "double" has a long history in psychoanalytic theory and more recent debates over postmodernism. First, the double is an important part of Freudian psychoanalysis. It is a central component of his theory of the conscious ego and unconscious id, and it also related to his concept of the uncanny, which blends the familiar (the self) and strange (what is not the self). Freud argued that the double initially functioned as a defender of the ego but at some point became a menacing harbinger of death, a "vision of terror," which underscores his highly ambiguous character. Freud also linked the double to repetition compulsion, the need to repeat traumas in order to master them. See Sigmund Freud, "The Uncanny," in *On Creativity and the Unconscious: Papers on the Psychology of Art, Literature, Love, and Religion*, ed. Benjamin Nelson, (New York: Harper and Row, 1958). Theorists of postmodernism are similarly interested in the idea of the double, but debate the implications of repetition. Frederic Jameson, for instance, argues that imitation no longer possess satirical potential and instead devolves into apolitical blank parody. In contrast, Linda Hutcheon argues that postmodern repetition can, in fact, function as parody when it reveals "how present representations come from past ones and what ideological consequences derive from both continuity and difference." See Linda Hutcheon, *The Politics of Post Modernism* (New York: Routledge, 1989), 93; see also Frederic Jameson, *Postmodernism, or, the Cultural Logic of Late Capitalism* (London: Verso, 1990).

57. *Ibid.*, 56.
58. *Ibid.*
59. *Ibid.*
60. *Ibid.*, 95–96.

61. George Dekker argues in his discussion of the historical romance that the "history" in historical romances affects the way audiences read them and that the recognition of the historical outcome provides a constrained space for modern novelists to present myth and legend, much like ancients like Aeschylus and Sophocles. Dekker writes that this genre results, "in a kind of fiction in which persons and events appear not only to be shaped in the mass by various impersonal conditioning forces but also to be, in their historical individuality, impenetrable and irrevocable, making us more poignantly aware than ever of the relentlessly serial nature of life in history." See George Dekker, *The American Historical Romance* (Cambridge: Cambridge University Press, 1987).

62. Joel M. Jones, "The Presence of the Past in the Heartland: *Raintree County* Revisited," *Myth, Memory, and the American Earth: The Durability of Raintree County*, David Anderson, ed. (East Lansing: Midwestern Literature Society, 1999), 25.

63. Ross Lockridge, Jr., *Raintree County* (Boston: Houghton Mifflin Company, 1948), 188.

64. *Ibid.*, 96.
65. *Ibid.*, 56.

66. Patricia Ward Julius, "The Southern Myth in Ross Lockridge Jr.'s Raintree County," *Myth, Memory, and the American Earth: The Durability of Raintree County*, David Anderson, ed. (East Lansing: Midwestern Literature Society, 1999), 9.

67. *Ibid.*
68. *Ibid.*, 58.
69. *Ibid.*

70. Concerning the relationship between John Shawnessy's daughter Eva and her fictional counterpart in Stowe's novel, the narrator remarks: "she would linger in the world of sentimental novels, where it wasn't necessary to be Eva Alice Shawnessy, a girl of twelve beginning to be ungracefully a woman. She would linger in the world of her namesake, the most famous child of the Nineteenth Century" (235). Shawnessy goes on to explain that Eva's second name, "Alice," was taken from the protagonist of Lewis Carroll's novel *Alice's Adventures in Wonderland*. When Shawnessy ponders the two courageous and noble girls from which his daughter's name traces, he ponders that his daughter Eva "would have to become a famous and beautiful woman to justify these names" (239).

71. Notable examples of this genre include: Bernie Babcock, *The Soul of Abe Lincoln* (Philadelphia: Lippincott, 1923); Clarence Archibald Bryce, *Kitty Dixon* (Richmond: Southern Clinic Press, 1907); James F. Caldwell, *The Stranger* (New York: Neale, 1907); Millard F. Cox, *The Legionnaires* (Indianapolis: Bowen-Merrill, 1899); John William DeForest, *Miss Ravenel's Conversion from Secession to*

*Loyalty* (New York: Harper, 1867); Mary Dillon, *In Old Bellaire* (New York: Century, 1906); Thomas F. Hargis, *A Patriot's Strategy* (Louisville: Charles T. Dearing, 1895); and Constance Cary Harrison, *The Carlyles* (New York: Appleton, 1905). These and other titles can be found at the Wilmer Collection of Civil War Fiction, Rare Books Division, The University of North Carolina at Chapel Hill.

72. *Ibid.*
73. *Ibid.*
74. *Ibid.*, 263.
75. *Ibid.*, 151.
76. *Ibid.*
77. *Ibid.*, 264.
78. *Ibid.*, 314.
79. *Ibid.*, 259.
80. Ross Lockridge, Jr., *Raintree County* (Boston: Houghton Mifflin Company, 1948), 285.
81. *Ibid.*
82. *Ibid.*
83. *Ibid.*, 284.
84. *Ibid.*
85. *Ibid.*
86. *Ibid.*, 406.
87. *Ibid.*, 318–319.
88. *Ibid.*, 319.
89. *Ibid.*
90. *Ibid.* See 331.
91. *Ibid.*
92. *Ibid.*, 353.
93. *Ibid.*, 432.
94. *Ibid.*
95. *Ibid.*, 438.
96. *Ibid.*
97. *Ibid.*
98. *Ibid.*, 440.
99. *Ibid.*, 440.
100. *Ibid.*, 439–441.
101. *Ibid.*
102. *Ibid.*
103. *Ibid.*, 442.
104. *Ibid.*
105. *Ibid.*, 443.
106. *Ibid.*
107. *Ibid.*
108. *Ibid.*
109. *Ibid.*
110. *Ibid.*
111. *Ibid.*
112. *Ibid.*
113. *Ibid.*
114. *Ibid.*, 446.
115. *Ibid.*
116. He remarks that he "didn't sleep at all well that night, and for the first time he began to want to leave the south." See 446–447.
117. *Ibid.*, 460.
118. *Ibid.*, 463–464.
119. *Ibid.*
120. *Ibid.*, 489.
121. *Ibid.*, 513 This tendency to privilege or to reconcile past personal pain as more significant to the cause of the union and the "emancipation of the negro race" appears throughout the novel. In a later passage following his second battlefield experience he makes similar connections: "it began to seem that the battle and his own search were enduring things, lasting for centuries, ages, perhaps forever" (531).
122. *Ibid.*, 542.
123. *Ibid.*, 544.
124. Despite cursory similarities, in *Raintree County* this process has much different implications than the argument made by John Stauffer in *The Black Hearts of Men: Radical Abolitionists and the Transformation of Race.* Stauffer posits that part of the abolitionist project involved white abolitionists, like John Brown, renouncing their whiteness and assuming a "black heart." Stauffer writes that white abolitionists developed an increasing awareness that "their self-conceptions and hopes for America depended upon their success in blurring and breaking down distinctions of race, religion, class, and gender" (3). By challenging the "static" assumptions of racial categories, Stauffer reasons, white abolitionists made conscious efforts to blur the social distinctions between themselves African Americans. See John Stauffer, *The Black Hearts of Men: Radical Abolitionists and the Transformation of Race* (Cambridge: Harvard University Press, 2002). In *Raintree County*, however, the process of assuming blackness and the ability of a white abolitionist like Shawnessy to occupy black subjectivity becomes a way to ultimately reinforce, and not blur, categories of privilege. A greater degree of empathy does result from temporarily taking on black subjectivity, but this new identification reifies and sets the abolitionist further apart from the slave and from the rest of the society.
125. Leonard Lutwack, "Raintree County and the Epicising Poet in American Fiction," *Ball State University Journal*, 1972, Vol. 131: 14–28; 27.
126. *Ibid.*
127. *Ibid.*, 545.
128. *Ibid.*
129. Elaine Scarry, *The Body in Pain: The Making and UnMaking of the World* (New York: Oxford Press, 1985), 124, 128.
130. Saidiya Hartman, *Scenes of Subjection: Terror, Slavery, and Self-Making in Nineteenth Century America* (New York: Oxford University Press, 1997), 4.

131. *Ibid.*
132. *Ibid.*, 4–5.
133. *Ibid.*, 19.
134. *Ibid.*
135. Jane Tompkins, *Sensational Designs: The Cultural Work of American Fiction, 1790–1860* (New York: Oxford University Press, 1985), pp.140–141.
136. Eric J. Sundquist, ed., *New Essays on Uncle Tom's Cabin: The American Novel* (New York: Cambridge University Press, 1986), pp.6–7.
137. *Ibid.*
138. Ross Lockridge, Jr., *Raintree County* (Boston: Houghton Mifflin Company, 1948), 546.
139. *Ibid.*, 546–547.
140. *Ibid.*, 639, 794.
141. *Ibid.*, 774.
142. *Ibid.*
143. *Ibid.*, 941.
144. Larry Lockridge, *Shade of Raintree: The Life and Death of Ross Lockridge, Jr* (New York: Viking, 1994), 295.
145. *Ibid.*, 933.
146. *Ibid.*, 1022.

## *Epilogue*

1. David W. Blight, *American Oracle: The Civil War in the Civil Rights Era* (Cambridge: Harvard University Press, 2011).
2. *Ibid.*, 2.
3. "President Adopts a Reformer: Garrison's 'I will not retreat' Inspires him for Parley," *New York Times*, 5 June 1961, 10.
4. *Ibid.*
5. Russell Contreras, "In North, Civil War Sites, Events, Long Forgotten," *Associated Press Report*, 17 April 2011.
6. Barack Obama, "Presidential Proclamation of the Civil War Sesquicentennial," Office of the White House Press Secretary, whitehouse.gov, 12 April 2011.
7. *Ibid.*
8. Russell Contreras, "In North, Civil War Sites, Events, Long Forgotten," *Associated Press Report*, 17 April 2011.

# Bibliography

## Archives

Boston Public Library, Boston, Massachusetts:
- Massachusetts Antislavery Society Papers
- New England Antislavery Society Papers
- Wendell Phillips Papers
- William Lloyd Garrison Papers

Harvard University, Cambridge, Massachusetts:
- Historical Textbooks Collection, Monroe C. Gutman Library

Library of Congress, Washington, D.C.:
- Frederick Douglass Papers
- James Birney Papers
- Newspapers and Periodicals
- Prints and Photographs Collection

University of North Carolina at Chapel Hill:
- Wilmer Collection of Civil War Fiction

## Primary and Secondary Materials

"Abolitionism Vs. Christianity and the Union." *Democratic Review*. July 1850. Print.

Alonso, Harriet Hyman. *Growing Up Abolitionist: The Story of the Garrison Children*. Boston: University of Massachusetts Press, 2002. Print.

Anderson, Benedict. *Imagined Communities: Reflections on the Origin and Spread of Nationalism*. London: Verso, 1991. Print.

Aptheker, Herbert. "The Event." Nat Turner: *A Slave Rebellion in History and Memory*. Ed. Greenberg, Kenneth. New York: Oxford University Press, 2003. Print.

*Atlantic Monthly*. January 1886, 121 ed. Print.

Augustine. *Confessions*. Ed. Pine-Coffin, R. London: Penguin, 1961. Print.

Azbug, Robert. *Cosmos Crumbling: American Reform and the Religious Imagination*. New York: Oxford University Press, 1994. Print.

———. "Garrisonian Abolitionists' Fears." *Cosmos Crumbling: American Reform and the Religious Imagination*. New York: Oxford University Press, 1994. Print.

Babcock, Bernie. *The Soul of Abe Lincoln*. Philadelphia: Lippincott, 1923. Print.

Ballou, Ellen B. *The Building of the House: Houghton Mifflin's Formative Years*. Boston: Houghton Mifflin Co., 1970. Print.

Barnes, Elizabeth. *States of Sympathy: Seduction and Democracy in the American Novel*. New York: Columbia Press, 1997. Print.

Barnes, Gilbert. *The Anti-Slavery Impulse*. Goucester: Peter Smith, American Historical Association, 1933. Print.

Barton, William E. *Pine Knot*. New York: Appleton, 1900. Print.

Baym, Nina. *Woman's Fiction: A Guide to Novels by and about Women in America, 1820–1870*. Urbana: Cornell University Press 1993. Print.

Bellah, Robert. "Civil Religion in America." *The Robert Bellah Reader*. Ed. Bellah, Robert N. Durham: Duke University Press, 2006. Print.

Benson, Mary. "A Letter to William Lloyd Garrison." William Lloyd Garrison Papers, Anti-Slavery Manuscript Collection, Boston Public Library, Boston, Massachusetts, January 14, 1837. Print.

Bercovitch, Sacvan. *The Puritan Origins*

*of the American Self.* New Haven: Yale University Press, 1975. Print.

Berlin, Ira. *Many Thousands Gone: The First Two Centuries of Slavery in North America.* Cambridge: Harvard University Press, 1998. Print.

Blight, David W. *American Oracle: The Civil War in the Civil Rights Era.* Cambridge: Harvard University Press, 2011. Print.

———. "If You Don't Tell It Like It Was, It Can Never Be as It Ought to Be." *Slavery and Public History: The Tough Stuff of American Memory.* Ed. Horton, James Oliver. New York: New Press, 2006. Print.

———. *Race and Reunion: The Civil War in American Memory.* Cambridge: Harvard University Press, 2001. Print.

Blue, Frederick J. *No Taint of Compromise: Crusaders in Anti-Slavery Politics.* Baton Rouge: Louisiana State University Press, 2005. Print.

Blumrosen, Alfred W., and Ruth G. Blumrosen. *Slave Nation: How Slavery United the Colonies and Sparked the American Revolution.* Napersville: Sourcebooks, Inc., 2005. Print.

Bolenius, Emma Miller, ed. *The Boys and Girls Fifth History Reader.* Boston: Houghton Mifflin, 1922. Print.

"Book Notes." *The Philadelphia Ledger.* February 11, 1889. Print.

"The Book of Acts." *The King James Version of the Holy Bible.* Nashville: Gideons International, 1971. Print.

*Book of Fables for the Amusement and Instruction of Children.* Hartford: Oliver D. Cooke, 1820. Print.

"Books and Authors." *Boston Daily Examiner.* December 1 0, 1889. Print.

Bowerstock, G.W. *Martyrdom and Rome.* Cambridge: Cambridge University Press, 1995. Print.

Bringhurst, Newell G. *Saints, Slaves, and Blacks: The Changing Place of Black People Within Mormonism.* Westport: Greenwood Press, 1981. Print.

Brodhead, Richard H. *Cultures of Letters: Scenes of Reading and Writing in Nineteenth Century America.* Chicago: University of Chicago Press, 1993. Print.

*Brooklyn Eagle.* January 28, 1870. Print.

Brown, Candy Gunther. *The Word in the World: Evangelical Writing, Publishing, and Reading in America, 1789–1880.* Chapel Hill: University of North Carolina Press, 2004. Print.

Brown, Ira V. *Mary Grew: Abolitionist and Feminist, 1813–1896.* Selinsgrove:

Brown, Joel. "An Abolitionist Recalled: William Lloyd Garrison to Be Honored at Literary Festival in Newburyport." *The Boston Globe.* April 24, 2011, sec. Local News. Print.

Brown, Katherine Holland. *The Father.* New York: Day, 1928. Print.

Brundage, W. Fitzhugh. *Where These Memories Grow: History, Memory, and Southern Identity.* Chapel Hill: University of North Carolina Press, 2000. Print.

Bruss, Elizabeth. *Autobiographical Acts: The Changing Situation of a Literary Genre.* Baltimore: Johns Hopkins University Press, 1976. Print.

Bryce, Clarence Archibald. *Kitty Dixon.* Richmond: Southern Clinic Press, 1907. Print.

Buckmaster, Henrietta. *Deep River.* New York: Harcourt, 1944. Print.

Bums, Paul. *Lives of the Saints.* Collegville: Liturgical Press, 2003. Print.

"The Burning of William: Slave Execution by Fire." *Daily South Carolinian.* October 24, 1856, 22 ed. Print.

Burstein, Andrew. *Sentimental Democracy: The Evolution of America's Romantic Self-Image.* New York: Hill and Wang, 1999. Print.

Bushman, Richard Lyman. *Joseph Smith: Rough Stone Rolling, a Cultural Biography of Mormonism's Founder.* New York: Vintage, 2005. Print.

Caldwell, James F. *The Stranger.* New York: Neale, 1907. Print.

Cardell, William Samuel. *Charles Ashton, the Boy That Would Be a Soldier.* Boston: N.S. and J. Simkins, 1823. Print.

Carleton, Will. *The Centennial Frog and Other Stories.* Philadelphia: Claxton, Remsen, & Haffelfinger, 1876. Print.

———. *Young Folks Centennial Rhymes.* New York: Harper and Brothers, 1876. Print.

Casper, Scott E. *Constructing American Lives: Biography and Culture in Nineteenth Century America.* Chapel Hill: University of North Carolina at Chapel Hill, 1999. Print.

Castle, Carl F. *Pillars of the Republic: Common Schools and American Society.* New York: Hill and Wang, 1983. Print.

Chapman, John Jay. *William Lloyd Garrison.* New York: Moffat, Yard, 1913. Print.

Child, Lydia Maria. "Book Review." *Na-*

*tional Antislavery Standard*. December 25, 1869. Print.

———. "A Letter to William Lloyd Garrison." Anti-Slavery Manuscript Collection, Boston Public Library, Boston, Massachusetts, May 15, 1835. Print.

———. "Through the Red Sea into the Wilderness." *The Liberator*. December 29, 1865. Print.

Christensen, Charles. "The Guilt of New England." *William Lloyd Garrison and the Fight Against Slavery*. New York: St. Martin's Press, 1995. Print.

Church, Robert L. *Education in the United States: An Interpretive History*. New York: Free Press, 1976. Print.

Cikovsky, Nicolai. "Winslow Homer's School Time: A Picture Thoroughly National." *Essays in Honor of Paul Mellon*. Ed. Wilmerding, John. Washington, D.C.: National Gallery of Art, 1986. Print.

Clark, Elizabeth B. "The Sacred Rights of the Weak: Pain, Sympathy, and the Culture of Individual Rights in Antebellum America." *The Journal of American History* 82.2 (1995). Print.

Cohoon, Lorinda B. *Serialized Citizenship: Periodicals, Books, and American Boys, 1840–1911*. Oxford: Scarecrow Press, 2006. Print.

"A Colossal Statue of Bronze, Nine Feet High, Will Be Erect." *The Christian Recorder*. March 29, 1883. Print.

Conforti, Joseph A. *Imagining New England: Explorations of Regional Identity from the Pilgrims to the Mid-Twentieth Century*. Chapel Hill: University of North Carolina Press, 2001. Print.

"The Conspiracy of Fanaticism." *Democratic Review*. May 1850: 391. Print.

Contreras, Russell. "In North, Civil War Sites, Events, Long Forgotten." *Associated Press*. April 17, 2011. Print.

Cox, Millard F. *The Legionnaires*. Indianapolis: Bowen-Merrill, 1899. Print.

Cremin, Lawrence A. *American Education: The National Experience, 1783–1876*. New York: Harper and Row, 1980. Print.

Cullen, Jim. *The Civil War in Popular Culture: A Reusable Past*. Washington: Smithsonian Institute Press, 1995. Print.

*Daily Richmond Enquirer*. September 27, 1864. Print.

Dalfume, Richard M. *Desegregation of the US. Armed Forces: Fighting on Two Fronts, 1939–1953*. Columbia: University of Missouri Press, 1969. Print.

Davis, David Brion. *Antebellum American Culture: An Interpretive Anthology*. Lexington: D.C. Heath, 1979. Print.

———. *Challenging the Boundaries of Slavery*. Cambridge: Harvard University Press, 2003. Print.

Davis, Jefferson. *Rise and Fall of Confederate Government*. New York: Appleton and Company, 1881. Print.

Deamer, Robert G. *The Importance of Place in the American Literature of Hawthorne, Thoreau, Crane, Adams, and Faulkner*. Lewistown: E. Mellen Press, 1990. Print.

DeForest, John William. *Miss Ravenel's Conversion from Secession to Loyalty*. New York: Harper, 1867. Print.

Dekker, George. *The American Historical Romance*. Cambridge: Cambridge University Press, 1987. Print.

Dillon, Mary. *In Old Bellaire*. New York: Century, 1906. Print.

Dillon, Merton L. *Benjamin Lundy and the Struggle for Negro Freedom*. Urbana: University of Illinois Press, 1966. Print.

Douglass, Ann. *The Feminization of American Culture*. New York: Knopf, 1977. Print.

Douglass, Frederick. *Frederick Douglass Papers*. July 24, 1851. Print.

———. "Oration at the Dedication to the Freedmen's Monument to Abraham Lincoln." *Frederick Douglass: Selected Speeches and Writings*. Ed. Foner, Stephen S. New York: Lawrence Hill Books, 2000. Print.

———. "Speech at the Death of William Lloyd Garrison." Frederick Douglass Papers, Library of Congress, Washington, D.C., June 2, 1879. Print.

DuBois, W.E.B. "As the Crow Flies." *Chicago Defender*. January 27, 1945. Print.

———. "As the Crow Flies." *Crisis*. June 1927. Print.

———. *Black Reconstruction in America*. New York: Russell, 1935. Print.

———. "National Negro Conference." *Horizons*. November 1909. Print.

———. "Opinion." *Crisis*. August 1922. Print.

———. "Opinion." *Crisis*. August 1922, 4 ed. Print.

———. "Triumph." *Crisis*. September 1911. Print.

Dumond, Dwight L. *Antislavery: The Crusade for Freedom in America*. Ann Arbor: University of Michigan Press, 1961. Print.

Dwight, Timothy. *Greenfield: A Poem in*

*Seven Parts*. Library of American Civilization, Gelman Library, the George Washington University, Washington, D.C. New York: Childs and Swaine, 1794. Microfiche.

Early, Jubal A. *Narrative of the War Between the States*. New York: Da Capo Press, 1991. Print.

Eaton, Clement. *Freedom of Thought in the Old South*. Durham: Duke University Press, 1940. Print.

"Editorial Pages." *Charleston Daily Courier*. October 25, 1864. Print.

Eggleston, Edgar. *The Ultimate Solution of the American Negro Problem*. New York: AMS Press, 1913. Print.

Ehrman, Bart D. *God's Problem: How the Bible Fails to Answer Our Most Important Question—Why We Suffer*. New York: HarperOne, 2008. Print.

Eliot, Charles W. Journal of the Proceedings and Addresses of the National Education Association, Session of the Year 1892. Cambridge: Monroe C. Gutman Library, Historical Textbooks Collection, Harvard University, Cambridge, Massachusetts, 1892. Print.

Elson, Ruth Miller. *Guardians of Tradition: American Schoolbooks for the Nineteenth Century*. Lincoln: University of Nebraska Press, 1964. Print.

*The Emancipator*. December 18, 1834. Print.

"The Execution of Washington Goode." *The Liberator*. June 1, 1849, 2 ed. Print.

Exman, Eugene. *The House of Harper: One Hundred and Fifty Years of Publishing*. New York: Harper and Row, 1967. Print.

Fahs, Alice. *The Memory of the Civil War in American Culture*. Chapel Hill: University of North Carolina Press, 2004. Print.

Faust, Drew Gilpin. *The Creation of Confederate Nationalism: Ideology and Identity in the Civil War South*. Baton Rogue: Louisiana State University, 1989. Print.

———. *The Ideology of Slavery: Pros Lavery Thought in the Antebellum South, 1830–1860*. Baton Rogue: Louisiana State University Press, 1981. Print.

———. *This Republic of Suffering: Death and the American Civil War*. New York: Vintage, 2008. Print.

Fehrenbecher, Don. *The Slaveholding Republic: An Account of the United States Government's Relations to Slavery*. Oxford: Oxford University Press, 2001. Print.

Filler, Louis. *The Crusade Against Slavery, 1830–1860*. New York: Harper and Row, 1960. Print.

Fitzgerald, F. Scott. *The Complete Stories of F. Scott Fitzgerald*. New York: Scribner, 1989. Print.

Fladeland, Betty. *James Gillespie Birney: Slaveholder to Abolitionist*. Ithaca: Cornell University Press, 1955. Print.

Foucault, Michel. *Discipline and Punishment*. New York: Vintage, 1979. Print.

Fox, Robin Lane. *Pagans and Christians*. New York: Alfred A. Knopf, 1987. Print.

Foxe, John. *Foxe's Book of Martyrs*. Grand Rapids: Zondervan, 1926. Print.

Franklin, John Hope. *The Emancipation Proclamation*. New York: DoubleDay, 1963. Print.

Frederickson, George M. *William Lloyd Garrison*. Englewood Cliffs: Prentice-Hall, 1968. Print.

Frend, W.H.C. *Martyrdom and Persecution in the Early Church: A Study of the Conflict from the Maccabees to Donatus*. Oxford: Basil Blackwell, 1965. Print.

Freud, Sigmond. "The Uncanny." *On Creativity and the Unconscious: Papers on the Psychology of Art, Literature, Love, and Religion*. Ed. Nelson, Benjamin. New York: Harper and Row, 1958. Print

Friedman, Lawrence J. *Gregarious Saints: Self and Community in American Abolitionism, 1830- 1870*. New York: Cambridge University, 1982. Print.

Garrison, Wendell Phillips. *Bedside Poetry: A Parent's Assistant in Moral Discipline*. Boston: D. Lothrop, 1887. Print.

———. "A Letter to William Lloyd Garrison." William Lloyd Garrison Papers, Anti-Slavery Manuscript Collection, Boston Public Library, Boston, Massachusetts, April 2, 1878. Print.

———. "A Letter to William Lloyd Garrison." William Lloyd Garrison Papers, Anti-Slavery Manuscript Collection, Boston Public Library, Boston, Massachusetts, February 7, 1875. Print.

Garrison, Wendell Phillips, and Francis Jackson Garrison. *William Lloyd Garrison, 1805–1879: The Story of His Life Told by His Children*. New York: The Century Company, 1885. Print.

Garrison, William Lloyd. *A Brief Sketch of the Trial of William Lloyd Garrison, for an Alleged Libel on Francis Todd of Massachusetts*. Boston: Garrison and Knapp, 1834. Print.

———. "Correspondence to Arthur Tappan

and the Association of Gentlemen." Garrison Family Papers, Sophia Smith Collection, Smith College, Northampton, Massachusetts, July 28, 1833. Print.

____. "A Covenant with Death, an Agreement with Hell." *The Liberator.* February 1, 1863. Print.

____. "The Death of Slavery." *The Liberator.* February 10,1865. Print.

____. "Declaration of the National Anti-Slavery Convention." *The Liberator.* December 14, 1833. Print.

____. "Editorial." *The Independent.* July 21, 1875. Print.

____. "Editorial." *The Liberator.* February 10,1865. Print.

____. "Editorial: Valedictory the Last Number of the Liberator." *The Liberator.* December 29,1865. Print.

____. "John Brown." *The Liberator.* October 21, 1859. Print.

____. "A Letter to Amos Phelps." William Lloyd Garrison Papers, Boston Public Library, Boston, Massachusetts, October 11, 1834. Print.

____. "A Letter to Anne Benson." William Lloyd Garrison Papers, Anti-Slavery Manuscript Collection, Boston Public Library, Boston, Massachusetts, February 4, 1837. Print.

____. "A Letter to Arthur Tappan." William Lloyd Garrison Papers, Anti-Slavery Manuscript Collection, Boston Public Library, Boston, Massachusetts, February 18, 1836. Print.

____. "A Letter to Francis Garrison." Garrison Family Papers, Anti-Slavery Manuscript Collection, Boston Public Library, Boston, Massachusetts, April 3, 1886. Print.

____. "A Letter to Francis Garrison." William Lloyd Garrison Papers, Anti-Slavery Manuscript Collection, Boston Public Library, Boston, Massachusetts, February 2, 1886. 123.49 vols. Print.

____. "A Letter to Garrison's Free Color Supporters in Boston." *The Liberator.* August 27, 1831. Print.

____. "A Letter to George Benson." William Lloyd Garrison Papers, Boston Public Library, Boston, Massachusetts, August 29, 1832. Print.

____. "A Letter to George Benson." William Lloyd Garrison Papers, Boston Public Library, Boston, Massachusetts, May 31, 1834. Print.

____. "A Letter to George Benson." William Lloyd Garrison Papers, Anti-Slavery Manuscript Collection, Boston Public Library, Boston, Massachusetts, January 12, 1835. Print.

____. "A Letter to George Benson." William Lloyd Garrison Papers, Anti-Slavery Manuscript Collection, Boston Public Library, Boston, Massachusetts, September 5, 1835. Print.

____. "A Letter to George Benson." William Lloyd Garrison Papers, Anti-Slavery Manuscript Collection, Boston Public Library, Boston, Massachusetts, September 12, 1835. Print.

____. "A Letter to George Benson." William Lloyd Garrison Papers, Anti-Slavery Manuscript Collection, Boston Public Library, Boston, Massachusetts, January 11, 1836. Print.

____. "A Letter to Harriet Farnham Horton." William Lloyd Garrison Papers, Boston Public Library, Boston, Massachusetts, May 12, 1830. Print.

____. "A Letter to Harriet Farnham Horton." William Garrison Papers, Antislavery Manuscript Collection, Boston Public Library: Boston Public Library, May 13, 1830. Print.

____. "A Letter to Harriot Plummer." William Garrison Papers, Anti-Slavery Manuscript Collection, Boston Public Library, Boston, Massachusetts, March 4, 1833. Print.

____. "A Letter to Harriot Plummer." Mission to England, Anti-Slavery Manuscript Collection, Boston Public Library, Boston, Massachusetts, November 4, 1833. Print.

____. "A Letter to Helen Benson." William Lloyd Garrison Papers, Boston Public Library, Boston, Massachusetts, April 5, 1834. Print.

____. "A Letter to Henry Benson." William Lloyd Garrison Papers, Anti-Slavery Manuscript Collection, Boston Public Library, Boston, Massachusetts, October 19, 1831. Print.

____. "A Letter to Henry Benson." William Lloyd Garrison Papers, Boston Public Library, Boston, Massachusetts, September 15, 1834. Print.

____. "A Letter to Henry Benson." William Lloyd Garrison Papers, Anti-Slavery Manuscript Collection, Boston Public Library, Boston, Massachusetts, January 26, 1836. Print.

____. "A Letter to Henry Thompson."

William Lloyd Garrison Papers, Anti-Slavery Manuscripts Collection, Boston Public Library, Boston, Massachusetts, May 30, 1830. Print.

———. "A Letter to Isaac Knapp." William Lloyd Garrison Papers, Anti-Slavery Manuscript Collection, Boston Public Library, Boston, Massachusetts, February 28, 1836. Print.

———. "A Letter to James Birney." William Lloyd Garrison Papers, Anti-Slavery Manuscript Collection, Boston Public Library, Boston, Massachusetts, April 6, 1836. Print.

———. "A Letter to James Miller Mckim." William Lloyd Garrison Papers, Anti-Slavery Manuscript Collection, Boston Public Library, Boston, Massachusetts, February 3, 1866. Print.

———. "A Letter to John Vashon." Mission to England Folder, William Lloyd Garrison Papers, Anti-Slavery Manuscript Collection, Boston Public Library, Boston, Massachusetts, November 1, 1833. 8 vols. Print.

———. "A Letter to Joseph T. Buckingham." Courier May 12, 1830. Print

———. "A Letter to Nathan R. Johnson." William Lloyd Garrison Papers, Anti-Slavery Manuscript Collection, Boston Public Library, Boston, Massachusetts, October 15, 1860. Print.

———. "A Letter to Nicholas Brice." William Lloyd Garrison Papers, Anti-Slavery Manuscripts Collection, Boston Public Library, Boston, Massachusetts, May 13, 1830. Print.

———. "A Letter to Oliver Johnson." William Lloyd Garrison Papers, Anti-Slavery Manuscript Collection, Boston Public Library, Boston, Massachusetts, December 18, 1835. Print.

———. "A Letter to Oliver Johnson." William Lloyd Garrison Papers, Anti-Slavery Manuscript Collection, Boston Public Library, Boston, Massachusetts, August 14, 1838. Print.

———. "A Letter to Oliver Johnson." William Lloyd Garrison Papers, Anti-Slavery Manuscript Collection, Boston Public Library, Boston, Massachusetts, December 23, 1865. Print.

———. "A Letter to Rev. George Shepard." William Lloyd Garrson Papers, Boston Public Library, Boston, Massachusetts, September 13, 1831. Print.

———. "A Letter to Samuel J. May." William Lloyd Garrison Papers, Anti-Slavery Manuscript Collection, Boston Public Library, Boston, Massachusetts, January 17, 1837. Print.

———. "A Letter to Sarah Douglass." William Lloyd Garrison Papers, Anti-Slavery Manuscript Collection, Boston Public Library, Boston, Massachusetts, March 5, 1832. Print.

———. "A Letter to Sarah Douglass." William Lloyd Garrison Papers, Boston Public Library, Boston, Massachusetts, March 5, 1832. Print.

———. "Letter to the Editor of the Newburyport Herald." *Newburyport Herald* May 21, 1822. Print.

———. "A Letter to Theodore Tilton." William Lloyd Garrison Papers, Anti-Slavery Manuscript Collection, Boston Public Library, Boston, Massachusetts, December 14, 1865. Print.

———. "A Letter to Wendell Garrison." William Lloyd Garrison Papers, Anti-Slavery Manuscript Collection, Boston Public Library, Boston, Massachusetts, April 4, 1868. Print.

———. "A Letter to Wendell Phillips Garrison." William Lloyd Garrison Papers, Anti-Slavery Manuscript Collection, Boston Public Library, Boston, Massachusetts, December 18, 1867. Print.

———. "A Letter to Wendell Phillips Garrison." William Lloyd Garrison Papers, Anti-Slavery Manuscript Collection, Boston Public Library, Boston, Massachusetts, March 23, 1868. Print.

———. "A Letter to William C. Nell." William Lloyd Garrison Papers, Anti-Slavery Manuscript Collection, Boston Public Library, Boston, Massachusetts, April 23, 1867. Print.

———. *Letters and Memorials of Wendell Phillips Garrison: Literary Editor of the Nation, 1865–1906*. Cambridge: Riverside Press, 1908. Print.

———. *The Mother's Register*. Boston: D. Lothrop, 1887. Print.

———. *The New Gulliver*. New York: Longman's, Green, and Company, 1898. Print.

———. *Parables for Home and School*. New York: Longman's, Green, and Company, 1897. Print.

———. *Sonnets and Lyrics of the Ever-Womanly*. Boston: D. Lothrop, 1897. Print.

———. "To James Woodbury." *The Liberator*. September 1, 1837. Print.

———. "To the Editor of the *Boston Courier.*" *The Liberator*. March 18, 1837. Print.

———. "To the Public." *Genius of Universal Emancipation*. November 29, 1829. Print

———. "To the Public." *Genius of Universal Emancipation*. November 29, 1829. Print.

———. *The Words of Garrison: A Centenary Selection, 1805–1905*. Boston: Houghton, Mifflin, 1905. Print.

Genovese, Eugene. *A Consuming Fire: The Fall of the Confederacy in the Mind of the White Christian South*. London: University of Georgia Press, 1998. Print.

Geselbracht, Raymond H. *The Civil Rights Legacy of Harry S. Truman*. Kirksville: Truman State University Press, 2007. Print.

Gilmore, William J. *Reading Becomes a Necessity of Life: Material and Cultural Life in Rural New England, 1778–1835*. Knoxville: University of Tennessee Press, 1989. Print.

*The Glen Beck Show.* CNN. November 3, 2006.

Glucklich, Ariel. *Sacred Pain: Hurting the Body for the Sake of the Soul*. Oxford: Oxford University Press, 2001. Print.

Goodman, Paul. *Of One Blood: Abolitionism and the Origins of Racial Equality*. Berkeley: University of California Press, 1998. Print.

Gordon, Sarah Barringer. "Blasphemy and the Law of Religious Liberty in Nineteenth Century America." *American Quarterly*, December (2000). Print.

Grant, Ulysses S. *Personal Memoirs of U.S. Grant*. 2 vols. New York: C.L. Webster, 1886. Print.

"Great Men: James Forten." *The North Star*. March 10, 1848. Print.

Greaves, Richard. "Bunyan and the Ethic of Suffering." *John Bunyan and His England, 1628–88*. Ed. Lawrence, Owen, and Sim. London: Hambledon Press, 1990. Print.

Greenberg, Kenneth. "Name, Face, Body." *Nat Turner: A Slave Rebellion in History and Memory*. Ed. Greenberg, Kenneth. New York: Oxford University Press, 2003. Print.

Greenblatt, Stephen. "The Circulation of Social Energy." *Shakespearean Negotiations: The Circulation of Social Energy in Renaissance England*. Berkeley: University of California Press, 1988. Print.

Guelzo, Allen C. *Abraham Lincoln: Redeemer President* Grand Rapids: William B. Eerdmans Publishing, 2003. Print.

H.M.R. "Review of Raintree County." *Christian Science Monitor*. January 5, 1948. Print.

Halbwachs, Maurice. *The Social Frameworks of Memory*. New York: Harper and Row, 1980. Print.

Hargis, Thomas F. *A Patriot's Strategy*. Louisville: Charles T. Dearing, 1895. Print.

Harper, Francis Ellen Watkins. *Poems on Miscellaneous Subjects*. Philadelphia: Merrihew & Thompson, 1857. Print.

*Harper's Weekly* February 18, 1865. Print.

Harrison, Constance Cary. *The Carlyles*. New York: Appleton, 1905. Print.

Harrold, Stanley. *The Abolitionists and the South, 1831–1865*. Lexington: University of Kentucky Press, 1995. Print.

Hartman, Sadiya. *Scenes of Subjection: Terror and Self-Making in Nineteenth Century America*. New York: Oxford University Press, 1999. Print.

Hilton, James. "Review of Raintree County." *New York Herald and Tribune Book Review*. January 4, 1948. Print.

Hix, Melvin. *The Approved Selections for Supplementary Reading and Memorizing*. Boston: Noble and Eldredge, 1905. Print.

Holt, Jean H. Baker, and Michael F. Holt. *The Civil War and Reconstruction*. New York: Norton Press, 2001. Print.

Homer, Winslow. *Country School*. 1873. Addison Gallery of American Art, Phillip Andover Academy, Andover, Massachusetts.

Horwitz, Tony. *Confederates in the Attic: Dispatches from the Unfinished Civil War*. New York: Vintage, 1998. Print.

Huntzicker, William E. *The Popular Press, 1833–1865*. Westport: Greenwood, 1999. Print.

Hutcheon, Linda. *The Politics of Postmodernism*. New York: Routledge, 1989. Print.

Hutton, Frankie. *The Early Black Press in America, 1827–1860*. Westport: Greenwood Press, 1993. Print.

Irons, Charles F. *The Origins of Pros Lavery Christianity: White and Black Evangelicals in Colonial and Antebellum Virginia*. Chapel Hill: University of North Carolina Press, 2008. Print.

Jameson, Frederic. *Postmodernism, or, the*

*Cultural Logic of Late Capitalism.* London Verso, 1990. Print.

Johnson, Oliver. "Testimonial: Valedictory: The Last Number of the Liberator." *The Liberator.* December 29, 1865. Print.

———. *William Lloyd Garrison and His Times.* Boston: Russell & Company, 1879. Print.

Johnson, Walter. Soul by Soul: *Life Inside the Antebellum Slave Market.* Cambridge: Harvard University Press, 1999. Print.

Jones, Howard Mumford. "Review of Raintree County." *Saturday Review of Literature.* January 3, 1948. Print.

Jones, Joel M. "The Presence of the Past in the Heartland: Raintree County Revisited." *Myth, Memory, and the American Earth: The Durability of Raintree County.* Ed. Anderson, David. East Lansing: Midwestern Literature Society, 1999. Print.

Joseph Seaman Cotter, Sr. "William Lloyd Garrison (1895)." *The Vintage Book of African American Poetry: 200 Years of Vision, Struggle, Power, Beauty, and Triumph from 50 Outstanding Poets.* Ed. Harper, Michael S. New York: Vintage, 2000. Print.

Kaplan, Amy. *The Anarchy of Empire in the Making of US. Culture.* Cambridge: Harvard University Press, 2002. Print.

Katz, Michael B. *The Irony of Early School Reform: Education Innovaton in Mid-Nineteenth Century Massachusetts.* Cambridge: Harvard University Press, 2001. Print.

King, John N. *Foxe's Book of Martyrs and Early Modern Print Culture.* Cambridge: Cambridge University Press, 2006. Print.

Kingsley, John. "A Slave Whipped and Burned to Death." *The Liberator.* January 23,1857, 4 ed. Print.

Komblith, Gary. *Slavery and Sectional Strife in the Early Republic.* New York: Rowan and Littlefield, 2010. Print.

Kraditor, Aileen S. *Means and Ends in American Abolitionism: Garrison and His Critics on Strategy and Tactics.* New York: Random House, 1967. Print.

Laurie, Bruce. *Beyond Garrison: Antislavery and Social Reform.* Cambridge: Cambridge University Press, 2005. Print.

Lavender, Caroline F. *Cradle of Liberty: Race, the Child, and National Belonging from Thomas Jefferson to WE.B. Dubois.* Durham: Duke University Press, 2006. Print.

Lee, Charles. "Review of Raintree County." *New York Times Book Review.* January 4, 1948. Print.

*The Letters of Catherine of Siena.* Ed. Noffke, Suzanne. Ithaca: Cornell University Press, 2001. Print.

Lewis, R.W.B. *The American Adam: Innocence, Tragedy, and Tradition in the Nineteenth Century.* Chicago: University of Chicago Press, 1955. Print.

*The Liberator.* November 8, 1834. Print.

*The Liberator.* November 8, 1834. Print.

*Life.* September 8, 1947. Print.

Lockridge, Larry. *Shade of Raintree: The Life and Death of Ross Lockridge, Jr.* New York: Viking Press, 1994. Print.

Lockridge, Ross. *Raintree County ... Which Had No Boundaries in Time and Space, Where Lurked Musical and Strange Names and Mythical and Lost Peoples, and Which Was Itself Only a Name Musical and Strange.* Boston: Houghton Mifflin Company, 1948. Print.

Loewen, James W. "Five Myths About Why the South Seceded." *The Washington Post.* January 9, 2011, sec. 1. Print.

Longstreet, Stephen. *Three Days.* New York: Messner, 1947. Print.

Lutwack, Leonard. "Raintree County and the Epicising Poet in American Fiction." *Ball State University Journal* 131 (1972). Print.

MacLeod, Anne Scott. *A Moral Tale: Children's Fiction and American Culture, 1820–1860.* Hamden: Archon Press, 1975. Print.

Maddow, Rachel."A Conversation with Rand Paul." Perf. Maddow, Rachel. The Rachel Maddow Show. *MSNBC May* 19, 2010.

Mann, Horace. *The Life and Works of Horace Mann, Volume IV.* Vol. 4. 4 vols 1867. Print.

Marten, James. *Children for the Union: The War Spirit and the Northern Home Front.* Chicago: Ivan Dee, 2004. Print.

———. *The Children's Civil War.* Chapel Hill: University of North Carolina Press, 1998. Print.

May, Samuel. *Some Recollections of Our Antislavery Conflict.* New York: Arno Press and the New York Times, 1968. Print.

Mayer, Henry. *All on Fire: William Lloyd Garrison and the Abolition of Slavery.* New York: St. Marten's Press, 1998. Print.

Mays, Benjamin E. *The Negro's God as Reflection in His Literature*. New York: Atheneum, 1975. Print.

McCarthy, Timothy Patrick, and John Stauffer, ed. *Prophets of Protest: Reconsidering the History of American Abolitionism*. New York: New Press, 2006. Print.

McGill, Meredith L. *American Literature and the Culture of Reprinting, 1834–1853*. Philadelphia: University of Pennsylvania Press, 2003. Print.

McIntosh, James T., ed. *The Papers of Jefferson Davis, Vol. 3: 1846–1848*. Vol. III. Baton Rogue: Louisiana State University Press, 1981. Print.

McKay, Ernest K. *The Civil War and New York City*. Syracuse: Syracuse University Press, 1990. Print.

McKivigan, John R., and Stanley Harrold. *Anti-Slavery Violence: Sectional, Racial, and Cultural Conflict in Antebellum America*. Knoxville: University of Tennessee Press, 1999. Print.

McPherson, James. *The Abolitionist Legacy: From Reconstruction to the NAACP*. Princeton: Princeton University Press, 1995. Print.

———. *The Struggle for Equality: Abolitionists and the Negro in the Civil War and Reconstruction*. Princeton: Princeton University Press, 1964. Print.

Meek, James Gordon. "Rand Paul's Civil Rights Remarks Are 'Misplaced' Say Rnc Chairman Michael Steele." *New York Daily News* May 23, 2010, sec. Washington Bureau Column. Print.

Mendehson, Jack. *Channing: The Reluctant Radical*. Westport: Greenwood Press, 1971. Print.

Meriwether, Elizabeth Avery. *The Sowing of the Swords*. New York: Neale, 1910. Print.

Merrill, Walter M. *Against the Tide and Wind: A Biography of William Lloyd Garrison*. Cambridge: Harvard University Press, 1963. Print.

Mills, Cynthia J., and Pamela H. Simpson, ed. *Monuments to the Lost Cause: Women, Art, and the Landscapes of Southern Memory*. Knoxville: University of Tennessee Press, 2003. Print.

Mitchell, Margaret. *Gone with the Wind*. New York: Warner Books, 1999. Print.

Mott, Frank Luther. *A History of Magazines Volume 3: 1864–1880*. Vol. 3. 6 vols. New York: D. Appleton and Company, 1930. Print.

Nash, Gary. *Race and Revolution*. Madison: Madison Horse, 1990. Print.

Nast, Thomas. *Emancipation*. 1867. Rare Prints and Photographs Divison, The Library of Congress, Washington, D.C., Philadelphia.

"New England Anti-Slavery Society Fall Quarterly Meeting Notes." New England Anti-Slavery Society Manuscripts, Anti-Slavery Manuscripts Collection, Boston Public Library, Boston, Massachusetts, 1832. Print.

"New York Diet Kitchen Association." *Social Service*. November 1903. Print.

*New York Times*. January 28, 1868. Print.

*New York Times*. September 8, 1869. Print.

Newby, A. *Jim Crow's Defense: Anti-Negro Thought in America, 1900–1930*. Baton Rouge: Lousiana State University Press, 1965. Print.

Newman, Lucretia H. "William Lloyd Garrison." *The Christian Recorder*. March 27, 1884. Print.

Newman, Richard S. *The Transformation of American Abolitionism: Fighting Slavery in the Early Republic*. Chapel Hill: University of North Carolina Press, 2002. Print.

*The North Star*. August 15, 1851. Print.

Nye, Russel B. *William Lloyd Garrison and the Humanitarian Reformers*. Boston: Little, Brown, and Company, 1955. Print.

*Pennsylvania Freeman*. June 25, 1851. Print.

Perkins, J. *The Suffering Self: Pain and Narrative Representation in the Early Christian Era*. London: Routledge, 1995. Print.

Perry, Lewis, ed. *Antislavery Reconsidered: New Perspectives on the Abolitionists*. Baton Rogue: Louisiana State University, 1979. Print.

Peterson, Merrill D. *Lincoln in American Memory*. New York: Oxford University Press, 1994. Print.

Phillips, Wendell. "A Letter to William Garrison, Jr.": William Lloyd Garrison Papers, Anti-Slavery Manuscript Collection, Boston Public Library, Boston, Massachusetts, April 16, 1880. Print.

———. *Remarks of Wendell Phillips at the Funeral of William Lloyd Garrison*. Boston: Lee and Shepard Publishers, 1884. Print.

Pillsbury, Parker. *Acts of the Antislavery Apostles*. Concord: Clague, Wegman, Schlicht & Co, 1883. Print.

Pope, Alexander. *Essay on Man and Other Poems*. New York: Dover, 1994. Print.

Potter, David. *Martyrdom as Spectacle: Theatre and Society in the Classical World.* Ed. Scudel, R. Ann Arbor: University of Michigan Press, 1993. Print.

Powell, Aaron M. *Personal Reminisces of the Anti-Slavery and Other Reforms and Reformers.* Westport: Negro Universities Press, 1970. Print.

Prescott, Orville. "Books of the Times." *New York Times.* October 10, 1944. Print.

Purvis, Robert. "A Letter to William Lloyd Garrison." William Lloyd Garrison Papers, Anti-Slavery Manuscript Collection, Boston Public Library, Boston, Massachusetts, September 12, 1835. Print.

Quarles, Benjamin. *Black Abolitionists.* New York: Oxford University Press, 1969. Print.

———. *Frederick Douglass.* New York: Da Capo Press, 1997. Print.

Ransom, Reverend. "An Oration on William Garrison." Garrison Centennial Collection, Boston Public Library, Boston, Massachusetts, December 11, 1905. Print.

Ravitch, Diane. *The Great School Wars: New York City, 1805–1973.* New York: Basic Books, 1974. Print.

Ray, Henrietta Cordelia. *Poems.* New York: Grafton Press, 1910. Print.

Reese, Charley. "Purge the South of It's Symbols? You're Barking Up the Wrong Flagpole." *Orlando Sentinel* February 20, 1997. Print.

Remini, Robert V. *Joseph Smith.* New York: Penguin, 2002. Print.

Reumann, Miriam G. *American Sexual Character: Sex, Gender, and National Identity in the Kinsey Reports.* Berkeley: University of California Press, 2005. Print.

"Review Clipping." *New York Tribune* February 9, 1889. Print.

Rich, Frank. "The Randslide and Its Discontents." *New York Times* May 22, 2010, sec. OP-ED. Print.

Richards, Leonard. *Gentlemen of Property and Standing: Anti-Abolition Mobs in Jacksonian America.* New York: Oxford University Press, 1970. Print.

Ripley, C. Peter. *The Black Abolitionist Papers: Volume 1, 1830–1865.* Vol. 1. 4 vols. Chapel Hill: University of North Carolina Press, 1985. Print.

Robertson, Stacy M. *Parker Pillsbury: Radical Abolitionist, Radical Feminist.* Ithaca: Cornell University Press, 2000. Print.

Robinson, David. "The Legacy of Channing: Culture Is a Religious Category in New England Thought." *Harvard Theological Review.* 74 (1981). Print.

Rohrbach, Augusta. *Truth Stranger Than Fiction: Race, Realism, and the U.S. Literary Marketplace.* New York: Palgrove Press, 2000. Print.

Rukeyser, Muriel. "The Soul and Body of John Brown." *The Collected Poems of Muriel Rukeyser.* New York: McGraw-Hill, 1978. Print.

Sanchez-Eppler, Karen. *Touching Liberty: Abolition, Feminism, and the Politics of the Body.* Berkeley: University of California Press, 1993. Print.

Sandage, Scott A. "A Marble House Divided: The Lincoln Memorial, the Civil Rights Movement, and the Politics of Memory, 1939–1963." *Time Longer Than Rope: A Century of African American Activism, 1850–1950.* Ed. Payne, Charles M. New York: New York University Press, 2003. Print.

Sandburg, Carl. *Abraham Lincoln: The Prairie Years.* New York: Harcourt, 1926. Print.

Sanders, James W. *The Education of an Urban Minority: Catholics in Chicago, 1833–1965.* New York: Oxford University Press, 1977. Print.

Savage, Kirk. *Standing Soldiers, Kneeling Slaves: Race, War, and Monument in Nineteenth Century America.* Princeton: Princeton University Press, 1997. Print.

Scarry, Elaine. *The Body in Pain: The Making and Unmaking of the World.* Oxford: Oxford University Press, 1985. Print.

Schodel, W.R. *Ignatius of Antioch: A Commentary on the Letters of Ignatius of Antioch.* Philadelphia: Fortress Press, 1985. Print.

Schwartz, Barry. *Abraham Lincoln and the Forge of National Identity.* Chicago University of Chicago Press, 2000. Print.

Scott, Lucy Jameson. *The Gilead Guards.* New York: Hunt and Eaton, 1891. Print.

Shackel, Paul A. *Memory in Black and White: Race, Commemoration, and the Post-Bellum Landscape.* Walnut Creek: AltaMira Press, 2003. Print.

———. *Myth, Memory, and the Making of the American Landscape.* Orlando: University of Florida Press, 2001. Print.

Sherwood, Robert E. *Abe Lincoln in Illinois.* New York: Dramatist Play Service, 1938. Print.

Silber, Nine. *The Romance of Reunion: Northerners and the South, 1865–1900.* Chapel Hill: University of North Carolina Press, 1993. Print.

Smith, Godwin. *The Moral Crusader: William Lloyd Garrison* New York: Funk & Wagnalls, 1892. Print.

Smith, John David. "Introduction." *Frederick Douglass' My Bondage, My Freedom.* New York: Penguin, 1993. Print.

Smith, Joseph. *The Complete Joseph Smith Translation of the New Testament.* Ed. Wayment, Thomas A. Salt Lake City: Deseret Books, 2005. Print.

\_\_\_\_. *Doctrine and Covenants.* Salt Lake City: The Church of Jesus Christ of Latter-day Saints. Print.

Snay, Mitchell. *Gospel of Disunion: Religion and Separatism in the Antebellum South.* New York: Cambridge University Press, 1993. Print.

Soderlund, Jean R. *Quakers and Slavery: A Divided Spirit.* Princeton: Princeton University Press, 1985. Print.

Southwick, Sarah H. *Reminisces of Early Anti-Slavery Days.* Cambridge Mass.: Privately Printed, Harvard University Library, 1893. Print.

Stauffer, John. *The Black Hearts of Men: Radical Abolitionists and the Transformation of Race.* Cambridge: Harvard University Press, 2002. Print.

Stem, Julia A. *The Plight of Feeling: Sympathy and Dissent in the Early American Novel.* Chicago: University of Chicago Press, 1997. Print.

Stewart, James Brewster. *William Lloyd Garrison and the Challenge of Emancipation.* Arlington Heights: Harlan Davidson, 1992. Print.

Stewart, James Brewer, ed. *William Lloyd Garrison at Two Hundred: History, Legacy, and Memory.* New Haven: Yale University Press, 2008. Print.

Strong, Douglass. *Perfectionist Politics: Abolitionism and the Religious Tensions of American Democracy.* Syracuse: Syracuse University Press, 1999. Print.

Sundquist, Eric J., ed. *New Essays on Uncle Tom's Cabin: The American Novel.* New York: Cambridge University Press, 1986. Print.

Susquehana University Press, 1991. Print.

Sweet, William Warren. *The Methodist Episcopal Church and the Civil War.* Cincinnati: Methodist Book Concern Press, 1912. Print.

Tabor, James. *A Noble Death: Suicide and Martyrdom Among Christians and Jews in Antiquity.* San Francisco: HarperCollins, 1992. Print.

Tate, Allen. *Stonewall Jackson: The Good Soldier.* New York: Minton, Blach, and Company, 1928. Print.

Terrell, Mary. *Garrison Centenary Program Speech.* Garrison Centenary Collection, Boston Public Library.

"Theological and Literary Intelligence." *The Unitarian Review and Religious Magazine* February 1886. Print.

Thomas, John L. *The Liberator: William Lloyd Garrison, a Biography.* Boston: Little, Brown, 1963. Print.

Tilton, Theodore. "Testimonial: Valedictory: The Last Number of the Liberator." *The Liberator.* December 29, 1865. Print.

"To William Garrison." *The Liberator.* January 16, 1836. Print.

Tompkins, Jane. *Sensational Designs: The Cultural Work of American Fiction, 1790–1860.* New York: Oxford University Press, 1985. Print.

Trend, W.H.C. *Martyrdom and Persecution in the Early Church.* Oxford: Blackwell Press, 1965. Print.

Tuveson, Ernest Lee. *Redeemer Nation.* Chicago: University of Chicago Press, 1975. Print.

Twain, Mark. *The Adventures of Huckleberry Finn.* New York: Norton, 1998. Print.

\_\_\_\_. *The Adventures of Tom Sawyer.* New York: Broadview, 2006. Print.

Tyack, David. *The One Best System.* Cambridge: Harvard University Press, 1974. Print.

Vanausdall, Jeanette. *Pride and Protest: The Novel in Indiana.* Indianapolis: Indiana Historical Society, 1999. Print.

Van Henten, and Jan Willem Friedrich Avemarie, eds. *Martyrdom and Noble Death: Selected Texts from Greco-Roman, Jewish, and Christian Antiquity.* London: Routledge, 2002. Print.

Villard, Fanny Garrison. *William Lloyd Garrison on Non-Resistance Together with a Personal Sketch by His Daughter Fanny Garrison Villard.* New York: Nation Press Printing, 1924. Print.

Villard, Henry. *Memoirs of Henry Villard: Journalist and Financier, 1835–1900.* Ed. Garrison-Villard, Helen. New York: Da Capo Press, 1969. Print.

Villard, Oswald Garrison. *The Disappearing Daily*. New York: Alfred A. Knopf, 1944. Print.

\_\_\_\_. *Prophets True and False*. New York: Alfred A. Knopf, 1928. Print.

"The Villard Will Fight." *New York Sun*. December 4, 1903. Print.

Voernberg, Michael. *Final Freedom: The Civil War, the Abolition of Slavery, and the Thirteenth Amendment*. Cambridge: Cambridge University Press, 2001. Print.

Ward, Patricia Julius. "The Southern Myth in Ross Lockridge Jr.'S Raintree County." *Myth, Memory, and the American Earth: The Durability of Rain Tree County*. Ed. Anderson, David. East Lansing: Midwestern Literature Society, 1999. Print.

Warren, Robert. *John Brown: The Making of a Martyr*. New York: Payson and Clark, 1929. Print.

West, Jessamyn. *The Friendly Persuasion*. New York: Harcourt, 1945. Print.

Whittier, John Greenleaf. "Oh None in All the World Before." *Poems in Wartime from Volume III: The Works of Whittier, Anti-Slavery Poems and Songs of Labor and Reform*. New York: Houghton and Mifflin, 1892. Print.

\_\_\_\_. "To William Garrison." *The Complete Poetical Works of John Greenleaf Whittier*. New York: Cornell University Press, 2010. Print.

Wiggins, William H. *O Freedom! Afro American Emancipation Celebrations*. Knoxville: University of Tennessee Press, 1987. Print.

"William Lloyd Garrison." *Afro-American*. December 9, 1905. Print.

"William Lloyd Garrison." *Farmer's Cabinet*. June 3, 1879,48 ed. Print.

Woodbury, James T. "A Clerical Appeal." *New England Spectator*. August 17, 1837. Print.

Woodward, C. Vann. "The Antislavery Myth." *The American Scholar* 31 Spring (1962). Print.

Yee, Shirley J. *Black Women Abolitionists: A Study in Activism, 1828–1860*. Knoxville: University of Tennessee Press, 1992. Print.

Yeocum, William H. "The Mind That Was in Christ." *Christian Recorder*. October 20, 1881: 1. Print.

*Young Mr. Lincoln*. Dir. John Ford. Perf. Henry Ford. Fox, 1939. Film.

# Index

Anderson, Benedict 98–99

Barnes, Gilbert H. 13–14
Benson, George 8, 34, 44–46
Benson, Helen 10
Birney, James 35–36, 41
Blight, David 4
*Book of Martyrs* 10–11, 30–32
Boston Unitarians 44–45
Buckingham, Joseph T. 1, 3

Channing, William Ellery 44
Child, Lydia Maria 29
*Christian Mirror* 8
Civil War Sesquicentennial 154–155

Davis, Jefferson 52
Denmark-Vessey Affair 48
Douglass, Frederick 6, 47, 56, 73, 76–78, 109
Du Bois, W.E.B 109–111

Ehrman, Bart 9

*The Father* 84–85
Faust, Drew Gilpin 7
*The Friendly Persuasion* 124

Garrison, Frank 13, 88–98, 103–105
Garrison, Wendell 13, 88–98, 103–105
Garrison, William Lloyd: public controversies 11–18; public eulogies 75–83; relationship with black abolitionists 36–39; relationship with black women activists 37–40; relationship with children 88–100, 106–108, 116; reports of slave suffering 47–52; scholarship on 11–18; Sesquicentennial Celebrations 115–116; "Valedictory: The Last Number of *The Liberator*" 60–65; violence towards 28–30; within historical Christian martyr tradition 32–36
*The Genius of Universal Emancipation* 1, 112
Grant, Ulysses S. 117–118
"Greenfield Hill" 58

*Harper's Weekly* 64–66
Hartman, Sadiya 20–22; 49
Homer, Winslow 100–102; *Country School* series 101–103

Kennedy, John F. 153–154

Laurie, Bruce 57–58
Lockridge, Ross 125–126
Lundy, Benjamin 3, 72

May, Samuel 35, 41, 57, 66–70, 86
McPherson, James 106

Paul, Rand 56–57
Phelps, Amos 8
Phillips, Wendell 60, 65, 74–78, 90, 111
Pickney, Henry 27–28
*Pilgrim's Progress* 29–35; 54
Pillsbury, Parker 57, 66, 86; *Acts of the Antislavery Apostles* 70–75
Pine Knot 82–83

Quarles, Benjamin 17–18

*Raintree County* (literary analysis) 126–152
Rukeyser, Muriel 124–125

Smith, Joseph 41–43; work on *Nauvoo Expositor* 42
*The Sowing of the Swords* 83
Stauffer, John 6

Tappan, Lewis 35
Thompson, George 26–27
Turner, Nat 48

*Uncle Tom's Cabin* 137, 148–149

Wilberforce, William 25–26

Yee, Shirley J. 38–39

www.ingramcontent.com/pod-product-compliance
Lightning Source LLC
Chambersburg PA
CBHW032059300426
44116CB00007B/811